# The Future of the Past

# The Future of the Past

## *When cultural heritage meets climate change*

Thijs Weststeijn

Translated by Liz Waters

polity

This publication has been made possible with financial support from the Dutch Foundation for Literature. The publisher gratefully acknowledges the support of the Dutch Foundation for Literature.

**Nederlands letterenfonds**
**dutch foundation for literature**

Polity Press
65 Bridge Street
Cambridge CB2 1UR, UK

Polity Press
111 River Street
Hoboken, NJ 07030, USA



ISBN-13: 978-1-5095-6784-3 – hardback

A catalogue record for this book is available from the British Library.

Library of Congress Control Number: 2025948161

Typeset in 11 on 14 Janson Text
by Cheshire Typesetting Ltd, Cuddington, Cheshire
Printed and bound in Great Britain by CPI Group (UK) Ltd, Croydon



For further information on Polity, visit our website:
politybooks.com

To my students

# Contents

# Prologue: A cry of nations o'er sunken halls

*Oh Venice! Venice! When thy marble walls*
*Are level with the waters, there shall be*
*A cry of nations o'er thy sunken halls,*
*A loud lament along the sweeping sea!*
Lord Byron, 'Ode on Venice', 1819

On 12 November 2019, the water in Venice rose higher than ever before, to almost 2 metres above its normal level. The famous square in front of St Mark's Basilica had quite frequently flooded, but now the sea was pouring in through the entry portal and even under the floor the water was rising. Never before had it reached the windows of the crypt holding the graves of the Venetian patriarchs (the equivalent of bishops). Stormy gusts, which also blew several sheets of lead from the roofs of the cupolas, drove even more of it inside. Persistent high water kept the church closed for a week. During the worst of the storm, more than three quarters of the city was under water.

Anyone visiting the basilica today can still see the consequences, even in good weather. Damp is not the biggest problem in a drama of this sort; worse is the salt. Brackish water is sucked into masonry and creeps upwards, and in 2019, in the mosaics and marble slabs of St Mark's, grains of salt could be found up to a height of 12 metres. Each time the seawater evaporates, the crystals expand and cause tiny explosions in the stonework. The salt then draws in water again, in a perpetual cycle. The far-sighted Venetians built their houses on a substrate of watertight limestone from Istria, but now water regularly rises above those foundations all over the city, causing bricks to disintegrate. 'The Serenissima is like a very sick person', one journalist wrote.[1]

*Acqua alta*, high water, was historically a recurring phenomenon that Venetians learned to live with, and to some degree it results from subsidence of the ground.[2] In 2020 a system of mobile gates was completed that can temporarily close off the lagoon from the Adriatic Sea. But its engineers failed to take account of one important factor: because of the continually rising sea level, the frequency and severity of floods is increasing. According to a recent report, even in a scenario in which the warming of the earth is limited to 2°C above pre-industrial temperatures, the water level in Venice will rise by more than 30 cm by the end of the century (and if warming is allowed to reach 4°C, the rise will amount to 1.8 metres).[3] In short, the likelihood that the city, founded in the year 421, will stand for as long as it has stood up to now is small.[4] Visit Venice while you can! In 2019 a photo went viral showing tourists with bulging bags from expensive Italian clothing brands wading up to their waists through the water on St Mark's Square. 'It seems easier to imagine the end of the world than the end of capitalism', the commentary ran (a quote from Marxist literary theorist Fredric Jameson). A virtuoso architecture student has since thought up a solution: a network of footbridges that will enable wealthy tourists to stand and stare as the city is slowly swallowed by the sea.[5]

However dramatic, the fate of Venice is merely a symptom of a larger problem that historical heritage is now having to contend with all over the world: the climate crisis. For me personally, images of the 2019 disaster made concrete something of which I had previously had only a vague suspicion. I was born in the 'Venice of the North', Amsterdam, a city of centuries-old canals that now faces severe climate-related problems. As an art historian, I have regularly guided students, schoolchildren and members of the public around the multiplicity of museums and historical buildings in my native city. I have often watched visitors experience their encounters with this heritage as an intense, emotional, almost physical immersion in history. But over the past few years I have noticed that a new dimension has been added to my students' view of the past. They have a grim awareness that this impressive patrimony may in fact have had its day.

I wrote this book in an attempt to grasp the confusing mixture of feelings and ideas that encountering heritage in the twenty-first century brings with it: the delights of art, an awareness of history, and climate-related uncertainty. There is an immense wealth of literature about the consequences of climate change for the natural world, but less has been written about its effects on heritage. How should the sense of history that contributes so much to the value of monuments and museums be considered afresh in a time when the fragility of our heritage confronts us with the future?

I begin with a look at the technical details, in chapter 1. How exactly is heritage worldwide, from New York to Easter Island, threatened by a climate crisis that is bringing not just floods but increasing heat, drought, fires, storms, damp, invasive species and thawing permafrost? In chapter 2 the central question concerns how serious the loss of artworks and architecture is, when set against damage to nature and the environment, to animals, humans and society. In the light of the ecological and economic devastation the climate crisis will inflict, especially in the Global South, it may seem perverse to focus on Renaissance villas in Tuscany. But love of heritage is not confined to Europe. Furthermore, the history of heritage conservation includes inspiring examples of our capacity as a species to address the challenges of climate change.

Chapter 3 presents a historical overview. For centuries, art and nature have interacted in fruitful ways. Some civilizations flourished during the climate change of the Little Ice Age. After the Industrial Revolution, however, artists closed their eyes to drastic transformations of the natural environment, and it is only recently that we have seen an end to this 'derangement' of the artistic mentality. Chapter 4 examines how, in a general sense, thinking about history is changing during the Anthropocene, with climate-related developments coming thick and fast. While in the previous century there was much theorizing about the end of art history, we are now having to deal with the actual loss of the past.

Finally, in chapters 5, 6 and 7, I present three solutions, three ways to preserve historical heritage in an era of climate change: transform, digitize and reconstruct. None of the three is entirely satisfying, but they do form a starting point for cultural triage over the coming decades. Heritage professionals, both in times of sudden calamity and in their long-term planning, will have to make choices. How, where and why should heritage be moved, adapted or abandoned?

To anyone who wonders why I have written a book about historical heritage rather than about polar bears, bees, coral reefs or nature more broadly, I would like to point out that we have known about the impact of the climate crisis on the environment since 1972. That was the year in which the report *The Limits to Growth* was published by a group of scientists who had gathered in Rome (the Eternal City, we used to think; a name we now know to be misguided, see chapter 1). Fifty years on, we have taken hardly any action in response and the worst-case scenarios seem to be playing out. This book therefore makes a fresh attempt to tell the most important story of our time.

By focusing not on nature but on historical heritage, I aim to address other sensitivities and perhaps even to mobilize new groups. As an art historian, I could never bring myself to glue my head to Vermeer's *Girl with a Pearl Earring* and then throw tinned tomatoes over it. But I can well understand the sentiments of the Belgian climate activist who decided to do exactly that in 2022, and whose protest was reported all over the world. So instead of a can of tomatoes, I opened up my computer and started to type.

# 1. Historical heritage threatened by the climate crisis

*The Collapse of Western Civilization* is the title of a 2014 book by Naomi Oreskes and Erik Conway. It opens with a map of 'the nation formerly known as the Netherlands', showing a strip of land along the German border as all that remains of the country in 2300.[1] Much of Belgium, too, has disappeared. The book is fictional but based on fact – the authors are renowned American science journalists – and it illustrates how interesting a case the Low Countries are when it comes to climate change. More recently, *The Economist* made a specific, non-fictional calculation: because of the climate crisis, houses in Amsterdam will become harder to insure and face a decline in value of 40 per cent.[2]

The Dutch capital is famous for the ring of canals around its seventeenth-century city centre, recognized by UNESCO as a World Heritage Site. With its tall gabled houses, arched bridges and impressive municipal buildings, Amsterdam has survived in a remarkably pristine condition the wars and urban development that have blighted many other European cities. But now the Dutch are the proverbial canaries in a global coalmine. They will have to accustom themselves to doing without not just their immaterial heritage, such as skating on natural ice, but much of their material heritage as well. Other low-lying parts of the country, including The Hague, Rotterdam and the old cities of the Dutch 'Golden Age', are no less vulnerable to rises in sea level. How much time is left before the existing system of dykes, drainage and artificially raised ground levels no longer suffices is unclear – decades, a century, two centuries or more? – but the bottom line is plain as day. Much of the country's heritage has stood for longer than it can hope to survive into the future.

## DUTCH CANARIES IN A GLOBAL COALMINE

Let us start by replacing science fiction with a proper historical and technical analysis.

Just as New Orleans was built in the Mississippi Delta and Venice in a lagoon where the Po flows into the Adriatic Sea, Amsterdam came into being in the delta of the Rhine, the biggest river in Western Europe. All three cities were made possible by drastic artificial 'terraforming'. Ever since the Middle Ages, the Dutch have drained land to form polders, efforts that culminated in the building of the huge Afsluitdijk in 1932, which transformed an open sea, the Zuider Zee, into the largest freshwater lake in Europe, the IJsselmeer. Artificial land reclamation has created a situation in which large parts of the Netherlands are now below sea level. Almost 60 per cent of the country would flood were it not for its extensive system of dykes and pumps.[3]

As a result of these historical interventions, the Netherlands regards itself as the best-protected delta in the world, but climate change is making the situation harder to control – and the consequences for heritage are already clearly visible.

Water management in Amsterdam requires the coordination of several factors, and the balance is becoming increasingly difficult to sustain. Like much of the western Netherlands, this region is a land of peat, its spongy and damp soils formed out of vegetable matter that has died and only partially decomposed. Heavier buildings sink irretrievably into them. Below the peat, however, are firmer layers of clay and sand. As early as 1493, an anonymous Carthusian monk described how in Amsterdam the churches and almost all the houses, as well as the city walls, were built on foundations of wooden piles between 11 and 17 metres long.[4] This method of creating an artificial underground forest was perfected in the seventeenth century by those who constructed the largest non-religious building in Europe at the time, the Town Hall on Dam Square (now the Royal Palace), a stately colossus in classical style (figure 1). As well as the blocks of German, Danish, French and Italian stone imported to build it, more than 13,659 wooden piles from Norway were shipped in. Those who commissioned the building liked to stress that they had achieved something truly great; in the classical splendour of the central hall, visitors still walk across marble floors inlaid with maps of the world, beneath Atlas carrying the globe on his shoulders, the planets orbiting around it – a representation of the vastness of space and time.

The Town Hall surpassed the Seven Wonders of the World of antiquity, claimed British art lover William Aglionby in his *Present State of the United Provinces of the Low-Countries* (1667). He was referring not just to its classical design but to its wooden foundations.[5] The Dutch were 'the most expert in Europe' at erecting large structures in marshy regions, wrote fellow Briton John Evelyn.[6] Men of the stature of Tsar Peter the Great of Russia, Tuscany's Prince Cosimo III de Medici and French minister Jean-Baptiste Colbert sent their engineers to the Netherlands to examine how it was done. In a popular emblem book of 1614 called *Sinnepoppen*, the technique was elucidated succinctly: '*Daer de natuer heeft ramp, Set het vernuft een klamp*' ('Where nature fails, ingenuity prevails').[7] An accompanying print shows how, with much collaborative labour, pile drivers were operated by hand (figure 2). Later extensions to the city were created in the same way as the ring of canals at its heart. Even the trees were planted on piles to prevent them from sinking under their own weight.[8]

The city's many thousands of piles can withstand the passing of centuries in a wet environment, but they begin to rot as soon as they come into contact with oxygen in the air. The risk of this happening increases as the groundwater level drops, which is precisely what happens nowadays as a result of sustained summer droughts. More and more Amsterdam homeowners find themselves forced to put new concrete foundations under their houses, an expensive operation that means the entire ground floor needs to be stripped out. Even tourists will not have failed to notice that many canal walls and bridges are suffering from unstable foundations and already need to be propped up with temporary structures. When timber piles are replaced by concrete and use is made of the opportunity to add a cellar, a new problem is created. Water could always flow fairly freely between the piles supporting the city, but concrete walls block it.

In the past, Amsterdam was able to regulate the water level by means of pumps and sluices in the surrounding polderland. But now periods of drought alternate with times when the groundwater is too high. It rains more often and for longer; the Royal Netherlands Meteorological Institute (KNMI) predicts that winter precipitation in the Netherlands will increase by almost 30 per cent by around 2085.[9] The same applies in neighbouring countries, which further magnifies the problem. The Netherlands as a whole is a large delta area for the vast body of water that drains from the Alps into the Rhine (figure 3). Three other major rivers, the Meuse, the Ems and the Scheldt, also make their way to the sea here. River water flows along the Amsterdam–Rhine Canal and across (and under) the city before eventually reaching the sea via the North Sea Canal. There its flow is regulated in both directions by the largest pumping station in Europe, at IJmuiden. Heavier rainfall already means that the level of the rivers can be up to a third higher in winter than in summer. This seasonal fluctuation is no small matter. Between the extremely wet January of 2018 and the subsequent record drought of the following summer, the level of the Rhine at the Dutch–German border fell by 8 metres.[10] Downstream, in Amsterdam, keeping the canals navigable is an increasing challenge.

As well as an unstable water level, the polders around the capital city are subject to a further change that compounds the problem. When peaty soil is stripped of its vegetation and drained by a network of ditches, it shrinks. Contact with oxygen causes bacteria to start breaking down the organic material that has built up over thousands of years. This rotting process, which incidentally releases a large amount of carbon dioxide ($CO_2$), means that the polders literally evaporate. The ground has been sinking by about a centimetre per year for several centuries. Over the past thousand years, the Netherlands has sunk by 6 metres and the problem is currently exacerbated by our hotter summers, during which farmers pump up groundwater for their crops. The land to the south of Amsterdam is now the lowest-lying in the country: 6.7 metres below sea level at its deepest point.

Not far away is the historic city of Gouda – world-famous for its cheese – which has been slowly sinking ever since it was founded in the eleventh century. It stands on a tidal river (the Hollandse IJssel), so it is in direct contact with the sea. The land surface is getting closer and closer to the level of the groundwater, but it is impossible to pump the water away because the centre of the city, as in Amsterdam, is supported by wooden piles. This combination of factors is disastrous, and the future of buildings like Gouda's Town Hall, its weighing house and its Church of St John, famous for its sixteenth-century stained-glass windows, is uncertain. In 2021, Museum Gouda asked an architecture bureau to come up with a vision of the future in which the church would stand on stilts and the rest of the town centre would become a paradise for divers. Although the accompanying film was intended as a joke (floating Gouda cheeses provide public transport), the underlying tone was deeply tragic.[11]

Even the higher-lying eastern part of the country is suffering from a shifting and settling of its sandy soils. One early victim was the fifteenth-century Oude Kerk in Borne. Its walls began to crack in 2018 and its rare frescos of the life of Christ, with unusual scenes such as the *Tree of Jesse* (Jesus' family tree), were damaged. Dramas of this kind inspired Slovenian researcher Sandra Fatorić to assess the risks facing all 64,000 Dutch buildings listed as nationally important, hazards resulting from a combination of the factors we have looked at: flooding, falling groundwater levels and subsiding land. Six thousand national heritage sites are exposed to the risk of flooding; 12,000 are very likely to suffer damage to their wooden foundations; and 1,000 are affected by subsidence of the soil. Fatorić advocated a national policy aimed at protecting heritage against climate change.[12]

The urgency of her plea became clear sooner than expected, when in 2021 exceptional rainfall in the southern Dutch province of Limburg caused the rivers to burst their banks. In Valkenburg, the thirteenth-century Church of St Nicholas and St Barbara took in so much water that the furniture floated. A life-sized statue of St Nicholas fell backwards into the water, and the right arm, its powerless fingers extended in blessing, broke off. Surveying the devastation sat a mourning Madonna, with the body of the dead Christ in her lap; her sizeable pedestal was all that prevented her feet from getting wet (figure 4). Elsewhere in Limburg too, because the water was unable to drain away into the province's rocky ground, the damage was great. The castles of Hoensbroek and Hartelstein, the remains of Roman bridges across the Meuse and even the collection of Museum Valkenburg were not spared. The Netherlands may be famous as the best-protected delta in the world, but the intensity and speed with which the water came surprised everyone. As the dyke wardens reported, despite ceaseless investment in dyke monitoring and drainage, the floods exceeded every imagined scenario.

## A BATHTUB SURROUNDED BY WATER

All this leaves aside the most fundamental change: more and more water is coming from the sea. The western part of the Netherlands is a 'bathtub surrounded by water', land that would flood were it not protected by dykes. Briefly put, the system is not designed to cope with a higher sea level. At this point we should be able to assume everyone knows the facts: the oceans are warming and therefore increasing in volume, so sea levels are rising worldwide, all the more so as the ice melts. The contribution of thawing ice is hard to quantify as yet, but probably with time most glaciers in mountainous regions and the ice sheets of Greenland and icecaps to the west of the South Pole will largely disappear.

In 2021 the IPCC (Intergovernmental Panel on Climate Change), an international consortium of climate scientists, summarized the research to date. By 2100, average global sea levels will have risen by between 0.5 and 1.1 metres, and 'due to deep uncertainty in ice-sheet processes' a rise of 2 metres by 2100 and 5 metres by 2150 'cannot be ruled out'.[13] This will not happen at the same rate everywhere. For the Dutch coast, the KNMI predicts that if $CO_2$ emissions are not drastically reduced, a sea-level rise of 1 metre will take place in the period 2090 to 2140. If the collapse of ice cliffs is taken into account, then that same 1-metre rise will occur by about 2070, reaching 2 metres within another twenty years after that. The rise will then continue for a long time, since climate change has set processes in motion that will affect the planet for millennia.[14]

The solution is not simply to raise the dykes. For a start, the mouths of the rivers currently form the 'holes' in the Dutch sea defences. So at every high tide in the North Sea, the water level in the rivers increases. The rise in the median sea level means that the water is pushed further inland. At around a rise of 2 metres, the limits of the system of polders, dykes and sand suppletion come within sight. It is technically possible to close off the mouths of the Rhine, the Meuse, the Scheldt and the Ems, and use bigger and bigger pumps to move the water flowing down the rivers, which will then be below sea level, over those coastal barriers. But that operation would be increasingly costly and energy-intensive, and at the same time become less and less effective as more salt water seeps under the dykes.

A second problem is that because of the dykes, the land cannot grow in response to the tides as it has done over millennia. In natural circumstances, a river flows less quickly as it approaches the coast, so sediment sinks to the bottom: first the gravel, then sand and finally, close to the mouth, clay and silt. When the sea advances, the rivers leave their deposits further inland, so a delta automatically adjusts to its changed coastline. This silting up process is obstructed by the existence of dykes, so more river water has to be pumped upwards to get it into the sea. As far back as 1996, the Dutch branch of the World Wide Fund for Nature (WWF) raised the alarm by publishing a report called *Meegroeien met de zee* (Grow along with the sea): 'It's true that higher dykes and larger pumps can turn the tide for a while, but ultimately this technology only brings us closer to Atlantis. Hard sea defences further disturb the balance between water, sediment and salt in the Dutch coastal zone.'[15]

Unfortunately, few of those 1996 recommendations have been acted upon, and the Netherlands is currently losing sediment more rapidly than it is deposited in the delta. As a result, more land is being lost than is being created. Dykes are clearly not a long-term solution. A diverse group of geo-scientists at Utrecht University therefore recently concluded that we need to consider other options. Sea-level expert Roderik van de Wal, who contributed to the IPCC report, and meteorologist Michiel van den Broeke write that we need to prepare for a future in which we withdraw to higher ground. Their colleague, sediment specialist Maarten Kleinhans, makes the following claim:

> We can cope with one metre, or maybe two, using a combination of sand suppletion, dikes and natural silting. So if governments were to actually abide by the Paris agreement [to stay below 1.5 degrees of warming], this is the scenario we'd use. . . . But if we continue on the current track, it's a completely unrealistic idea. I totally agree with the projection that, if the sea level rises by more than one and a half or two metres, we're not going to make it with this country. We can spray sand onto the beach to protect the Randstad [the metropolitan area around Amsterdam], but that would be ignoring the salt water ingress under the dunes, the low-lying peat areas, . . . and above all: the fact that the sea doesn't stop at the Dutch border! Rising sea levels will impede the outflow of rivers, resulting in high river-water levels as far inland as the border with Germany, and sand suppletion in the port of Rotterdam wouldn't be very useful at that point, to cite just one example.[16]

Some of what are now the primary dykes will be cut through and older dykes further back will take over their role. (The

Dutch traditionally distinguish between dykes called *wakers* [watchers] and, further inland, *dromers* [dreamers] and *slapers* [sleepers].) Physical geographer Kim Cohen has sketched a new coastline in which the north-west of the Netherlands and parts of Belgium are given back to the sea – including the historical cities of Amsterdam, The Hague, Rotterdam, Antwerp and Ghent (figure 5).

Unsurprisingly, hydraulic engineers have not been standing still. They have seized upon the physicists' prediction to draw up detailed plans for projects such as the 'Haakse Zeedijk', a wide sea dyke to be placed a maximum of 25 kilometres off the current Dutch coast. To achieve the full effect it would need to start at the cliffs of Calais and run past Belgium, the Netherlands, northern Germany and Denmark all the way to the high ground at Gothenburg in Sweden. A good deal more ambitious yet is the plan for a Northern European Enclosure Dam (NEED), a system that would close off the English Channel between Britain and France and the sea between Scotland and Norway, turning the entire North Sea and Baltic Sea into one big freshwater lake (figure 6).[17] This lake might even be drained, enabling immense land reclamation. Such vastly expensive projects are so utopian in character that they actually serve to illustrate the gravity of the problem: if radical measures are not taken, the continued existence of all the land at or below the current sea level is at risk.

Leaving aside all the social and economic costs of these new plans, for a story about the future of the past, the bottom line is that much of our historical real estate – including the cities associated with what is still known as the Dutch 'Golden Age', from Leiden where Rembrandt was born to Delft where all the members of the Dutch royal family are interred – has seen its best days. It should be clear that whatever technical solutions are developed over coming decades, however much is invested in dykes, in artificial means of raising the ground level and in drainage, and no matter how else we adjust to the changing sea, some of our heritage will have to be adapted, relocated or abandoned. I look at several possible strategies for achieving this in chapters 5, 6 and 7.

## HERITAGE WORLDWIDE UNDER THREAT

All over the world, heritage is threatened by the climate crisis. As well as increasing drought and rainfall, and rising sea levels, we face higher air humidity, stronger winds, more frequent fires and storms, new invasive plant and animal species, more ultraviolet light and worse air pollution. The alarm was first raised in 2005, when the UN's World Heritage Committee published a warning that we must 'seriously consider the potential impacts of climate change' and 'take early action in response to these potential impacts'.[18] Other institutions followed its example, including the International Council on Monuments and Sites (ICOMOS), which in 2020 announced a climatological and ecological emergency.[19] In 2024 the World Monuments Fund made a considerable sum (15 million dollars) available for repairing damage caused by climate change.

The following summary of risks is no doubt incomplete, and not all predictions are equally likely to be borne out.[20] Nor do Old Testament-style scenarios make for cheerful reading. But anyone willing to face the facts will benefit from this global survey.

## HIGHER TEMPERATURES, MORE DROUGHTS AND RAIN

We begin with those things that are currently most vulnerable: archaeological relics, especially at underwater locations that are affected by changing currents and higher temperatures. The wrecks of Viking ships in the Baltic Sea, undisturbed for centuries, are now being consumed by shipworms that thrive in warmer water. Objects deliberately left underground by archaeologists to conserve them are becoming unstable because the soil is experiencing greater extremes of wetness and dryness, and its chemical composition is changing. In the peatlands of Britain, for example, which are rapidly drying out, more than 20,000 sites from the Stone Age, Bronze Age and Roman periods are under threat. Particularly dramatic is the condition of sites next to Hadrian's Wall, the barrier built to protect the Roman Empire from attack by the Picts; over the next few years, archaeologists will scramble to save as many of the buried artefacts as they can.[21] Another example is the classical Greek city of Sybaris in southern Italy, founded in the seventh century BCE. The extensive, partially excavated site is being severely damaged by rising groundwater. In 2013 it turned into a quagmire when a nearby river burst its banks, and experts believe it has suffered 'inestimable, irreparable' damage.[22] In that same year the excavations at nearby Metapontum, Pythagoras' city, were also flooded.

Even Rome can no longer be called the 'Eternal City', now that the climate crisis has started to hit home. During a storm in 2024, when the metro system filled with rainwater, the Arch of Constantine, a triumphal arch next to the Colosseum, was struck by lightning, causing fragments of stone to fly off it. As far back as 2016, a section of the ancient city walls from the time of Emperor Aurelian collapsed in heavy rain, and two years later the same happened to the legendary Tarpeian Rock on the slope of the Capitoline Hill. The Roman Triglio Aqueduct (near Taranto) met a similar fate. The historical Italian fortified towns in particular, sited on hilltops, run the risk of severe subsidence of the kind that occurred in 2014 at Volterra, when dozens of metres of its mediaeval city walls disappeared into the depths, at the Fortress of San Leo (near Rimini), which stands on a clifftop the north side of which gave way, and at the picturesque Civitā di Bagnoregio.

The Italian Institute for Environmental Protection and Research (ISPRA) periodically carries out a risk analysis of landslides and floods, which are happening more frequently because of increasing rainfall. In 2021 it estimated that of the more than 213,000 Italian historical monuments, 38,000 are in danger of suffering landslides and 50,000 at risk of flooding (figure 7). In Rome alone, 2,000 monuments are exposed to the possibility of floods that predictions used to say would occur 'once in 500 years', especially in the low-lying zone of the Campus Martius, where famous sites include the Pantheon and the Piazza Navona.[23]

Greater extremes of moisture and dryness bring another risk with them too: an increase in salt, which is especially threatening to the even older heritage of Mesopotamia in what is now Iraq, home to the most ancient of cities. The United Nations estimates that mean annual temperatures in the region will rise by 2°C by 2050, with more days when the thermometer tops 50°. The soils and groundwater of Mesopotamia have always been naturally rich in salt. Since the rivers are bringing less water, the concentration of salt in the architectural monuments is rising to the point where they become unstable. One example is the World Heritage Site of Babylon, where the 2,600-year-old bricks of the Temple of Ishtar, the Sumerian goddess of war and love, are already covered in a layer of salt. Salt is also accumulating in the depths of the thick walls, and when it crystallizes, it causes the bricks to crack and break apart.[24]

Most vulnerable to the new extremes, however, is Africa. In Egypt, which is warming at twice the rate of the global average, the once pink granite of many of the monuments built by the pharaohs has already turned grey. Drought and heat are causing subsidence and cracks.[25] The combination of desertification and increased rainfall is damaging the centuries-old adobe architecture of Mauritania and Mali, including the famous Sankoré Mosque in Timbuktu. In Sudan the pyramids of the Kush kingdom, which was dominant from the eighth century BCE to the fifth century of our era (also known as the World Heritage of al-Bajrawiya), need protection against more severe flooding of the Nile. Another site recognized by UNESCO is Sana'a in Yemen, one of the oldest cities in the world, occupied continually for more than 2,000 years. According to legend, it was founded by Shem, one of the sons of Noah. Because the architecture is largely made of mud, it is literally washing away under increasingly extreme rainfall.

## THAWING PERMAFROST

The High North is plagued by a different problem, namely the thawing of the permafrost that used to remain frozen throughout the summer. Since 2007, rising temperatures in Canada have disrupted the historical whaling settlements on Herschel Island (Qikiqtaruk in Inuit). In a cold, dry climate, their wooden structures have lasted for well over a hundred years, but they are now being affected by rot and mould, while gravestones are toppling and coffins floating to the surface.[26] Entire cities have been built on permafrost, such as Yakutsk in Russia, and now the thaw has set in. The icy cold of Siberia has preserved a landscape of grave mounds and rock paintings created by the Scythian nomadic culture since 1500 BCE. Rising temperatures are expected to have damaged the frozen graves irrevocably by the middle of this century.[27]

## STORMS AND FIRES

Worldwide risks that are harder to predict, but no less harmful, take the form of storms and fires. Much of the old centre of New Orleans was destroyed in 2005 by Hurricane Katrina, and seven years later Hurricane Sandy caused the Statue of Liberty and the nearby Ellis Island Museum to be closed to the public for months. In 2017, Hurricane Maria was relentless in its assault on the cultural institutions of Puerto Rico, including the Museum of Contemporary Art. The director eventually had holes drilled in the galleries to protect them against mould.[28]

The 2019 forest fires in California came dangerously close to the famous Getty Museum in Los Angeles, and a year later Canberra's National Gallery had to close its doors to prevent smoke from wildfires from damaging the collection. It will eventually become harder to protect heritage in more isolated locations against fire, such as the impressive cities of the Pueblo culture in Cliff Palace, Colorado, which were abandoned in about 1300 CE after long periods of drought. Those involved with their preservation dread to think what might happen in this highly flammable landscape.

## THE RISING SEA

Then there is the rising level of the sea. As things stand, coastal locations worldwide, whose treasures include fortresses, temples and graveyards, are the most directly threatened. Examples include the ruins of the Gereza Fort on Kilwa Kisiwani in Tanzania and the imposing Moai, the monolithic human figures on Easter Island (called Rapa Nui in the local Polynesian language).[29] The 5,000-year-old prehistoric village of Skara Brae on Orkney, Scotland, which once stood a kilometre from the coast, is now on the beach, with winter storms pushing seawater higher and higher up the specially built dyke. In the winter of 2021 the sea swallowed part of Hurst Castle in Milford on Sea in England, built by Henry VIII. The Tower of London and the Palace of Westminster are protected for the time being against unusually high tides by the Thames Barrier. When it was completed in 1982, estimates suggested the barrier would have to be closed two or three times a year, but in 2013 it was raised fifty times in a single winter, and it will soon be in need of a substantial technical upgrade.[30]

The best-known victim, however, was described in the prologue: Venice. Since 2020 the city has been protected against storm surges by a moveable barrier with the biblical name of Moses; in Italian it is called Mosè, which is also an acronym for Modulo Sperimentale Elettromeccanico (Experimental Electro-Mechanical Module). Unfortunately, this huge, technically ambitious project, for which planning started in 1975, was not designed with a view to rising sea levels and it will alleviate the problem only temporarily. In fact it is possible that by 2100 the historical city will be under water for good. One solution is to permanently close off the lagoon from the sea, but that would mean the loss of the area's unique ecosystem. As things stand, the wetland vegetation in the lagoon forms a buffer against flooding, while at the same time absorbing a large amount of $CO_2$ from the atmosphere.[31] Another practical problem is that Venice does not have a sewerage system; human waste goes straight into the water and washes out into the open sea with the tides. Closing off the lagoon might preserve the city for tourism, but it would spell the end for its residents.

In 2018 the authoritative scientific journal *Nature Communications* published an estimate of the risks to World Heritage around the Mediterranean Sea between now and 2100.[32] Researchers at the University of Kiel modelled what would happen by 2100 to the region's UNESCO sites under four possible sea-level-rise scenarios. It became clear that no fewer than thirty-seven sites are at risk of flooding and forty-two of being damaged by coastal erosion (figure 8). After Venice, it will be the turn of neighbouring Aquileia, and of Ravenna, the former capital of the Western Roman Empire, famous for its Byzantine mosaics. Next comes the Croatian coast, with the ancient cathedral city of Poreč and the palace of Emperor Diocletian in Split. The ruins of Carthage in Tunisia, the crusaders' chief port of Acre in Israel, the ancient Temple of Artemis at Ephesus in Turkey and even the modernist architecture of Tel Aviv are likewise vulnerable to rising sea levels. Incidentally, the research did not look at places for which countries have never applied for World Heritage status, such as the Aegean coast of Turkey, an important archaeological region (think of ancient Troy) that unquestionably finds itself in the risk zone.

An area that faces a comparable threat is the south-eastern United States. According to a survey in the scientific journal *PLOS One*, a rise in the sea level of just 1 metre would flood more than 13,000 heritage locations, from the 7,000-year-old archaeological remains left by Native Americans in Florida to the colonial settlement of Jamestown Island in Virginia (figure 9).[33] One example of a site that is currently at critical risk is Pockoy Island in South Carolina, where since 2017 archaeologists and volunteers have been engaged in a battle to salvage artefacts 4,300 years old. The island is eroding at a rate of 15 metres a year.

It is the lower-lying regions of Asia, however, that will be worst hit by flooding. If current projections are realized, Bangladesh, Thailand and Vietnam will barely be able to hold their own against rising waters over the coming decades. As early as 2011, for instance, floods in Thailand reached hundreds of temples in the province of Ayutthaya (figure 10). The fifteenth-century city of Hội An, recognized by UNESCO as World Heritage, has suffered extensive flooding every year since 2017, and if dykes are not built it will be unable to withstand the expected rise in the sea level.[34]

## MUSEUMS

Ultimately, even objects conserved by prestigious institutions cannot be safeguarded against damage by climate change. Of all European cities, Florence is probably the best prepared to defend itself against flooding. The Bardini Museum, for instance, with its Renaissance artworks, close to the Arno River, has already been provided with a moveable plastic dyke that comes into operation when the water rises. In the Santa Croce Museum, paintings are now attached to an ingenious pulley system, so that they can be lifted several metres within seconds. The Louvre in Paris, sited dangerously close to the River Seine, actually resorted to moving 250,000 artworks to a safe location in northern France in 2021 – so it is somewhat ironic that one of the biggest sponsors of the museum is oil company Total, against which activists have repeatedly demonstrated in vain.[35] No less ironic is the fact that the Koch family in America, vastly rich oil barons and climate-change deniers, are the main sponsors of the museum of natural history in Washington, the Smithsonian, which continually has to monitor the threat to its collection from flooding.[36]

Temperature fluctuations and even the increase in ultraviolet light increasingly disturb the meticulously adjusted climatic conditions needed to conserve paintings and sculptures, as became clear during a heatwave in 2017 that, as is the tradition in Italy, was given a telling name: Lucifer. When its air-conditioning failed, the world-famous Uffizi Gallery in Florence had to close its doors. In 2022 the same fate struck the British Museum, generously sponsored for decades by British Petroleum (BP).

## COMBINATIONS OF FACTORS

For many locations the future is hard to predict, since they are facing a combination of threats: heatwaves, downpours, floods, fires and air pollution. Moreover, climate change can be a multiplier of the threats that cultural heritage has always had to combat. This is the case for the twelfth-century Cambodian temple complex Angkor Wat, famous as the biggest religious monument in the world. Mass tourism has used so much groundwater that the earth has subsided, destabilizing the architecture as well as making the site more susceptible to flooding. Such combinations can create a situation in which the deterioration of heritage becomes exponential. When an ecosystem is out of balance, its local heritage will not remain intact. Take for example the thousand or more rock paintings in the Serra da Capivara in Brazil, the most extensive and oldest prehistoric site in the Americas, which UNESCO has declared to be World Heritage. As well as fires, drought and erosion, termites and other insects are a growing threat to the painted figures, which date from between 6,000 and 12,000 years ago.[37]

It is hard to make predictions about fatal tipping points in this ongoing deterioration, or to anticipate all potential new technical methods of protecting, transforming and relocating objects. But it is certainly possible to think about what these changes mean for our assumptions about cultural heritage and its future. The next chapter poses a question: Why do we want to focus on historical patrimony at all, when the consequences of the climate crisis for nature and society are so much more profound?

# 2. Why heritage?

Why does cultural heritage matter? Is it not far more important to concern ourselves with animals that are dying out? We are probably talking about dozens, perhaps hundreds of species per day, which means we are living through the sixth mass extinction, the first since the loss of the dinosaurs.[1] Should we not be concentrating on disappearing coral reefs, desertification, crop failures, forced human migration, and all the related economic and social harms, especially in the Global South? To clarify the importance of historical heritage we can look back to an episode during the Second World War.

When in 1944 American and British troops were attempting to chase the Nazis out of southern Italy, their advance stalled just below Rome, at the Monte Cassino monastery. Built in the foothills of the Apennine Mountains, the monastery provided a view across dozens of kilometres of the Latin Valley, all the way to the coast. Allied high command believed it was functioning as a lookout post in the Gustav Line, the German defensive line that ran right across Italy. On the morning of 15 February, Allied aviators dropped more than a thousand tonnes of explosives on the sixth-century monastery, leaving it and its church and collection of paintings a smoking ruin. A film held by British Pathé shows the power of the explosions. The voice-over states that 'the whole civilized world will regret the destruction of the monastery on Monte

Cassino, one of the most interesting buildings, possibly, in the whole of Europe'.[2]

A few days later, a passionate article appeared in the conservative British periodical *The Spectator*. Sir Harold Nicolson MP (1886–1968), famous as a historian, journalist and novelist, fulminated against the bombardment. Monte Cassino was a great work of art that could never be replaced. It would have been morally preferable, he believed, to have tolerated thousands of deaths. He made no exception of his own son, Nigel (1917–2004), who at the time was a serving soldier in the Eighth Army at Monte Cassino:

> It is to my mind desirable that such works [of major artistic value] should be preserved from destruction, even if their preservation entails the sacrifice of human lives. I should assuredly be prepared to be shot against a wall if I were certain that by such a sacrifice I could preserve the [famous thirteenth-century] Giotto frescoes; nor should I hesitate for an instant (were such a decision ever open to me) to save St. Mark's [Basilica in Venice] even if I were aware that by so doing I should bring death to my sons. . . . My attitude would be governed by a principle which is surely incontrovertible. The irreplaceable is more important than the replaceable, and the loss of even the most valued human life is ultimately less disastrous than the loss of something which in no circumstances can ever be created again.[3]

There is no reason not to take seriously Nicolson's readiness to sacrifice his life and those of his offspring. In the Second World War, the Allies as a rule took great care to spare historical heritage, for example in their extremely meticulous bombing of Florence. Nicolson was a sensitive soul, and it is no surprise to find that his youngest son, Benedict (1914–78), became a prominent art historian after the war and was appointed editor-in-chief of the stylish professional journal *The Burlington Magazine*. His studies of baroque painter Caravaggio are still regarded as standard works, and his phenomenal collection of photographs is held in the Netherlands Interuniversity Institute for Art History (NIKI) in Florence.[4]

That Florence was largely spared the devastation that befell Monte Cassino was not purely a result of the accuracy of the Allied pilots, incidentally. The Nazis too exhibited a remarkable reverence for historical heritage. When they withdrew from the city shortly before the British-American advance, they destroyed several bridges over the River Arno. General Albert Kesselring (1885–1960) could not, however, bring himself to blow up one particularly picturesque mediaeval bridge, the Ponte Vecchio, even though by doing so he could have delayed the enemy advance significantly. He limited himself to placing booby traps at the extreme ends of the bridge.

In reality there were no Germans in the monastery on the day Monte Cassino was bombed. The story goes that an error of translation had arisen. The British are said to have intercepted a coded message that included the abbreviation 'Abt' and interpreted it as a reference to an *Abtei*, abbey, instead of an *Abteilung*, battalion. It was precisely out of respect for heritage that the Nazis had not made Monte Cassino part of their fortified defensive lines, despite its advantageous strategic position. In all his Italian campaigns, Kesselring carefully avoided destroying historical heritage in cities such as Rome, Siena and Orvieto. He even had some of his own men shot after they were caught looting, and assumed that artworks would be better off under the control of the German central government than left in Italian hands. (He believed the Italians were all too ready to sell their heritage to foreign dealers.) When in 1945 the Allies drew up records of what had been lost in Italy, they concluded that its heritage had indeed suffered relatively little under German occupation. It seems Kesselring shared Nicolson's conviction that it was worth sacrificing human lives to preserve irreplaceable artistic and historical artefacts.

At the same time, this reverence for heritage ensured that the warring parties had no hesitation in attacking with great ferocity monuments belonging to the opposing side, precisely because they realized the extent to which this would hurt the enemy. The Nazis famously undertook 'Baedeker raids', in which pilots carrying the travel guides of that name sought out historical attractions in the south-east of England with the aim of reducing them to rubble; the little books conveniently indicated with one or two stars the importance of each site. The Allies in their turn had no compunction at all about carpet-bombing German heritage sites, and were in fact eager to see the total destruction of Dresden, as the ultimate culture-rich German city. In bombing it, according to Thomas Mann (1875–1955), the British became 'the apprentice who surpasses the master'.[5] The desolate prospect presented by the centres of so many German cities nowadays is a lasting reminder of this attitude towards the fundamental importance of historical heritage.[6]

## THE HERITAGE CRUSADE CONTINUES

Nicolson's accusation illustrates the extent to which, even in times of war (or indeed precisely then), people have felt emotionally committed to heritage. The eccentric aristocrat was not alone. In more recent years too, heritage has been at stake in military conflicts. One memorable example is the Stari Most, a bridge connecting two parts of the multi-ethnic city of Mostar in what is now Bosnia-Herzegovina, formerly part of the Ottoman Empire. Built in 1557 by a court architect to Sultan Suleiman the Magnificent (1494–1566), the bridge was seen as an outstanding example of Islamic architecture in the Balkans and a symbol of centuries-long ethnic harmony. During the Bosnian Civil War, residents of the city therefore tried to protect it against unguided projectiles with mattresses, planks of wood and car tyres. But on 9 November 1993, Croat paramilitaries used the Stari Most as a target (describing it as 'worth less than a Croat soldier's little finger'), and during a firefight lasting a day and a night it completely collapsed. The bridge was later rebuilt, with the financial support of UNESCO and countries including Turkey and the Netherlands.

Nowadays, Islamic heritage is under particular threat from the Chinese Communist Party, which is targeting mosques and graveyards in the western province of Xinjiang, of which two thirds have now been damaged or destroyed. The Party sees the presence of a Muslim minority as a threat to the country's cultural unity.[7] In Chinese history, this destructive tendency is not new, incidentally. The animosity used to be mainly a matter of class warfare: the material heritage of the top social class was smashed to bits during Mao's Cultural Revolution (or clandestinely sold abroad). Even Beijing's fifteenth-century city walls were ruthlessly demolished, and only two steadfast conservationists, Liang Sicheng (1901–72) and his wife Lin Huiyin (1904–55), both educated in the United States, managed to save the Forbidden City from even more widespread urban renewal. The tide now seems to have turned as far as the Chinese past is concerned, and the Party views with suspicion other ancient civilizations, such as that of Egypt, intent as it is on deploying Chinese heritage to highlight its own status on the world stage.[8] In one of the former imperial capitals, Datong, the modern city centre has been knocked down so that city walls and pagodas in the eleventh-century style can be erected again.

The term 'heritage crusade', coined by historian David Lowenthal (1923–2018) with his magisterial book *The Heritage Crusade and the Spoils of History* (1996), expresses rather well the intensity with which individuals, political groupings, minorities and states all over the world have focused upon historical heritage as a matter of life and death.[9] Lowenthal analyses the many possible, often contradictory arguments underlying the way objects and locations from the past have later been appropriated by specific groups to support the stories they tell about their own identities. A similar sacred fire has motivated those who, precisely in order to obviate the deployment of cultural heritage for political purposes, have tried to claim that there is such a thing as a shared heritage that belongs to all of humankind. With the Baedeker raids and Monte Cassino fresh in the memory, the United Nations decided in 1945 to set up a cultural organization, UNESCO (United Nations Educational, Scientific and Cultural Organization), to protect heritage worldwide in peaceful collaboration and thereby to reduce the likelihood of the outbreak of new wars.

The term 'World Heritage' was first used in 1965, at a conference in the White House. The American futurist R. Buckminster Fuller (1895–1983), famous for his theory of 'spaceship earth', where humans can survive only by sharing the planet's resources in concert, introduced it along with a renowned art historian at Yale University, Vincent Scully (1920–2017), and artist John McHale (1922–78). The threesome proclaimed that the cultural diversity of the earth must be protected as a universal resource comparable to oil or gas.[10] This fossil metaphor, used to characterize World Heritage as a global common good, testifies to a well-honed capacity to look ahead. The fact that there is a limit to the use of fossil fuels is now just as broadly accepted as the fragility of historical heritage. But the insight that fuel use can be a *cause* of the loss of heritage still belonged in those days to the relatively distant future.

The 'common goods', or more briefly the 'commons', are resources that can be used by all members of a group or society. Nowadays the term 'global commons' usually refers to the oceans, the atmosphere or the polar regions. In the 1960s the United Nations was referring to a wider, more idealistic principle that was also applied to a clean environment, stable financial markets, peace, security and health – and, according to Buckminster Fuller, cultural heritage. The ideal of World Heritage was intended to create a global reservoir of knowledge about all the cultural achievements of humankind that would be accessible to everyone. In 1972, at its World Heritage Convention, UNESCO established a mechanism for protecting heritage worldwide. In an introductory statement, it laid down that 'deterioration or disappearance of any item of the cultural or natural heritage constitutes a harmful impoverishment of the heritage of all the nations of the world'.[11]

Over the decades since then, more than 800 locations have been given the status of World Heritage, with Italy and China the best-endowed countries. Since 2005, UNESCO has based its decisions on ten criteria that an object or site must meet to be considered for such a status. The first five are as follows. Nominated properties must:

(i) represent a masterpiece of human creative genius;
(ii) exhibit an important interchange of human values . . . on developments in architecture or technology, monumental arts, town-planning or landscape design;
(iii) bear a unique . . . testimony to a cultural tradition or to a civilization which is living or which has disappeared;
(iv) be an outstanding example of a type of building, architectural or technological ensemble or landscape which illustrates (a) significant stage(s) in human history;

(v) be an outstanding example of a traditional human settlement, land-use, or sea-use which is representative of a culture . . . especially when it has become vulnerable under the impact of irreversible change.[12]

The remaining five criteria relate, among other things, to immaterial and natural heritage; UNESCO has given World Heritage status to more than 200 natural landscapes. These fall outside the scope of this book, which focuses primarily on historical heritage, which is to say on heritage with both a material and a cultural component. We will, however, look at several relevant differences between cultural and natural heritage in chapter 4. Suffice it to say, for now, that the essence of heritage resides in the existence of good reasons for insisting it must be preserved; objects, monuments and locations deserve to be cared for so that they can be passed on to subsequent generations in good condition. Clearly, for each of the UNESCO categories given above – from individual masterpiece to urban design or cultured landscape – the climate crisis can be a disturbing factor.

## INHERITING AND BEQUEATHING: THE NEW CHALLENGE

Lowenthal studied various threats to material heritage, such as war, mass tourism and commerce, recognizing that many centuries-old locations are barely able to cope with the way in which they are currently exploited as amusement parks. But in his 1996 book he makes not a single reference to climate change! This is a good illustration of the blind spot that experts on heritage had until recently where the climate is concerned. That same eleventh-century St Mark's Basilica for which Harold Nicolson was willing to sacrifice his sons' lives now stands in the front line of the climate crisis.

Lowenthal's blinkers in respect to climate change are particularly remarkable given that the rising sea level does not merely conflict with the preferences of British aesthetes; it represents a threat to the native soil of people all over the world. It is often the case that the oldest heritage is the most vulnerable to changes in the climate. The pre-Christian burial sites of Brittany and the Orkney Islands are disappearing as a result of coastal erosion. In Canada higher temperatures threaten thousands of locations that are important to the archaeology of the Inuit. In the south-east of the United States, rising sea levels threaten the heritage of Native Americans and the earliest European settlements.

The native soil, Lowenthal writes, is generally the most important element from which identities are derived. In *The Heritage Crusade* he pays a great deal of attention to the argument from *Blut und Boden* (blood and soil). For centuries the Europeans regarded their identities as profoundly wedded to the locations where they believed their bloodlines originated, not just land that was cultivated by their forebears but land they had defended with life and limb against foreign enemies. As Lowenthal indicates, identities are mental constructs and fabrications; in other words, self-images are all too often contrived or entirely invented. We therefore have a profound need of physical locations to which we can attach the stories we want to tell about ourselves. But how can that need be satisfied if the native lands and graves of our ancestors are flooded?

When in 2019 Notre Dame went up in flames, Parisians gathered on the street weeping, and sang hymns in a despairing choir. Their sorrow was not motivated by religion alone but by a sense of history: this was the church in which Napoleon crowned himself emperor. Venetians identify in a similar way with St Mark's Basilica, the traditional place where the newly elected ruler of their city state, the Doge, showed himself to his subjects. In the Netherlands a similar emotion attaches to the Nieuwe Kerk in Delft, where members of the Royal House of Orange-Nassau inter their dead.

In Venice and Delft, the future of this heritage is uncertain because of climate change. But an even more topical example of far-reaching damage to ancestral land is Togoru, a village on Viti Levu Island, Fiji, in the Pacific Ocean, founded in 1835 by an Irish migrant called James Dunn. The centuries-old graveyard, with the graves of the original founder of the settlement and his family, used to lie on the coast but is now under the sea. Only the largest tombstones and a few obelisks can still be seen above the surf, their inscriptions covered in barnacles or worn away by the waves (figure 11).[13] As early as 2004, descendant Kini Dunn, patriarch of the village, said, 'Our family has lived here in Togoru for as long as anyone can remember, and we cannot see ourselves moving – even though the ground our ancestors trod is gradually disappearing into the sea.'[14] Since then, the inhabitants of five neighbouring villages have sought refuge elsewhere. Kini's relative Anne Dunn, a former Miss Pacific Islands, also laments the loss of her roots in Togoru: 'Climate change to me means that we couldn't bury my father and my uncle at our traditional burial grounds. . . . It affects our identity. We are islanders, our unique way of living is being threatened.'[15] Anne has emerged as an eloquent activist; she spoke at the climate conference in Bonn in 2017, for example, which was chaired by Fiji.

A related topic in Lowenthal's book is that of *lieux de mémoire* (a concept coined by French historian Pierre Nora), meaning 'places of memory', locations that are associated with specific historical events. Statues or other monuments can be erected with the purpose of emphasizing such associations, for example on a former battlefield to commemorate those who fell in a war. Museums that house the historical collections of their region are often deliberately designed as *lieux de mémoire*. It has become obvious that many places of memory will not be spared climate-related destruction. One good example is the Statue of Liberty in New York, originally a gift from France in recognition of the American attempt to put the ideals of the French Revolution of 1789 – liberty, equality and fraternity – into practice. For the Americans, and for many others who decided to emigrate to that promised land, it has taken on a further significance as a symbol of the American way of life and the role of the United States as a defender of democracies worldwide. However, in 2012, as a result of Hurricane Sandy, the statue and the nearby Ellis Island Museum were closed to the public for several months. In his Oscar-winning film *An Inconvenient Truth* (2006), presidential candidate Al Gore pointed out that the location of the Twin Towers in Manhattan, place of memory of the terrorist attacks of 11 September 2001 in which both towers of the World Trade Center collapsed, is particularly vulnerable to any slight rise in the sea level. In chapter 7 we will look at the huge effort the Americans have made to move, in its entirety, an old lighthouse, a relic of the founding fathers, that was threatened by coastal erosion.

Because of the sensitivity to climate change of native soil and of *lieux de mémoire*, the concept of heritage itself is in the balance. Concepts such as 'testate' and 'legatee' require reassessment in the light of the climate crisis. In pre-modern patriarchal societies it was the eldest son who, by keeping and protecting his heritage, took responsibility for his father's reputation after his death. The continued physical existence of a country estate, ancestral portraits or an art collection was tangible proof of greatness. The French and Italian terms for heritage, *patrimoine* and *patrimonio*, are derived from the Latin *pater* (father) and explicitly stress that it was originally a matter of inheritance (*patrimoine* also means 'inheritance') through the male line (in southern Europe at least – in other places, including the Low Countries, women too could inherit).[16] The erudite aesthete Harold Nicolson must have been aware of these associations when, in *The Spectator*, he turned the argument on its head – a device that was highly effective rhetorically. Instead of placing heritage at the service of his family, he was prepared to sacrifice the perpetuation of his family line for the sake of material heritage. (His declaration was not as exceptional as we might think: British aristocrats were traditionally obliged, by membership of their class, to send their sons to the battlefront as officers in time of war.)

Sigmund Freud (1856–1939), often seen as one of the founders of the modern European conception of the human being, believed that in the twentieth century people were full of a desire for patricide, a radical wish to break with the line of tradition. This is the famous Oedipus complex. According to Freud, every man has been through a phase during childhood in which he wanted to kill his father. This turned out to be an apt description of many modernist writers and artists who attempted a complete break with tradition. The futurist poet Filippo Marinetti (1876–1944) would have liked to close all Italian museums, and his Russian colleague Vladimir Mayakovski (1893–1930) wanted to put the works of the old masters up against a firing squad.[17] Civil servants and politicians, more even than poets, ultimately followed the Freudian model. In the 1950s and 1960s, many Europeans responsible for urban renewal sacrificed the historical fabric of cities to motorways. In Amsterdam some even advocated filling in the canals. But what remains of that modernist rationale, now that climate change is placing the Oedipus complex in a radical new light? For those who are young today, given the circumstances sketched in chapter 1, it no longer goes without saying that passing heritage on to future generations will be possible. In that regard it is of course their fathers and grandfathers who have failed. Because of their excessive use of fossil fuels, their children have nothing to inherit; or rather, sons and daughters are now faced with the task of coming up with ways to avoid or amend the destruction.

Heritage theory and heritage practices are actually at the forefront of thinking in terms of generations, for which there is now increasing attention as the future becomes so much more uncertain. Back in 1997, UNESCO formulated a Declaration on the Responsibilities of the Present Generations Towards Future Generations. The countries and organizations that signed the declaration agreed to make efforts to 'identify, protect and safeguard the tangible and intangible cultural heritage and to transmit this common heritage to future generations'.[18] In that same year the Foundation for the Rights of Future Generations was established in Stuttgart, and in 2007 Hungary appointed an ombudsman for future generations, as did Wales, Gibraltar and the Netherlands. Traditions outside Europe set an example in this sense. It is a basic assumption of the Iroquois (a Native American group), for example, that in making any decision they must consider the consequences for the next seven generations. In other words, what they do today must be sustainable for anyone living around 140 years from now. Meanwhile, the climate problem has become so urgent that it is increasingly prompting legal action.[19] When in 2020 catastrophic forest fires tore across Portugal, children lodged a complaint with the European Court of Human Rights. Their example was followed by young people from another five countries, including Greta Thunberg (b. 2003), who brought a case against the United Nations, arguing that by failing to do enough to tackle climate change, their governments were violating the rights of the child.[20] The children were protesting against the loss of the natural environment, but their case is in keeping with arguments used for decades by those whose job it is to ensure the preservation of historical monuments.

## SOLASTALGIA

The very concept of heritage is therefore in need of an overhaul, now that an ability to hand it on to subsequent generations can no longer be taken for granted. The accompanying emotional turmoil is food for psychologists. It is arguable that we are talking here about a trauma resulting from something that has yet to happen, while great uncertainty exists around the timing and severity of the actual event ('pre-traumatic stress').[21] Unlike the destruction caused by a war, earthquake or tsunami, climate change is as yet a matter of long-term concern. The residents of Hội An, Venice and Amsterdam are currently seeing only the early symptoms. In fact predictions about the future are still largely speculative. We can be certain that much of our historical heritage has already been affected, that more of it is threatened and that some will ultimately have to be abandoned, but few scientists are willing to say anything about the period of time in which climate damage will increase in severity, and furthermore there is considerable disagreement between them. Climate models are continually being adjusted in the light of new facts that can accelerate, delay or complicate the processes involved.

Meanwhile, plenty has been written about this uncertainty factor. It explains in part why few people are taking concrete action in response to climate change. In his book *The Water Will Come* (2017), American journalist Jeff Goodell concludes that people lack the mental wherewithal needed for taking decisions about barely perceptible threats that accelerate only gradually.[22] Our brains react differently to climate change than to acute dangers, such as the hypothetical prospect of being hit by a comet. Even the problem of the hole in the ozone layer was sufficiently urgent in nature for it to be solved over a few years by means of the Montreal Protocol of 1989. Global warming, by contrast, gives off none of the unambiguous signals that would mobilize our innate sense of threat.

An astute reviewer of Goodell's book, Meehan Crist, has attempted to explain the situation based on the well-known 'five phases of mourning' derived from psychology: denial, anger, bargaining, depression and acceptance, writing that many people are in the first or second phase in relation to climate change.[23] Crist, however, questions whether this model of five stages, in which the beloved person or object has entirely disappeared, is appropriate to 'the experience of living in an area threatened by a rise in sea levels'. She therefore prefers another term from psychiatry, 'ambiguous loss', which is applied, for example, to the family of a soldier who fails to return from a mission and is not found. Relatives go through a particular form of mourning that follows a loss without closure. There are two kinds of ambiguous loss:

> When the object is physically absent but psychologically present (as with soldiers missing in action), and when the object is physically present but psychologically absent (as with Alzheimer's disease). The first helps illuminate the arrested mourning often experienced by climate refugees. How do you mourn a home that is sinking into a faraway sea, but remains psychologically present? The second type of ambiguous loss is appropriate to the experience of living in an area threatened by a rise in sea levels. The object of attachment is there but not there – still present, but slowly disappearing. How do you mourn the loss of someone whose hand you can still hold? How do you mourn a home increasingly prone to flooding, but

> not submerged, yet? The parallels aren't perfect, but even the disjunctures reveal how wickedly hard the problem of climate grief can be. When a beloved person is slowly disappearing into the fog of senescence, the endpoint is known. With rising seas, the endpoint remains unknown. Three feet? Eight feet? Grief is stalled by uncertainty.

In relation to climate change, a complex emotion of this kind is central to the work of Australian philosopher Glenn Albrecht (b. 1953). He has coined the term 'solastalgia', derived in part from 'nostalgia', or longing for the past.[24] Based on the Latin word *solacium* (solace) and the Greek *algos* (pain), it refers to the phenomenon of feeling homesick while you are still at home. A person who has never lived in a house that is subject to climate-related threats can understand the term by thinking of the emotion that sometimes takes hold of you as a traveller. On arrival at an attractive destination you might find yourself immediately overwhelmed with nostalgia for that very place, because you know that you will be staying there for only a short time.

In 2015, the leading medical journal *The Lancet* adopted 'solastalgia' as a useful concept in determining the impact climate change can have on a person's mental health.[25] It can be useful for art historians too. Perhaps it might assist me in trying to understand the feelings of my students during a guided tour of Amsterdam: they are overwhelmed by the experience of historical heritage in the knowledge that in the long term it will no longer be there.

## HERITAGE: BETWEEN MICRO AND MACRO

The emotions we experience when historical heritage is lost can also be of importance at a cognitive level, by making the extent and significance of the climate crisis more tangible and 'digestible'.

One feature of climate change is the unprecedented magnitude of the problem, which is difficult for an individual to grasp. After all, only collaboration between different countries, regions and supranational organizations has any chance of rectifying the situation. Moreover, it will be necessary not just to think beyond the next election, but to think in terms of generations – our grandchildren and their grandchildren – and even in terms of the survival of animal and plant species that have evolved over many thousands of years. Looking so far into the future and back in time, and on a global scale, represents a unique cognitive challenge. Writers and scholars have therefore tried to understand climate change with reference to Freud's psychoanalytical ideas about the uncanny (*das Unheimliche*, literally a thing with which you do not feel at home) or the classic philosophical concept of the sublime, which stresses the insignificance of humankind in relation to nature.[26] American literary critic Timothy Morton (b. 1968) has even invented an entirely new term. He calls global warming a 'hyperobject', something so widespread that it eludes normal description in time and space (other examples of hyperobjects, according to Morton, are polystyrene foam and radioactive plutonium).[27] If these three terms make anything clear, it is that we find it hard to relate our own human scale to the scale on which the climate crisis is taking place.

Here is a good example of a fact that is hard to grasp: the amount of anthropogenic material (which is to say stuff made by humans) is now greater than the amount of biomass in the world. On average, for each human being, the amount of anthropogenic mass produced each week is equivalent to his or her bodyweight, and sometimes even exceeds it.[28] To what extent does such a numerical insight create clarity? Does it actually contribute rather more to an undirected sense of powerlessness?

The reality is that our confrontation with the disappearance of historical heritage takes place on a meso-level, occupying as it were a position in between the micro-level of personal experience and the macro-level of a problem that stretches right across the world and far outwards in time. Historical heritage connects us as individuals in a tangible way to previous generations, sometimes centuries into the past. But however ancient or extensive it is, it never attains the impalpable character of a 'hyperobject'. (While I do sometimes hear people discussing the negative sides of heritage, such as the way it encourages tourism and gentrification, I have never heard anyone complain about the *unavoidability* of heritage.)

Because of this difference in scale, the focus on heritage can offer a new perspective on the capacity of human beings with regard to climate change. All cultural heritage was once made by human hands, drawing upon the expertise of artists, architects and craftspeople. Human creativity will likewise enable us to save it, adapt it or, as a last resort, reconstruct it.

This insight touches upon what Swedish climate activist Greta Thunberg has described as 'cathedral thinking'. We have an admirable ability to commence work that cannot be completed until several generations have come and gone. It took more than two centuries to build Notre Dame in Paris, from 1163 to 1345; the cathedral in Cologne, begun in 1248, was not finished until 1880. In 2019 Thunberg used the following words to urge the European Parliament to take action in light of the climate crisis:

> Our house is falling apart. The future as well as what we have achieved in the past is literally in your hands now. . . . It will take a far-reaching vision. . . . It will take fierce determination to act now, to lay the foundations when we may not know all

> the details about how to shape the ceiling. In other words, it will take cathedral thinking. . . . We must all do the seemingly impossible.[29]

The use of an architectural metaphor was very effective rhetorically. In the past, humans as cathedral builders have shown themselves to be good ancestors, and this gives us a framework for action to combat climate change. Thunberg was using architecture in a metaphorical sense, to talk about ecology; in this book, by contrast, we dwell upon the literal consequences of climate change for heritage.

In chapter 4 we will look further at the distinction between nature and culture, and the two different timescales against which they are generally evaluated. While we may fall prey to a feeling of impotence when faced with the loss of coral reefs, entire animal species and landscapes all over the globe, the rescue of works made by humans can inspire fresh creativity in us. Three possible ways of saving heritage in the future – transformation, digitization and reconstruction – will be examined in the last three chapters of this book. A good understanding of the situation, however, would not be complete without a look back over history.

# 3. Art and nature: fertile cross-pollination?

We might nowadays find that witnessing the disappearing of Venice is the main reason for enjoying a visit there, so it is obviously an illusion to see heritage as a separate domain, immune to natural factors. A glance back in time, however, makes clear that this situation is in no sense new. The history of heritage is closely bound up with historical changes in climate.

Down through the ages, periods of cultural flourishing and decline have been a function of changes in natural phenomena and of human activities aimed at dealing with those changes, as historian Peter Frankopan (b. 1971) recently argued in his comprehensive tome *The Earth Transformed* (2023).[1] Perhaps the best example of this reciprocity is the Little Ice Age, the period of cold that affected Western Europe and parts of North America from the fourteenth to the eighteenth century. Frankopan and his colleagues do not agree on the causes of the Little Ice Age. Perhaps volcanic eruptions were to blame, or reduced solar radiation, or changes in the ocean currents and the position of the earth's axis, or even the slaughter of the indigenous inhabitants of America after the arrival of the Europeans. However that may be, historical data, based on sources such as diaries, municipal financial accounts and tree rings, clearly show that the temperature in both regions was some 1 to 2 degrees lower than the values seen in the twentieth century up to 1990. This brought about the collapse of several civilizations. When Greenland, for example, was hit by the Little Ice Age, the Vikings who had settled there disappeared. Other residents of the continent managed to adjust. In the sixteenth century the Iroquois in north-eastern America abandoned their farmlands in favour of a more flexible existence in smaller settlements.

Conversely, humans have been intervening in nature for the past 12,000 years at least.[2] It is more than possible that, for millennia, the agricultural revolution actually had a stabilizing effect on the climate. Before the development of farming, the earth went through a cycle of ice ages (these were 'major' ice ages in which large parts of the earth were completely covered in ice) and periods of warming, a pattern caused by fluctuations in the planet's orbit. But when forests were burned on a large scale to clear arable land, $CO_2$ was released that delayed the return to an ice age. So humans themselves contributed to the stability of the Holocene, the geological period in which they were able to flourish.[3]

With the burning of fossil fuels, even more carbon was released into the atmosphere. Fossil fuels are a store of solar energy; photosynthesis had made plants grow and their remains had been squeezed together over hundreds of millions of years. That energy now came free in one great burst. The highly advanced classical Roman and Chinese civilizations initiated the digging of coalmines and the use of natural gas, but when the Industrial Revolution took off in Europe these activities gained momentum, and the landscape was changed radically by mining and by the fossil fuel industry. A worldwide impact soon eventuated. Steamships enabled European colonization of much of the globe and the colonies then contributed fossil fuels that increased Western prosperity.

One artwork that encapsulates the situation is a lithograph by Sir Leopold George Heath (1817–1907) (figure 12).[4] An admiral in the British Royal Navy, Heath was not without merit as an artist. In 1837 he depicted the discovery of a coal seam on the island of Labuan off Borneo (today's Malaysia), an ideal location for the refuelling of steamships on their way to Hong Kong. In a lush forest, as relaxed as if on a tourist excursion, stand two white men. The tropical paradise is rather spoilt by the fact that several trees have been felled, revealing a coal seam. One of the men is possessively clutching the tree roots that have forced their way into and around the coal. The other, in the uniform of a British army officer, points upwards, as if to say: here a new era must begin. He can already see the fossil fuel industry that will inevitably arise at this spot.

A new era indeed. Much of the oil industry that still exists today is rooted in European imperialism. The origins of British Petroleum (BP) lie in Teheran, headquarters of the Anglo-Persian Oil Company. Those of Shell are on the island of Sumatra – Royal Dutch Shell was a creation of the Dutch colony in what is now Indonesia. This colonial heritage means that two Western European countries are the biggest historical culprits when it comes to their total emissions of $CO_2$. Carbon Brief (a British non-governmental organization for climate-related journalism) has calculated that if these emissions were apportioned based on the present-day population, the Netherlands would find itself at the top, because of its Asian colony, at 2,014 tonnes of $CO_2$ per person. Coming a close second is another colonizer, the United Kingdom (1,922 tonnes). Some way behind come Russia and the United States (with respectively 1,655 and 1,560 tonnes of $CO_2$).[5] The Labuan picture is therefore a kind of 'Urbild of the fossil economy', in the words of Andreas Malm (b. 1977), a Swedish activist academic who specializes in human ecology:

> First the fuel was in the ground, still and unstirred; then someone came to the scene and, eyeing profit and power,

> commenced its exploitation. . . . It is, if you will, a picture of the Fall. . . . The uncountable repetitions of the same act over the past two centuries form the defeated time now pouring down from the sky.[6]

The $CO_2$ released from fossil fuels now wraps the entire globe like a blanket. We have added more carbon molecules to the atmosphere by weight than the sum total of everything ever built by humans that is still standing on the surface of the planet.[7] So a colossal cloud of waste, an enduring monument to the Industrial Revolution, hangs over all the world's cathedrals, citadels and cities.

## MANKIND'S BEST MOMENT?

At the same time, those very cities, castles and cathedrals are exposed to floods and other climate-related destruction, as we saw in the previous chapter. In this chapter, therefore, we will attempt to enlarge upon Frankopan's story of how natural phenomena, including climate change, have altered the course of human history by adding a third dimension to the narrative: heritage.

One starting point for this analysis is, once again, the Low Countries. After all, there is probably no other region in which heritage is so closely interwoven with the centuries-old battle against water. This was made clear several decades ago in the Jefferson Lecture by American historian and Pulitzer Prize winner Barbara Tuchman (1912–89) who, in her struggle with the challenges of her own day such as 'the energy problem', summed up three of 'mankind's better moments'. At number three was the founding of the United States, 'the sheer grit it took to leave the known and set out across the sea'; at number two, the mediaeval cathedrals that required several generations to complete; and at number one, the building of the Afsluitdijk in the Netherlands in 1932, which made it possible to turn the Zuider Zee into a polder. 'The will to do the impossible, the spirit of Can-Do that overtakes our species now and then was never more manifest than in this earth-altering act by the smallest of the major European nations.'

> For centuries, ever since the first inhabitants, fleeing enemy tribes, settled in the bogs where no one cared to bother them, the Dutch struggled against water and learned how to live with it: building on mounds, constructing and reconstructing seawalls of clay mixed with straw, carrying mud in an endless train of baskets, laying willow mattresses weighted with stones, repairing each spring the winter's damage, draining marshes, channeling streams, building ramps to their attics to save the cattle in times of flood, gaining dike-enclosed land from the waves in one place and losing as much to the revengeful ocean somewhere else, progressively developing methods to cope with their eternal antagonist. . . . Today, the Afsluitdijk, or Zuider Zee road, is a normal thoroughfare. To drive across it between the sullen ocean on one side and new land on the other is for that moment to feel optimism for the human race.[8]

The creation of the Dutch polder landscape from the Middle Ages onwards was indeed a tremendous feat, evidence of the human capacity to think several generations ahead (philosopher Roman Krznaric calls it an example of 'being a good ancestor').[9] In the eighteenth century the dykes were reinforced with huge megalithic stones taken from prehistoric graves, cromlechs older than Stonehenge. Nowadays the dykes themselves are heritage. UNESCO has recognized the windmills of the Kinderdijk, a popular tourist attraction, as World Heritage because of the 'outstanding contribution made by the people of the Netherlands to the technology of handling water'.[10] The former island of Schokland symbolizes, according to that same organization, 'the heroic, age-old struggle of the people of the Netherlands against the encroachment of the waters'.[11] Similar considerations were behind the awarding of World Heritage status to the ring of canals in Amsterdam, the impoldering of the Beemster in North Holland and the D.F. Wouda pumping station in the Dutch province of Friesland (the largest steam-powered pumping station ever built).

It is therefore more than a little ironic that the survival of this heritage is now threatened by climate change (or in some cases given new relevance; the D.F. Wouda pumping station, built in 1920, needs to be turned on increasingly frequently because more modern pumping systems are unable to cope). Not just this industrial heritage but the exceptional number of Dutch paintings produced in the seventeenth century – the so-called 'Golden Age' of Rembrandt and Vermeer – can be linked to the way in which people have attempted to take control of nature. In fact humans produced both artificial nature and what might be called natural art, which capitalized on specific climatological conditions.

## THE LITTLE ICE AGE

It is more than possible that the economic and cultural flourishing of the Netherlands in the seventeenth century is directly attributable to a climatological development and the reaction to it, as seen in energy use. American climate historian Dagomar Degroot (b. 1985) uses a wide range of factual materials to argue in his innovative book *The Frigid Golden Age* (2018) that without the Little Ice Age, the Netherlands would have developed very differently.[12] From about 1530 onwards, the winters brought more ice and snow, and lasted until March or April. Even in summer the weather remained autumnal, complete with storm tides. Historical research by the Royal Netherlands Meteorological Institute (KNMI) shows that the last quarter of the sixteenth century was probably the coldest in a thousand years. It was the nadir of the Little Ice Age.

Degroot claims that the Dutch Republic succeeded in profiting from this changing natural environment. Other European states, being more dependent on agriculture than the Netherlands, suffered terribly. By adapting their economic policies to weather that brought neighbouring countries to a standstill, Dutch merchants managed to cash in on failed harvests. Financial innovation could turn a crisis into an opportunity; the world's first bond was issued by the water board of the Lekdijk Bovendams, to raise capital for the repair of the dyke between Amerongen and Vreeswijk, which had given way in 1624 (the water board is still paying off the interest to this day). Seafarers took advantage of changing wind directions, and inventors thought up techniques for benefitting from the lower temperatures. This was possible because, while the Dutch Republic's economy was focused on trade with other regions, the Dutch were also in a position to deploy accessible energy sources, peat and wind, in such a way that they could break through the boundaries that neighbouring economies came up against. Windmills made the polder landscape possible, and in harsh winters isolated villages were connected by the ice of frozen waterways.[13] As Degroot puts it:

> To some extent, the Republic's successes were partly a product of Dutch resilience to the Little Ice Age. People in coastal cities, for example, had diverse diets and could therefore cope with shortages in a particular food. Urban charities provided

> for the poor, who were particularly vulnerable to harvest failures in other countries. Climate change also seems to have benefitted the Dutch. Much of the Republic's economic dynamism stemmed from activities at sea, where complex changes in patterns of prevailing wind mattered more than cooling. These changes shortened Dutch commercial voyages and often helped Dutch war fleets more effectively harness the wind when sailing into battle. Climate change did pose severe challenges for the Dutch and, when it did, the Dutch often adapted creatively. When storms sparked a series of urban fires across Europe, for example, Dutch inventors developed and then exported new firefighting technologies and practices. When winter ice choked harbours and halted traffic on essential canals, the Dutch invented skates and refined icebreakers. Merchants set up fairs on the ice that attracted thousands from afar, and pioneered insurance policies that protected them from the risks of storms at sea.[14]

Degroot points to one clearly recognizable cultural consequence of all these successes: the development of the winter landscape as a genre in painting. Pieter Bruegel the Elder (*c.* 1525–69) was probably the first European artist ever to depict a winter landscape without giving it any explicit religious significance (figure 13). His famous work leads the viewer's gaze over the shoulders of hunters with their dogs into a snowy valley where villagers are enjoying themselves on the ice. After Bruegel, other Netherlandish painters began to specialize in everyday winter scenes, the most famous among them being Hendrick Avercamp (1585–1634). So in art, the cold was presented not as a threat but as an opportunity for pleasure, social contact and an aesthetically pleasing image.

Furthermore, a parallel can be perceived between the way in which the Dutch managed their land and water and the organization of financial flows on the art market. The Low

Countries had traditionally been a loose federation of cities and regions. When it came to building and maintaining dykes, however, they were forced to collaborate closely. This produced a mentality that makes itself felt to this day in what is known as the 'polder model', according to which decisions are taken based on intensive consultation between politicians of different persuasions and other interested parties, such as businesses and social organizations. Everyone's interests are taken into account as far as possible – with the obvious disadvantage that nobody is ultimately accountable. From a cultural point of view, the consequence of this political constellation was that in the seventeenth century a bourgeois elite could arise that was able to spend money on art but did not want to stand out from the crowd by exhibiting ostentatious behaviour.[15] The harsh winters in which the different social classes engaged in amiable recreation on the ice contributed to the egalitarian character of Dutch society. This, for example, is how philosopher and legal expert Hugo Grotius (1583–1645) described a skating festival:

> Here nobody asks about class, here all are free and frank,
> Here a farming lass has a nobleman at her flank,
> There you see a farmer's boy with a host of ladies in tow,
> There a courtly gentleman and a burgher woman go,
> For that which no great monarch, nor even philosopher could
> achieve,
> Happens here because the wet has solidified in the freeze;
> Ask from the bottom of your heart who here is truly wise,
> And I'll say from the bottom of my heart: only the ice.[16]

In short, while great philosophers had aspired in vain since antiquity to create a Platonic republic in which the people were to a large extent in charge, it was only the levelling effect of the ice that made that ideal a real possibility, or so Grotius believed. It was indeed true that while the extreme temperatures in the rest of Europe increased social polarization (and encouraged, for example, the persecution of women believed to be witches), in the case of the Dutch they actually contributed to its reduction.

As far as the buying and selling of artworks is concerned, whereas elsewhere in Europe aristocratic patrons were relied upon, in the Low Countries an extensive free market in art flourished, with paintings of accessible scenes that because of their low prices many people could buy. Foreign visitors were amazed to find that paintings could be admired in the houses of ordinary citizens, even peasants.[17] Many painters focused on a specific genre, such as the still life, achieving immense virtuosity or indeed mass producing works for a broad public. Their paintings often depicted the everyday environment, landscapes by Van Goyen and Avercamp and their many imitators being an obvious example.

## LANDSCAPE INTO ART

The new genres of painting, in which religious elements faded into comparative irrelevance, are characteristic of the development of Dutch art. This is also clear from treatises the painters wrote, in which an Aristotelian principle is fundamental: *ars imitatur naturam*. Art imitates nature. According to Michelangelo, Dutch painters set themselves apart from the Italian tradition by the fact that they could accurately depict so many details of the visible world. Masters from the Netherlands who settled elsewhere, in Rome for instance, were therefore popular above all for their skill at painting background landscapes. Their medium – a slow-drying oil paint said to have been invented by Jan van Eyck (1390–1441) – was particularly suitable for producing the atmospheric effects that were impossible using the Italian fresco and tempera techniques.[18]

In the seventeenth century, demand for paintings of the flat Dutch landscape surged and they developed into a distinct genre, in which eventually the narrative elements became entirely absent (although human figures were always included, and landscape painters could hire specialists to paint them). Art was nothing more nor less than a 'mirror of nature', as Samuel van Hoogstraten (1627–78), a pupil of Rembrandt who wrote a voluminous treatise on painting, famously declared.[19] While writing by his contemporaries in Italy and France stressed the importance of subject matter from biblical history and of aspiring to imitate classical antiquity, attitudes were different in the Netherlands. The unadorned depiction of God's creation was, after all, a religious activity. Van Hoogstraten wrote that he did 'not want to maintain that the sole objective of our Painting should be to prepare the mind for Virtue, since we know a more direct and certain way' of achieving that, namely by reading the Bible. He did believe it was undeniable, however, that painting 'keeps no one away from virtue': indeed, that it 'brings the sincere practitioner, through his sublime contemplation of God's miraculous works, closer to the Creator of all things'.[20] Creation, as Calvin himself had said, was the Book of Nature, and it therefore deserved to be studied meticulously and explored. It was probably this religious belief that caused the simultaneous, and exceptional, flourishing of landscape art and natural sciences in the Netherlands in the seventeenth century.[21]

## THE ARTIFICIAL LANDSCAPE

Van Hoogstraten made no reference to the fact that nature, so fervently imitated by the Dutch masters as 'God's miraculous works', was in fact manipulated by human beings to a great degree. Farmland had been created in place of lakes and marshes, by means of dyke-building and drainage, and artists were often involved in this process. Many painters of the sixteenth-century Low Countries were skilled at surveying land and drawing maps, including Lanceloot Blondeel (*c.* 1496–1561), Pieter Pourbus (1523–84), Jan de Hervy (?–1509) and Cornelis Anthonisz (1505–53).[22] Jan van Scorel (1495–1562) in particular interwove his artistic skills closely with his work in land reclamation and water management.

Van Scorel was one of the masters who laid the basis for the later flourishing of painting in the Dutch Republic. He was among the first Dutch artists to visit Rome, the artistic and scientific centre of Europe in his day. There he joined the retinue of Pope Adrian VI, born in Utrecht, who appointed him keeper of the Vatican art collections. He later travelled to Venice and on by sea to the Holy Land. When he returned to the Netherlands, his ambitions were no longer confined to art. He had technical innovation in mind too, specifically an ingenious dredging machine and a new construction method for dykes, based on his study of the classical Roman texts. He needed them in order to found a 'New Rome' in the Netherlands.

This 'Nova Roma' was to be built on new land that would be reclaimed from the Zijpe, a large area of mud flats and salt marshes in West Friesland, between Den Helder and Petten. If the plan were brought to fruition, it would be the first time that an area of considerable dimensions had been won back from the sea. On a map of the new land, Van Scorel had already drawn seven churches, each of them bearing the name of one of the seven main churches of the Holy City (figure 14). For their foundations he intended to reuse material from the old Roman fort at Katwijk, the Brittenburg, the ruins of which emerged from the water in 1552, during an exceptionally low tide, and had attracted a great deal of interest among Dutch antiquarians. Van Scorel took several stone blocks to Brussels, to show them in person to Emperor Charles V, who gave him a patent that same year for the building of Nova Roma.

His travels had clearly made Van Scorel a man of the world. At the Antwerp stock exchange he managed to interest a group of merchants in his scheme. They were seeking new investments for the money they had earned from global trade. The artist could also count on support from the men in charge back in Holland, since they had for a long time hoped they might be able to turn the Zijpe into a polder. As early as the fourteenth century, the abbot of Egmond had put a huge amount of energy into the building of dykes, but by this time the resulting land had been lost to the waters again.

The 'New Rome' became in the end a rather more modest project than Van Scorel had in mind, although one that took half a century to complete. Among other things, it needed to combat the storms that the most extreme years of the Little Ice Age brought with them. In 1555 the dykes broke for the first time. Then in 1573 the polder was deliberately inundated to obstruct the Spanish army during the Siege of Alkmaar. The financiers in the Southern Netherlands had meanwhile gambled away a fortune, and they withdrew from Van Scorel's scheme. It was not until 1597 that the land reclamation project was brought to a satisfactory conclusion. Nevertheless, the ultimate success of the impoldering was an important victory. It whetted the appetite, and in Holland it marked the transition from a defensive to an offensive battle against the water. From the end of the century onwards, the conquest of lost land accelerated rapidly.

Van Scorel's own paintings show us nothing of this new polder landscape. They do, however, give us an impression of his experiences while crossing the Alps: craggy rock formations allow for abruptly shifting views. But for the painters who imitated him in the first half of the seventeenth century, it was precisely the new, flat land that they found attractive as a subject: the straight horizon with more space for sky than for land. From 1600 onwards, the horizon came to lie lower and lower in the picture plane, and painters set to work creating spectacular cloudscapes. Typical is a work by Jan van Goyen (at one time in the collection of Shell director Henri Deterding) (figure 15), in which the viewer's gaze is led off into the distance by a series of windmills built to pump groundwater out over the river dykes.

By limiting his palette to relatively cheap earth pigments such as ochre and umber and using them sparingly, Van Goyen was able to produce paintings in prodigious quantities. As American poet Lytle Shaw elegantly suggests, his paint was essentially oily mud, spread strategically over the canvas, and Van Goyen's activity as a painter in that sense bore some similarity to the literal shifting of land masses and draining of marshes. In the wet-in-wet brushstrokes of his quagmires, we find the aesthetic recapitulation of land reclamation.[23]

This comparison ties in with the insight of Van Goyen's contemporaries that, while landscape painters wanted to honour Creation, the Dutch engineers had in fact given the Lord a hand with his creative activities: 'God made the world, but the Dutch made Holland', as René Descartes (1596–1650) is supposed to have said. The French philosopher would know. He was familiar with the landscape of polder, river and coast. Attracted by press freedom in the Dutch Republic, he spent twenty years in various cities in Holland, Utrecht, Gelre and Friesland.

Descartes lived for a while close to Egmond aan Zee, which of all Dutch settlements was the most sorely tested by the water. As a painting by Van Goyen of the coast at Egmond shows, the village, including the squat tower of its St Agnes's

Church, lay close to the shore of the North Sea, where fishing boats were readied for departure (figure 16). When admiring this work, in which sea and land touch each other so directly, the public must have recalled how Egmond had been hit by the most disastrous flooding in Dutch history, the All Saints' Flood of 1570, when the Little Ice Age was at its most extreme. After a lengthy storm had pushed the water up to unprecedented heights, a great many dykes gave way and the entire coast from Flanders to north-western Germany was inundated. The island of Bosch disappeared into the Wadden Sea for ever and Van Scorel's New Rome was not spared. The total number of dead must have exceeded 20,000. Another 10,000 people were made homeless, livestock were engulfed and winter stocks of food destroyed.

The All Saints' Flood affected the entire country; in a letter to King Philip II of Spain, the Duke of Alba wrote that five sixths of Holland was under water. Ultimately the disaster had far-reaching political consequences. Because the duke had been attempting to push through tax reforms that same year, political tensions in the country had risen. The catastrophic flooding reinforced dissatisfaction with Spanish rule and the desire to make the Low Countries independent. In 1579 the regions joined forces in the Union of Utrecht, marking the start of the successful war of independence. With a bit of imagination, Van Goyen's painting of the proud church tower of Egmond can therefore be interpreted as a homage to the Dutch nation, which had prevailed against the forces of both the sea and the Spanish occupier.

The scene depicted by Van Goyen was not destined to last. In 1717 a flood swept away so much of the coastal dune landscape that St Agnes's Church found itself on the beach. To protect both the church and the village, the people raised a dam, but a fresh storm (in 1741) undermined the building and split the tower down its full length. The entire village was then moved inland. The situation remained so fragile that, even in the twentieth century, large sections of dune were washed away. The coast is now regularly reinforced by pumping sand up onto it.

Landscape paintings are of course first of all artistic creations, and we always need to question to what extent they accurately depict the true circumstances. Nevertheless, paintings such as Salomon van Ruysdael's *River Landscape with Ferry* (1649) give an atmospheric impression of the way in which Dutch people tried to enter into a symbiotic relationship with water (figure 17). The busy rivers were the most important transport routes between cities, and within the artificial landscape there was space for the water that flowed into it from the sea.

Other painters, by contrast, show just how precarious the balance between land and sea was. On 4 March 1651, the St Peter's Flood inundated much of Amsterdam and its surroundings. Dykes built on the eastern side of the city to protect it against the Zuider Zee broke. Eyewitness Jan Asselijn (1610–52) painted the sea pouring in through a large breach in the St Anthony's Dyke (figure 18). His colleague Willem Schellinks (1623–78), looking from the far side of the water, depicted the consternation of powerless Amsterdammers. Less dramatic is a work by Matthias Withoos (1627–1703) showing the flooded land at Schardam after a new All Saints' Flood in 1675 (figure 19). Painted on commission from the organization responsible for repairs (the Committee of Councillors of West Friesland and the Northern Quarters), it shows the dyke being reconstructed a year after the breach. To the right stand two pile drivers, ready to hammer a triple row of piles into the ground. On the horizon we see the neighbouring town of Hoorn, with its great coming and going of ships on the Zuider Zee. Once again, the water had been transformed from enemy to friend.

These paintings plainly show that the Dutch Republic produced landscape art as well as artificial land.

## FROM WIND AND PEAT TO COAL AND OIL

Works by Withoos, Van Goyen, Van Ruysdael and their fellow painters illustrate how, during the Little Ice Age, the Dutch managed to exploit the wind as an accessible energy source and by doing so, according to Degroot, to rise above the limitations of neighbouring economies. The most important supplement to wind energy, however, was non-renewable in nature: peat, or dried slabs of the peaty soil that was abundant in the Low Countries and commonly burned as fuel. Given the scale on which it was consumed, the Netherlands could be referred to as the world's first fossil fuel economy. Traces of the trade are visible in the landscape to this day, since the cutting of turfs contributed to reductions in ground level on a significant scale in areas where it took place. When the surface of the land came to lie at practically the same level as the groundwater, windmills were built from the sixteenth century onwards to pump the water over the dykes and turn lakes into polders. These areas now lie well below sea level.

In the marshy landscape that resulted, grass was the only crop that thrived, so the land was used for the grazing of cows. The large amount of milk they produced led to the intensification of the production of cheese, it being the only way to make milk last. It is no coincidence that the lowest lying city in Holland, Gouda, is synonymous with a Dutch cheese exported all over the world. Given the city's uncertain future, with the ground sinking and the sea level rising (see chapter 1), it has become clear that the limits of this centuries-old economic model have been reached.

As well as peat, charcoal and even coal were used as fuel in the early-modern Low Countries. Historian Richard Unger has shown that industry in the major Dutch cities used coal from England, Scotland and the area around Liège. In 1710, for instance, 25,000 tonnes of British coal were imported.[24] Anyone looking closely at the details of Jacob van Ruisdael's *A Panoramic View of Amsterdam Looking towards the IJ* (1670) will see in the foreground the Bentheim sandstone and scaffolding poles of a town hall still under construction, while in the background plumes of smoke rise from a forest of chimneys on houses, and on local industrial works, which ran partly on fossil fuels (figure 20).

At the same time, however, the painting shows that it was old-fashioned wind power that connected the Dutch capital with the rest of the world. From the scaffolding of the Town Hall, Amsterdam's then orientation towards its harbour is obvious. The city lay right on the sea, and ships could sail along the canals to Dam Square at its heart; it was not until the twentieth century, with the building of the Afsluitdijk, that Amsterdam lost direct access to the world's oceans.

If the painter had been able to turn around and face the facade of the Town Hall, he would have seen how these overseas trading connections were stressed in the architecture of the grand new building. On the triangular tympanum we see the personification of Amsterdam standing in front of a large ship with a reefed sail, while to the left and right four women representing Europe, Asia, Africa and America humbly offer their produce. The global pretensions of the Dutch capital were explicitly emphasized once again by the figure of Atlas, erected directly above Amsterdam, bearing a sizeable globe on his shoulders (figure 21).

The wide Dutch landscape could therefore contain the promise of colonial adventures on an even more distant horizon, in the Dutch East Indies. On the island of Java in what is now Indonesia, the Dutch founded their colonial capital, Batavia, deriving its Latin name from a marshy Dutch region called the Betuwe. From there, good business was done as far away as Taiwan (a Dutch colony from 1624 to 1668) and Japan (which limited its relations with the Western world to the Netherlands in the period 1639–1854). Batavia was also the base from which the Australian coast was mapped. But without the cooling climate of the Little Ice Age, if we are to believe Degroot, the maritime innovations required for this overseas project would never have been so successful.

It was the East Indies adventure that ultimately changed energy management in the metropolis radically. The Dutch East Indies (today's Indonesia) were not conquered in full as a colony until the early twentieth century. Fossil fuels motivated that conquest. The first paraffin-rich oil was discovered in 1885 in the Sultanate of Langkat, on the border with Aceh, and the establishment of the Koninklijke Nederlandsche Maatschappij tot Exploitatie van Petroleumbronnen in Nederlandsch-Indië (KNMEP) soon followed. When the well in Langkat dried up in 1897, the company found rich oil reserves in nearby Perlak. That was part of the Sultanate of Aceh, however, which had not yet come under the authority of Queen Wilhelmina of the Netherlands. It was not until 1914 that the Dutch emerged victorious from the bloody Aceh War. At that point the colonial authorities were able to secure not just the fossil fuels but also transport by sea to Europe, through the Malacca Strait. Around the turn of the century, oil was found elsewhere in the archipelago too and a British firm, the Shell Transport and Trading Company, set up a refinery in Balikpapan. To gain a monopoly, the two companies merged in 1907 to become the Royal Dutch Shell Group.

The founding of Shell placed a firm pillar under the economy of the modern Netherlands. Its energetic director Henri Deterding (1866–1939), nicknamed The Petrol Napoleon, was supported in his efforts by his adjutant Hendrikus Colijn (1869–1944), who had made a career for himself as a commanding officer in the Aceh War. Under the leadership of these two men, the company grew to become the biggest rival to America's Standard Oil, and by the late 1920s Shell was the most important oil company in the world, producing 11 per cent of all crude oil. Because Deterding was an admirer of National Socialism, and because Reichsmarschall Hermann Göring was a regular guest at his German hunting lodge, the Dutch prefer not to be reminded of him.[25] But the prestige of Shell itself has never been tainted by its fascist prehistory. This is remarkable, especially since the Japanese allies of the Nazis, precisely because of the presence of oil, which they needed to enable their imperialist expansion, eventually invaded and conquered the Dutch East Indies.

When the Netherlands lost its colony for good after the Second World War, Shell remained active in Indonesia. Today it is still involved in the development of the huge Abadi gas field.[26] The importance of Shell for the Netherlands became greater, if anything, in the second half of the twentieth century. The country's biggest quoted company remained extremely profitable. This had major consequences when, towards the end of the twentieth century, the need for a far-reaching climate policy became increasingly clear.

## SHELL AND THE CLIMATE MOVEMENT

In the 1980s the Netherlands was still extremely advanced in its thinking on climate change, and in 1989 it hosted the first international climate conference. Ministers from sixty countries came together in a hotel in Noordwijk that has a view of the sea, to talk about saving the earth. With the end of the Cold War and the proven success of the banning of CFC gases, which were causing a hole in the ozone layer, there was optimism about the prospects for laying down a legal basis for a reduction in $CO_2$ emissions. We have never been so close to solving the climate problem. But because the United States refused to commit to concrete action of any kind, agreements ultimately proved impossible. More than half of all $CO_2$ emissions since industrialization have in fact occurred since 1989.[27]

It took until 2015 for international agreements to be made, at the Climate Conference in Paris (COP). But they were not legally binding. By that point the Netherlands had already fallen back towards the rear of European countries as regards climate-friendly policy, whether judged by its promises or by what it was actually doing. The governing liberal party, Volkspartij voor Vrijheid en Democratie (VVD), even advocated discontinuing subsidies to the KNMI, claiming the meteorological institution was paying too much attention to the disaster scenarios of the IPCC. For years the Netherlands has been among the 20 per cent of nations with the biggest $CO_2$ emissions in terms of absolute quantity, and within that group the Dutch are also in the top ten when it comes to highest emissions per head of population.[28] Change is agonizingly slow. As recently as 2020, the Netherlands was fifth from bottom in a European league table showing the share of each country's energy coming from renewable sources (only Hungary, Belgium, Luxembourg and Malta did worse).[29] That it has been left behind to such a degree is all the more surprising in light of the country's extreme vulnerability to climate change.

The failure of the 1989 conference is largely attributable to the oil industry, an important sponsor of the then American president George Bush Sr. But in the Netherlands the interests of politicians and those of the fossil fuel industry, in other words Shell, are perhaps even more tightly interwoven than in the US. Shell is a 'state within a state', with a greater income than the national government (in 2018 the income of the Dutch state was 274 billion and Shell's income 282 billion euro); this clearly suggests that the Netherlands deserves a place in the ignominious list of 'petrostates' that includes Venezuela and Saudi Arabia.[30] Dutch diplomats are regularly sent on secondment with the oil giant. The state even collaborates with Shell structurally on extracting natural gas in the northern Dutch province of Groningen. From extraction and transportation to use and research, along the entire fossil fuel chain, the Dutch government is either a player or has a financial interest.[31]

Politicians of all stripes started off with Shell or switched to it later, beginning with the abovementioned Hendrikus Colijn, who after a career in the fossil fuel industry was five times premier for the Christian Democrats in the 1920s and 1930s. His example looms large in Dutch history even to this day. From the recent past, Labour prime minister Wim Kok is the best known, but many ministers and junior ministers on all sides have worked for that particular oil company (one of them, who as a Christian Democrat minister promoted the interests of aviation, eventually became European Commissioner for Climate Action). All this is despite the fact that Shell has been far and away the country's biggest emitter of greenhouse gases for years. It emits more than twice as much $CO_2$ as the whole of the Netherlands.[32] Even on a global scale, Shell is a blatant malefactor. Of all the oil companies that are in the hands of shareholders (rather than of states, like Saudi Aramco and Russian Gazprom), Shell is responsible for the second largest share of total $CO_2$ emissions since the start of industrialization.[33]

The company itself, incidentally, has been more aware than anyone of what is at stake. In an internal memo written in 1986, Shell researchers warned of 'relatively rapid and dramatic changes' in the climate on earth, 'with impacts on the living environment for humans . . . and the potentially great social, economic and political consequences that will follow'.[34] In response, Shell's engineers changed the design of a drilling platform in the North Sea, making it 2 metres higher to take account of the expected rise in the sea level. In 1991 Shell even produced a film called *Climate of Concern*, to be shown in schools. It warned that if policies did not change, the fossil fuel industry would be responsible for extreme weather, flooding, famine and the migration of countless climate refugees. The warning was 'endorsed by a uniquely broad consensus of scientists', according to the film. 'If the weather machine were to be wound up to such new levels of energy, no country would remain unaffected. . . . Global warming is not yet certain but many think that to wait for final proof would be irresponsible. Action now is seen as the only safe insurance.'[35]

The 'green' arm of Shell did not find favour with investors, however, and in 2014 Ben van Beurden took the helm and gained notoriety for stating, 'I'm going to pump all I can pump'.[36] Journalistic platform *De Correspondent* has calculated that less than 1 per cent of all investment in Shell has gone on renewable energy, while the company has at the same time spent tens of millions a year on thwarting unwanted climate policy.[37] But in 2021 Greenpeace and the Dutch branch of Friends of the Earth won a case in court, which ruled that the oil giant must adapt its policy to comply with the demands of the Paris climate conference.[38] Not long after that, Shell decided to move its head office to London. The editor-in-chief of the Netherlands' most business-oriented daily newspaper concluded that panic would be justified if branches of business were to leave that would be of value in the future, but 'not an oil company that in the coming ten years will mainly be busy trying not to get overtaken by history'.[39]

## ARTISTS VERSUS THE FOSSIL FUEL INDUSTRY

*The Great Derangement* is a brilliant 2016 essay by Indian writer Amitav Ghosh (b. 1956).[40] In it he claims that the development of modern literature in Europe – especially the novel, on which he focuses – is characterized by an incapacity to relate in a meaningful way to the Industrial Revolution and the climate change that resulted from it. Broadly speaking, he concludes that since the seventeenth century, when the philosopher Descartes (whom we met earlier in this chapter) made a fundamental distinction between humans and nature (or between mind and body), Europeans have taken to concentrating on their own experiences as if they were isolated from the animal world and from natural processes. So at the very time when scientific developments were making the Industrial Revolution possible, changing the physical world drastically, cultural life switched its focus to the subtleties of the inner world of human beings.

The long-term consequence was that the effects of industry on nature, if they were observed at all, were ignored in new literary genres such as the novel. Because of their obsession with bourgeois interiors, novelists made it impossible for themselves to address protracted global developments. To appreciate those you need to focus on people as a collective. Worldwide, Ghosh complains, self-declared socially engaged writers have emulated the European model. Only over the past decade does this seem to be changing: many writers now, mindful of Ghosh's plea, have started to take an interest in climate change, although it receives most attention in science fiction, a genre generally regarded as marginal.[41]

Artists may feel the appeal of Ghosh's plea. As we have already seen, in the seventeenth century painters kept up with the most modern industrial developments and regarded the new polders, windmills and even pile drivers as attractive subjects, but in the art of the nineteenth and twentieth centuries the consequences of the Industrial Revolution remained largely invisible. Like the writers all over Europe who became absorbed in bourgeois concerns, painters concentrated on snapshots of everyday life. Their preference was eloquently described in the famous essay 'Le peintre de la vie moderne' ('The Painter of Modern Life', 1863) by Charles Baudelaire (1821–67). The fictional central character, artist Constantin Guys, tries to capture Parisian life in rapid sketches. In the chapter 'Modernity' he says, 'By "modernity" I mean the ephemeral, the fugitive, the contingent, the half of art whose other half is the eternal and the immutable. . . . This transitory, fugitive element, whose metamorphoses are so rapid, must on no account be despised or dispensed with.'[42] By losing themselves in such fashionable transience, artists wilfully shut their eyes to what actually made the new urban societies possible: large-scale industry that changed the world irrevocably.

Oddly, in the Low Countries it was precisely the landscape painters who donned blinkers of a similar kind. Like the French Impressionists, the painters of the Hague School did not hesitate to set up their easels somewhere out on the land or the beaches and record directly what they could see. But in doing so they limited themselves to nostalgic scenes that recalled a pre-industrial era. The focus was overwhelmingly on the North Sea coast and the historic polder landscape, complete with old-fashioned sailing ships and windmills. The new infrastructure remained invisible, including the railways, viaducts, cranes and factories that set in motion the industrialization of the Netherlands and that, as photographers of the time understood perfectly well, presented a visual spectacle in their own right.[43]

A letter from Vincent van Gogh (1853–90), who before he became a painter believed his calling was to be a missionary among Belgian miners, speaks volumes. In 1879 he went down into the coalmine at Marcasse (which can still be visited to this day) and gazed in astonishment at the impoverished miners, many of them still children – both boys and girls. At a depth of 700 metres 'the most hidden corners of that underworld' opened up to him, he wrote to his brother. 'It's a sombre place, and at first sight everything around it has something dismal and deathly about it. The workers there are usually people, emaciated and pale owing to fever, who look exhausted and haggard, weather-beaten and prematurely old. . . . If anyone were to try and make a painting of the *maintenages*, that would be something new and something unheard-of or rather never-before-seen.'[44] It was apparently unthinkable that an artist would take it into his head to depict the fossil landscape and its inhabitants (and Van Gogh limited himself to one forgettable pencil sketch).[45]

Van Gogh, in short, who was familiar with Baudelaire's work, stuck to the belief that the modern artist swears by brief experience and subjective spontaneity. Even he, so often praised for his capacities as a visionary, could not, it seems, wrest himself out of the collective Great Derangement. This was no less true of the generations that came after him. As recently as the final decades of the twentieth century, when the visual arts gradually developed to become performances that included social commentary, climate change was a subject remarkably rarely addressed in the European art academies. When in 1961 the Dutch conceptual artist Wim T. Schippers, during his famous *Manifestation on the Beach at Petten*, literally carried water to the North Sea and emptied a lemonade bottle into the waves ('carrying water to the sea' being the Dutch equivalent of carrying coals to Newcastle), it was to him merely a matter of art as a diversionary tactic, foolishness as a way to avoid being confronted with the pointlessness of existence. In 1979 Schippers made the *Steeple of Drienerlo* on the campus of the university in Enschede (figure 22). The tip of a church steeple sticks up out of a lake (and calls to mind Lake Reschen in Italy, of which more in chapter 5). Neither of these works had anything to do with rising sea levels. Schippers may perhaps have intended to address the increasing irrelevance of religion, but he was mainly making a joke. The unbearable lightness of such conceptual art prompted philosopher Arthur Danto (1924–2013) to claim in the 1990s that the visual arts worldwide, having degenerated into intellectual tomfoolery that did not go much beyond self-commentary, had reached the end of their historical development.

A noteworthy exception to this artistic navel-gazing was in the context of land art, large sculptural works that make a direct intervention in the landscape. One early example that stresses the precarious condition of the Dutch landscape is by American sculptor Richard Serra with his work *Sea Level* (1996) at Zeewolde in Flevoland, a province that consists entirely of reclaimed land. Serra set two concrete walls 200 metres long at an angle to the canal, on either side of the water, aligned with each other as if continuous. Dead level in an artificially undulating landscape, closest to the canal both walls are several metres high, while at their other ends they penetrate the slopes.[46] If the dykes around Flevoland were to be breached, the water would rise to the top of the walls. Visitors walking downwards past the cool concrete may have the impression of becoming immersed.

A more recent project that addresses the perishability of the Low Countries involves the scale models at the Waterloopkundig Laboratorium (Hydraulic Laboratory) in Marknesse. The models were built to test the effectiveness of major projects including the Delta Works, the system of dams, sluices and dykes built from 1954 onwards to protect the south-west of the Netherlands (the huge delta of the Rhine, Meuse and Scheldt) against the sea. The largest of the models was the Delta Flume, a pool used for experiments with waves. After the laboratory was closed, artists' collective Atelier de Lyon/RAAAF dug out the concrete basin so that it now towers 7 metres above the level of the groundwater. The artists sawed large blocks out of the walls and tilted them, thereby highlighting questions about the durability of the Delta Works, which were designed for a rise in sea level of a maximum of 40 centimetres. The most recent report by the IPCC predicts that by 2100 this safety margin will no longer be sufficient.

When the real Delta Works were completed, the American Society of Civil Engineers – unconsciously repeating what had been said of the wooden-pile foundations of the Amsterdam Town Hall in the seventeenth century – declared them one of the seven wonders of the modern world. But in fact the vast project has failed. The Delta Law of 1958 lays down that the Dutch state is obliged to protect its citizens against storm surges, and the annual likelihood of flooding must be no greater than 1 in 1,000, or as low as 1 in 100,000 for the most important dykes. It is questionable to what extent the government, which has already (in 2021) proven unable to comply with a demand made by a judge, namely to reduce greenhouse gas emissions by 25 per cent, will be able to comply with Dutch law in this respect.

## THE ROBBER BARONS AND THEIR ART PATRONAGE

In the nineteenth and twentieth centuries, artists shut their eyes to the fossil fuel industry, but the fossil fuel industry certainly did not shut its eyes to art. The American robber barons and their descendants, who accumulated huge fortunes in heavy industry, including the extraction of oil and coal, acted as patrons of the arts to an impressive degree. The most famous example is John D. Rockefeller Jr (1874–1960), director of one of the largest oil companies in the world, founded by his father, the aforementioned Standard Oil (which later changed its name to Esso and is currently known as ExxonMobil). Rockefeller succeeded in becoming famous mainly for his philanthropic activities, including the large sums he spent on historical heritage. He financed the collection held by The Cloisters, the well-known museum of mediaeval art in New York, and the building in which it is housed. He also paid almost the entire cost of the reconstruction of colonial Williamsburg (we will look at the ethics of such large-scale reconstruction in chapter 7). This particular magnate was no less active in the 'Old World', sponsoring excavations of the Agora in Athens and Luxor in Egypt. He eventually became an honoured guest of the French president after donating part of his fortune to the restoration of Rheims Cathedral and the palaces of Fontainebleau and Versailles. Visitors to Versailles today, as well as seeing statues of Louis XIV, can admire Rockefeller's name, immortalized in gold lettering carved into marble.

Rockefeller's great rival, Shell director Henri Deterding, was no less generous to Dutch museums. Many of the most important works in the Rijksmuseum in Amsterdam, including the famous *Little Street* by Vermeer and winter landscapes and river views by Avercamp, Van Ruysdael and Aert van der Neer, were donated by Deterding in the 1920s and 1930s. The Mauritshuis in The Hague benefitted from his generosity too, with masterpieces including Ter Borch's *Woman Writing a Letter* and landscape paintings by Van Ruysdael, Van Goyen and Jan van de Cappelle.

If Deterding's enthusiasm for National Socialism had not disqualified him as a national hero, his importance for Dutch heritage would no doubt be far better known.

It is clear in any case that Deterding wanted to operate somewhat in the background in comparison to the notorious 'robber barons'. With his modest profile he distinguished himself from one of the other founders of Shell, the Armenian Calouste Gulbenkian (1869–1955). Possessing a fortune based on oil shares, Gulbenkian compiled a dazzling art collection, including two Rembrandts, which was initially kept in his house in Paris. During the war he moved to Portugal, where the works can still be admired in the Calouste Gulbenkian Museum in Lisbon.

The fossil fuel industry was also at the root of the richest art institution in the world, the J. Paul Getty Trust. Getty (1892–1976) was the founder of the Getty Oil Company, an energy empire that stretched from Mexico to Saudi Arabia. Part of his profits went on art, and in the 1970s he had a copy of a Roman villa in Pompei built among the California cactuses. It became the improbable setting for a display of more than 600 paintings by artists including Rembrandt and Rubens. He appointed Wilhelm Valentiner (1880–1958) as director of the museum, a specialist in the Dutch masters who had trained in The Hague. To this day the Getty Trust invests generously in art-historical research and conservation sciences; I myself received one of his subsidies in 2007 for the writing of a book.[47]

The fact that the continued existence of the Getty Museum is now threatened by the increasingly destructive California wildfires, caused by persistent drought, and was forced to close for a while in 2019 and again in 2025 for that reason, can only be described as ironic. I should mention here that the Trust owes its wealth purely to profits from the fossil fuel industry in the past – the institution does not currently have any links to that industry. The same goes for the collection of Thomas Kaplan (b. 1962), an investor in precious metals who was also the founder of a successful company (Leor Energy) that prospected for oil and gas in Texas. Kaplan has emerged as the most active living collector of works by Rembrandt. His Leiden Collection is one of the biggest private collections of Dutch seventeenth-century art in existence, and it loans them to museums all over the world.

## ARTWASHING WORLDWIDE

In more recent times, in the wake of Rockefeller and Getty, oil companies – Shell, BP, Total, Aramco – have cynically tried to connect their names with the world's great museums. These attempts to give malodorous fossil-oil-based activities a coating of civilization by sponsoring the arts has become known as artwashing, by analogy with greenwashing, or the way companies try to placate their critics by seemingly adopting environmentally aware policies.

Since the 2010s, several artists' collectives have succeeded in taking up the matter of artwashing with those who visit art museums. The best-known are the United Visual Artists, based in London, who caused an 'oil spill' in the Tate Modern, the city's well-known museum of contemporary art, to draw attention to twenty years of subsidy from BP. An even greater impression was made by *The Gift*, a 16-metre-long wind-turbine blade that the activists managed to smuggle into the museum's Turbine Hall. In 2017 the Tate ended its sponsorship deal with the oil giant.

The example proved infectious; the United Visual Artists have sympathizers worldwide. The glass pyramid at the Louvre in Paris was daubed with thick molasses by French activists to highlight the museum's connection with Total.

In 2017 eight women in white dresses climbed the steps of the Van Gogh Museum in Amsterdam and theatrically drank an oily substance out of shells. One of them read out a letter from Vincent van Gogh in which he writes about courage in dangerous times. They also set out 411 shells holding coal-black ink between the paintings, pointing to the 411 parts per million (ppm) of $CO_2$ that were present that day in the atmosphere (as measured at the Mauna Loa weather station on Hawaii; since then a peak of 430 ppm has been reached). Shortly afterwards, the museum severed its links with Shell, although it denied that the protest had anything to do with its decision.

The activists may, however, have been barking up the wrong tree. European art institutions constitute a perpetually ailing sector. Since the economic crisis of 2008 many governments have introduced neoliberal reforms. Museums need to strive for financial independence through cultural entrepreneurship, and as a result many have dutifully sought sponsorship contracts with commercial companies. The fossil fuel industry has taken the opportunity, sometimes with minimal investment, to gain immense visibility and influence in museum programming.[48] The fact that the oil companies boost their image through artwashing is reprehensible in the light of the damage climate change inflicts, upon cultural heritage among other things, but a far more substantial problem is the vast amount of government subsidy given to the fossil fuel industry. If heritage is really such a matter of life and death that even large multinationals cannot do without it, there is a shorter route: invest the taxpayers' money now spent as state support for businesses directly in museums and the cultural sector. According to the International Monetary Fund, 7,000 billion dollars each year worldwide is used to subsidize the fossil fuel industry (in the UK the sum is 18 billion dollars, in the Netherlands 49 billion dollars), which comes to more than 7 per cent of global domestic product. That is far more than the amount spent by governments annually on education (4.3% of global GDP).

As far as artwashing goes, however, it seems the trend is unlikely to be reversed. If anything the opposite may happen. The Museum of Modern Art in New York is planning to open a branch in Abu Dhabi, capital of petrostate the United Arab Emirates, which already hosts impressive dependencies of the Louvre and the Guggenheim Museum. Another Louvre is planned for Riyadh, capital of Saudi Arabia.

## ANOTHER COLONIAL DIMENSION: BRITAIN, INDIA, MYANMAR, IRAN, IRAQ

The most impertinent example of artwashing, which shows how tightly interwoven are colonial history, modern energy imperialism, the fossil fuel industry, climate change, heritage and museums, is the collaboration between BP and the British Museum.

From the founding of the multinational Royal Dutch Shell, Britain was a stakeholder in the Dutch East Indies. In order to produce oil on the Indian subcontinent as well, in 1871 the Rangoon Oil Company was established in Glasgow, followed in 1886 by the Burmah Oil Company and in 1890 by the Assam Oil Company. The big bang came in 1909, when in Iran (then still called Persia) a major oilfield was discovered at Masjed Soleyman. It was developed by the Anglo-Persian Oil Company, out of which, after a merger with the companies focused on India, British Petroleum eventually arose.[49]

BP (like Shell) is still a major player in the Middle East, a situation that could be described as 'neo-imperialist'. In the months leading up to the Second Gulf War, the American–British invasion of Saddam Hussein's Iraq in 2003, BP lobbied the British government for access to the local oil reserves. After the war, the oil giant was the first Western company to return to Iraq. Although the British government has always denied that oil was the motivation, the war certainly did not do this showpiece of national industry any harm. In the years since the Iraq War, BP has extracted at least 15 billion pounds' worth of oil in Iraq.[50]

During the First Gulf War (1990–1) President George Bush Sr consulted a team of archaeologists, with the aim of ensuring his invasion of Iraq would involve as little damage to heritage as possible. Mesopotamia is the cradle of human civilization, they assured him. It was here that handwriting was first developed and the earliest surviving fictional story written, the Gilgamesh epic. It is also the setting of the biblical book of Genesis. Sumerians, Acadians, Babylonians, Assyrians, Chaldeans, Persians, Greeks, Romans, Parthians and Sassanians have each in turn left archaeological traces there.

But in 2003 George W. Bush and the British prime minister Tony Blair were a good deal more reckless. Their coalition set up Camp Alpha, for example, complete with a helicopter base, right in the middle of the ruins of Babylon. The biggest city in the world in the second millennium BCE, Babylon is one of the most important sites of antiquity. King Nebuchadnezzar II built his famous Hanging Gardens there, one of the Seven Wonders of the World. In laying out Camp Alpha, US military vehicles crushed brick floors 3,000 years old. American and Polish troops filled sandbags with archaeological soil, brutally disturbing the integrity of the site. Vibrations from helicopters caused the Temple of Nabu and the roof of the Temple of Ninmah to collapse (both date from the sixth century BCE). A theatre from the time of Alexander the Great was used as a parking area. Although experts on heritage pointed out to the commanding officers and to the general public how egregious the effects of all this were, the base was not dismantled until after the American troops had left.

Far more damaging, however, was the looting of the museums of Iraq. In their 'Joint Statement on Iraq's Future' of 8 April 2003, Bush and Blair stressed their 'commitment to protect Iraq's natural resources, as the patrimony of the people of Iraq, which should be used only for their benefit'.[51] By 'patrimony' they meant only petroleum. When they captured Baghdad, coalition troops protected the Ministry of Oil but not the National Museum, which housed the country's archaeological heritage. It was looted. During and after the invasion, countless Iraqi antiquities (an estimated 600,000 items) found their way onto the illegal art market.[52] The museum in Baghdad is currently full of replicas. The originals have been scattered – as has Iraq's oil wealth, which has mostly ended up in the pockets of foreign companies.

It is particularly ironic that so much Babylonian heritage can currently be found in London, in the British Museum, which is generously sponsored by BP. This collaboration resulted, among other things, in a blockbuster exhibition in 2018 about the Assyrian king Ashurbanipal. Many of the objects on show had originally been taken from Iraq as loot. To this day the museum's website makes proud mention of its partnership with BP, which 'represents one of the most significant corporate investments in UK arts and culture'. After all, 'BP has a history in Iraq, stretching back to the 1920s'.[53]

The term irony actually seems inadequate. Since the war, the carbon released by the burning of petroleum has led to extreme rises in temperature in the region that includes ancient Mesopotamia. As touched upon in chapter 1, the United Nations estimates that by 2050 average annual temperatures will have risen by 2°C. Iraq will experience more heatwaves (temperatures of 50° or more) and its average rainfall will reduce by 9 per cent. The soils and groundwater in

Mesopotamia have always been highly saline. With the rivers bringing less water, the salt concentration in local architecture is rising and the walls of the Temple of Ishtar are already covered in a layer of salt. When the salt crystallizes, it can crack the stones of the World Heritage Site of Babylon, the largest city of the classical world, which is almost 4,000 years old.

## MUSEUMS AS BATTLEGROUNDS FOR CLIMATE ACTION

It was a protest watched all over the world. One of the most popular paintings in the Mauritshuis in The Hague – Johannes Vermeer's *Girl with a Pearl Earring* – was crudely affronted in her timeless dignity. In 2022 a Belgian climate activist attempted to superglue his bald head to the glass that protects the painting. A companion opened a can of tomatoes and poured the contents over his head. 'How do you feel when you see something beautiful and priceless being apparently destroyed before your eyes?' one of the pair called out to the art lovers present, who clutched their pearl necklaces in shock. In museums in Italy and the UK too, the soup-throwers of Just Stop Oil mounted protests.

Even though the activists limited themselves to paintings that were protected by glass, it was difficult to share their conviction that their actions were completely non-violent; they had a notable impact on the mental wellbeing of the museum attendants. A year later, taking their lead from the suffragettes, who attacked the same painting in 1914, Just Stop Oil broke the glass of Velázquez's *Rokeby Venus* in the National Gallery in London, and on that occasion the painted surface was (slightly) damaged. But it is at least as difficult to have no sympathy at all for their objective. The activists targeted the paintings they found most beautiful, such as Van Gogh's *Peach Trees in Blossom* or Botticelli's *Primavera*. Precisely because of the great attachment to these artworks, they understand perfectly well the 'punch to the stomach' that most of us will feel when witnessing an attack on a much-loved painting. That punch is highly effective in propagating an activist message. In the words of a member of Extinction Rebellion (XR), 'The soup on the painting was an extraordinary experiment concerning our relative attention to the world. . . . It is striking that our culture takes it for granted that we can conserve art – insured, behind armoured glass, with a red rope in front and under the watchful eye of an attendant – and at the same time simply watch with sorrow the ubiquitous pollution and destruction of our world.'[54] A more prosaic comment would be that the value of these paintings is easier to express in monetary terms than the value of nature.

When *Girl with a Pearl Earring* was targeted, the most obvious comment to make was that the whole of The Hague would be flooded if no action was taken against climate change. Glenn Albrecht, the philosopher who invented the concept of 'solastalgia', looked even further into the future when he defended the activists who smeared orange paint on Stonehenge: 'A couple of people on foot use non-violence and biodegradable means to bring attention to the need to stop this fossil-fuel generated madness. If we do not stop this madness, visiting Stonehenge will be done only by rooks . . . and only if they survive the desolation that comes next.'[55]

Such protests also produced a good deal of self-reflection in the international museum world. When a British judge sentenced the activists who had thrown soup over Van Gogh's *Sunflowers* to substantial jail sentences, a collective of artists, curators and art historians wrote in defence of what they had done. They saw it as performance art, and part of a long iconoclastic tradition (their main objection being that the activists would have done better to use Campbell's soup, famous from the work by Andy Warhol named after it).[56] The penny dropped even with some museum directors. In the Netherlands the chair of the national museum association, Vera Carasso, expressed support for the activists; she understood that the social role of museums makes them the scene of action for climate activism.

The shock effect could not last, however. When in 2024 Leonardo da Vinci's *Mona Lisa* in Paris was hit by soup, it made hardly any impression (this was perhaps the first time that the *Mona Lisa* failed to overshadow Vermeer's *Girl*). There was criticism of a different kind from the Global South. The polemic of European young people who got excited about paintings, and their circumspect tango with museum attendants, was seen as extremely elitist in countries like Colombia and the Philippines, where climate activists face brutal violence daily. Every few days, one of them is killed.[57]

The most important consequence of the museum protests may be a shift in the 'Overton Window'. Polls show that after witnessing extreme protests, the general public has a greater tendency to appreciate more moderate action.[58] How rapidly this shift can occur was seen in 2023, when Dutch activists from Extinction Rebellion occupied a motorway in The Hague, the seat of the national government, month after month. Compared to attacking beloved artworks, this was a lot less threatening. Their demand, a steady reduction in fossil fuel subsidies, eventually gained broad support among the population. When the government decided to agree to it, XR was able to suspend its protests.

For this book, it is above all of importance that the man who glued his head to the *Girl with a Pearl Earring*, probably without knowing it, focused attention on a historical cycle. Without the climate change of the Little Ice Age there would have been no Golden Age of Dutch art, but in the twenty-first century the Netherlands is a frontline nation when it comes to the 'collapse of Western civilization'. The protest therefore made Vermeer's *Girl* the perfect poster girl for the interlinkage between heritage and climate. Her future, along with that of the Netherlands, will after all depend on the degree to which the climate crisis can be averted in the coming decades. It seems quite likely to me that in the long term, Vermeer's image will remain famous above all as an icon of human helplessness in the face of climate change.

For art lovers and art historians, it will be increasingly important to turn their gaze not just to the past but to the future. This realization might prompt reflection on how, in the light of the climate crisis, we must start to think differently about the course taken by the history of art and about the passage of time in general. More about this in the next chapter.

# 4. The historical sensation in the Anthropocene

'Stop using the word Holocene. We're not in the Holocene any more. We are in the . . . the . . . the Anthropocene!' So Utrecht climatologist and Nobel Prize winner Paul Crutzen (1933–2021) is said to have remarked angrily during an earth sciences conference in Mexico.[1] The term Anthropocene has since become established. Derived from the Greek words *anthropos* (human) and *kainos* (new), it expresses the idea that the Holocene, the warm period that followed the last Ice Age, has given way to a new period in which humans indisputably have an influence on the climate. In 2002 Crutzen argued as follows in the authoritative journal *Nature*:

> Because of these anthropogenic emissions of carbon dioxide, global climate may depart significantly from natural behaviour for many millennia to come. It seems appropriate to assign the term 'Anthropocene' to the present, in many ways human-dominated, geological epoch, supplementing the Holocene – the warm period of the past 10–12 millennia. The Anthropocene could be said to have started in the latter part of the eighteenth century, when analyses of air trapped in polar ice showed the beginning of growing global concentrations of carbon dioxide and methane. This date also happens to coincide with James Watt's design of the steam engine in 1784.[2]

His article caught the attention of scholars in the humanities, who realized that this new era was significant for them too. In 2009 Indian historian Dipesh Chakrabarty (b. 1948) wrote an article that has since become famous, called 'The Climate of History'. Recognition of the geological and climatological consequences of human behaviour, he believes, forces those studying the history of humankind and of nature to see them as interconnected.[3] This may seem obvious, but for centuries the humanities have done precisely the opposite.

According to Neapolitan philosopher Giambattista Vico (1668–1744), often seen as one of the founders of the humanities, people can only truly know what they themselves have made. Vico therefore claimed that the humanities clearly have a different character from the natural sciences, despite being no less rigorous and sound. We can fully understand culture and history, in which people have always been the guiding force. He believed this distinguished them from nature, whose secrets we will never entirely discover.

Now that we live in the Anthropocene, however, we need to recognize that human and natural history cannot be considered in isolation from each other. What is nature, if it has been fundamentally altered by human actions? What is history, if it no longer deals exclusively with human development but patently has an effect on the natural environment on a planetary scale – and in doing so causes events that escape human control? Vico, who lived in the pre-industrial era, will have had predominantly positive associations in mind when contemplating human creations, with the exception perhaps of cannonballs and warships. Now that more concrete, asphalt and steel exist on earth than biomass (by weight), his philosophical preference for human as against natural products seems outdated.

In our own day, the humanities have taken to heart the interweaving of human and natural factors, and historians, literary theorists and others, full of conviction, have thrown themselves into the new discipline of the environmental humanities. One good example is Dagomar Degroot, whom we met in the previous chapter. He studies the connection between socio-economic history and meteorology. Philosophers too are eager to join the conversation. Traditionally, the branch of philosophy known as aesthetics, which asks what beauty is, studied both nature and the arts; after all, the experience of nature, like the experience of art, can bring us a sense of beauty or the sublime. How does such appreciation change in a time of climate crisis?

The experience of beauty or the sublime need not have anything to do with history; if we are to believe Plato, for instance, true beauty is eternal and unchanging. In this book, therefore, we focus on a different, more specific issue. Heritage always has a relationship with the passage of time. We value it not merely because we find it beautiful or impressive, but primarily because it connects us, or at least puts us in touch, with the past. The nuances of this confrontation – does heritage bring the past closer, or does it show us the unbridgeable distance between the past and us? – will be examined in the next chapter. But first, with Crutzen and Chakrabarty in mind, we look at the question of how, in the Anthropocene, our attitude to historical heritage relates to our attitude to nature.

## HUMAN AND NATURAL HISTORY: A MATTER OF SCALE

This book is about heritage fashioned by human hands, which is to say historical or cultural heritage. There is also something we could call 'natural heritage'. UNESCO places it in a separate category, that of landscapes that merit preservation, irrespective of human involvement. Of course there are intermediate forms, making it hard to draw a firm line between cultural and natural heritage. 'Cultured landscapes' testify to the ways in which humans have shaped the landscape. The former island of Schokland, for example, is one of the UNESCO World Heritage Sites in the Netherlands. Human intervention caused it to be surrounded by polders as time went on, and it is now part of Flevoland, a new Dutch province made up of three huge land reclamation projects completed between the 1940s and the 1960s. Recent archaeological research suggests that humans have been interfering in nature for 10,000 years, and that in many cases there is therefore little point in distinguishing between nature and culture.[4] But in a broad sense, the timescales in which they have developed present an important distinction between cultural heritage and natural heritage. The time over which cultural production has taken place is considerably shorter than that of geological or other natural processes, often referred to as 'deep time' (of which more later in this chapter).

Here are the numbers. The timescale of cultural heritage covers a period from the oldest surviving cave painting, created 50,000 years ago on the Indonesian island of Sulawesi, to our material keepsakes of our parents and grandparents. A landscape too, of course, shows the passage of time. Take for example the sediment layers of the Grand Canyon in the US, eroded over millennia. But then we are looking at developments of a very different temporal order: estimates of the age of the landscape of the Grand Canyon range from 5 to 55 million years. This is a considerably longer period than the timescale within which mammals evolve. Fossil remains show that the maximum lifespan of an animal species, if we limit ourselves to mammals, is no more than a million years. *Homo sapiens* probably came into existence 200,000 years ago.

Cultural heritage, unlike nature, can therefore confront us with the historical development of our species and of our own capacities, and this determines to a great extent our appreciation of it – even, or perhaps especially, in an era of climate disruption. Nature will continue to exist, even if humankind disappears, although it will be different, whereas the continued existence of the human species cannot be taken for granted. Climate change now presents a risk to heritage from all phases of the timeline of human existence. As regards prehistory, the cave paintings on Sulawesi have already been seriously damaged by increasing temperatures.[5] Rising sea levels are threatening a cave complex on the east coast of Gibraltar that contains the artistic traces of Neanderthals who lived more than 39,000 years ago.[6] If we then look at the recent past, which is to say the places and objects associated with our parents and grandparents, cemeteries are a telling example. We see dramatic images of the aforementioned graveyard in Togoru in the Pacific Ocean, which comes to lie further under the sea every year (see p. 34 and figure 11).[7]

Heritage made by human hands confronts us with the course of our own history, and in this respect it differs from natural heritage. In chapter 2 we looked at how global warming is beyond the human capacity to imagine space and time, making it a 'hyperobject'. The consequences of warming for historical heritage, by contrast, are increasingly observable in ways that are entirely concrete. It is therefore meaningful to focus on heritage, even though the Anthropocene demands an integrated approach to the history of humankind and that of the natural environment. To put it another way, historical monuments can take an intermediary position (a meso-level) between the micro-level of individual human experience – the memory of one, two or perhaps three generations – and the macro-level, the 'deep time' within which the evolution of species and geological developments occur.

## THE HISTORICAL SENSATION IN THE LIGHT OF THE FUTURE

For a better understanding of the relationship between heritage and the scale, direction and speed of the passage of time, it is helpful to begin with Dutch historian Johan Huizinga (1872–1945). Regarded as the founder of cultural history as a discipline, he is best known for his concept of 'historical sensation'. He experienced this sensation for the first time at an exhibition of fifteenth-century paintings by Jan van Eyck and Rogier van der Weyden, held in Bruges in 1902. Looking at these artworks, exceptionally rich in everyday details and painted with dazzling virtuosity, was for him more deeply affecting than reading the historical sources, and it inspired him to write his world-famous book *Herfsttij der Middeleeuwen* (*Autumntide of the Middle Ages*), first published in Dutch in 1919. He writes of material heritage that 'a feeling of immediate contact with the past is a sensation as deep as the purest enjoyment of art; it is an almost ecstatic sensation of no longer being myself, of overflowing into the world around me, of touching the essence of things, of through history experiencing the truth'.[8]

Huizinga belongs in the same category as famous visually oriented intellectuals such as Johann Wolfgang von Goethe (1749–1832), Jacob Burckhardt (1818–97) and Mario Praz (1896–1982), who could experience a historical sensation at the sight of a piece of furniture, a cityscape or a room untouched for hundreds of years.[9] In the twentieth century, scepticism arose among historians, who increasingly doubted that it was possible to experience and even 'touch' the past so directly through the senses. For some people, however, the idea is still very much alive, including the notion that the historical sensation 'pulls the faces of past and present together in a short but ecstatic kiss', as philosopher of history Frank Ankersmit (b. 1945) puts it. He even defines it as a 'sublime experience'.[10] Within heritage practice too, there is a prevailing belief that only carefully regulated sensory perception can give access to the past. UNESCO, for example, demands that the locations it recognizes as World Heritage must be surrounded by a buffer zone that corresponds visually and materially with the authentic historical remains.

Looking back, it is striking that Huizinga's ideas about the importance of the historical sensation cannot be seen in isolation from the way in which the Western world has dealt with natural resources. His desire to touch history was inspired by his realization that there is a fundamental break between past and present. This outlook is not universal. It is associated with historicism, a worldview that emerged in nineteenth-century Europe. Before that time, Westerners assumed they were still in direct contact with the world of their ancestors. The Amsterdammers who built the city's ring of canals, for example, believed they were the descendants of the Batavians, a Germanic tribe that lived in the Low Countries at the time of the Roman occupation.[11]

Around 1800, however, traumatic political and scientific developments occurred that changed the world to such an extent that a return to the previous situation seemed impossible. This was what is known as the 'dual revolution', when the French Revolution of 1789 coincided with the Industrial Revolution, sparked in 1784 by James Watt's invention of the steam engine. Those two mutually reinforcing developments created an insurmountable barrier between past and present.[12] In 1830 German philosopher Georg Wilhelm Friedrich Hegel (1770–1831) recalled the excitement of that time, then just a few decades back, in terms of a cosmological change such that humans gained command of their environment for the first time:

> As long as the sun stands in the firmament and the planets revolve around it, has it not happened that man stood on his head, that is, on Thought, and built up actuality in conformity to it. . . . Only now has man come to the insight that Thought should govern spiritual actuality. This was, consequently, a glorious sunrise.[13]

From our present-day perspective, the disruptive consequences of the Industrial Revolution are obvious. We are all now aware that the development Hegel pointed to also heralded a shift from wood and other renewable energy sources to the use of fossil fuels on a large scale – first coal, later oil and gas. His suggestion of a radical about-turn can from this perspective be read as advance notice of the Anthropocene, the age in which humans have themselves become a geological and climatological factor of significance. It seems that the sunrise of which he wrote, when human beings came to govern nature, is now being followed by a sunset, with nature proving less and less governable. It is therefore appropriate to look at the historicism of Hegel and Huizinga afresh in the light of the climate crisis. Whereas until recently the confrontation with historical structures and artefacts entailed above all reflection on the past, as a result of climate change the timeline now runs in two directions: the vulnerability of heritage inspires us to look ahead, into the future.

## THE END OF PROGRESSIVISM

Hegel's optimism – seeing the French and Industrial Revolutions as having made an irreversible contribution to progress – proved to have a limited shelf life. It appears that history does not simply move in one direction, towards modernity. In the humanities this perspective is not new, and the validity of the 'modernist narrative' has been subjected to scrutiny for some time already, even by authors who are not at all interested in the climate crisis. As far back as the 1990s, postmodern philosophers Francis Fukuyama (b. 1952) and the aforementioned Arthur Danto announced, respectively, the 'end of history' and the 'end of art'. According to Fukuyama, the entire world would slowly but surely adopt the model of Western liberal democracy.[14] According to Danto, as concepts and critical reflection gradually gained the upper hand over form, art, 'having finally become vaporized in a dazzle of pure thought about itself', would remain 'as it were, solely as the object of its own theoretical consciousness'.[15] Meanwhile, it has become clear to what extent these postmodern notions testify to an almost unbearable intellectual lightness. Firstly, in the 1990s precious few of the self-declared socially engaged thinkers and artists realized what was actually happening in terms of fundamental climate disruption. Secondly, this disruption had as its consequence more of a practical than a theoretical 'end' of art and art history.

While the end of history has been contemplated for some time by philosophers, it is striking that the idea of progress within heritage studies is still very much alive. It is a generally accepted idea that with the help of more refined scientific techniques, we are increasingly in a position to conserve and future-proof material heritage. Moreover, every year UNESCO gives more and more buildings and locations the status of World Heritage, thereby reinforcing the technical, legal and ethical framework for protecting heritage against future decay. Climate change is so disruptive, however, that such optimism is coming to an end, now that architecture, ancient cities and entire cultured landscapes are having to be abandoned.

Both scientifically inspired optimism (progress) and postmodern scepticism (stasis) therefore fall short for those wishing to contemplate historical developments in the Anthropocene. It would be more accurate to say that history moves in different directions, at different speeds. Is there any structure left in this new disorder?

## PROGRESS IN THE WEST = DECLINE IN THE GLOBAL SOUTH

Writing history in the Anthropocene means first of all, mindful of Crutzen and Chakrabarty, becoming conscious of the increasing climatological damage that we will suffer in the twenty-first century. Kathryn Yusoff in London, a self-declared professor of 'inhuman geography', observes that we are fairly late in arriving at this insight. Europeans and Americans have already left a trail of destruction behind them. Waving the banners of Enlightenment, progress and modernization, Westerners have for decades exported petrochemical and other industrial damage to the Global South. We may deplore the fact that we are no longer able to understand our history in terms of progress, and that the end of the world may perhaps be coming into view, but we would do well to realize that the Western ideal of progress has been hastening the end of worlds elsewhere ever since its inception.[16]

When Crutzen first came up with the concept of the 'Anthropocene', he concluded that the effects he was describing 'have largely been caused by only 25% of the world population'.[17] For that 25 per cent, the use of fossil fuels made possible modernization of a kind never seen before. The rest of the world did not merely lag behind in this development; in many cases it was left with ravaged landscapes and other ecological devastation. Meanwhile, it is precisely the Global South that is being hit disproportionately hard by the consequences of climate change.

The term 'Anthropocene' is therefore misleading. It places the responsibility for the current situation at the door of all human beings, whereas in fact it lies only with the Western industrialized elite, Yusoff claims. (Nowadays, according to the latest IPCC report, the richest 10 per cent of humankind is responsible for half of all greenhouse gas emissions.[18]) A better alternative might be the term 'Capitalocene', which suggests large companies are the culprits – or even, feminists suggest, the 'Patriarchalocene', because men, the patriarchy in other words, have a larger ecological footprint than women.[19]

In her book *A Billion Black Anthropocenes or None* (2019), Yusoff stresses the interwoven histories of the fossil fuel industry and the trans-Atlantic slave trade. On the one hand it is arguable that the abolition of slavery was possible only because fossil fuels made much human labour unprofitable (as they did beasts of burden, and wood, wind and water as sources of power). Towards the end of the twentieth century, 85 per cent of all the energy used by humans came from fossil fuels.[20] On the other hand it is obvious, Yusoff claims, that one evil has now been exchanged for another. Black communities in the US, after abolition as before it, sustained the fossil fuel industry. The Tennessee Coal, Iron and Railroad Company and the Alabama Iron Ore Company, for instance, used forced labour by predominantly African-American prisoners. They kept the coalmines of the US Steel Corporation, one of the mainstays of the national economy, running. To this day, the fossil fuel industry relies on the exploitation of minorities at home and of populations in the Global South.[21] Particularly illustrative in this sense is the continual clash between American oil companies and Native Americans. Protests against the Dakota Access Pipeline, which runs past the Standing Rock reservation and threatens not just the quality of the drinking water but ancient Native American burial places and other sites of historical significance, have been going on since 2016.

To authenticate her claim, Yusoff points to parallels between oil and another form of energy extraction, nuclear energy, of which the dark side – nuclear weapons and radioactive waste – was obvious from the very start. The Americans developed these technologies by experimenting in Asia and Oceania, with immense ecological and social consequences. For nuclear tests on Bikini Atoll (part of the Marshall Islands), all residents were forced to move to other islands. The 1954 hydrogen bomb, called Castle Bravo, the most powerful nuclear weapon ever detonated by the US – the explosion was far bigger than expected – amounted to a spine-chilling foreshadowing of the tragic fate now faced by the region. With a rise in sea level of 1 metre, several islands will disappear entirely, and the continued existence of several others is threatened. As poet Kathy Jetñil-Kijiner, who comes from the Marshall Islands, puts it, 'These two issues – they're so much bigger than us, nuclear issues and climate change and yet we [the Marshall Islands] are at that crossroad.'[22] Meanwhile, the large amount of nuclear waste stored on these islands (partly the result of nuclear testing that the US carried out elsewhere) is in danger of being swallowed by the ocean as sea levels rise; the consequences are expected to be disastrous.

The Americans are not the only culprits. The Dutch have grubby hands too. Leaky oil pipelines belonging to Shell have caused extremely damaging pollution in the Niger Delta in Nigeria, for which in 2021 the company was found liable to pay damages. But an even more tragic fate, if such a thing is possible, has struck the former capital of the Dutch East Indies, where Shell developed the world's biggest oil company, beginning in 1900. Of all today's cities, low-lying Jakarta now runs the greatest risk of destruction by sea-level rise, largely caused by global warming. In 2022 a start was made on the building of an entirely new Indonesian capital, in the interior of Borneo. The cause of the vulnerability of Jakarta lies in its history as the successor to Dutch Batavia. Like other colonial capitals, including Mumbai, New York and Hong Kong, the location of Batavia in the Java Sea was chosen with a view to its accessibility from the European metropolis, but without any thought being given to its ecological safety in the long term. (This is in contrast to cities such as Amsterdam and London, which were not built right on the coast.) The situation is now calamitous, and Jakarta's days are numbered.[23]

## CYCLICAL HISTORY

Kathryn Yusoff laments the blinkered view of Westerners with regard to their concept of time, which presumes their own progress at the price of decline elsewhere. Unfortunately she says nothing about what alternatives to the white, Western model of progress she would propose. Alternative 'time regimes' – which is to say, other ideas about where history is going and how quickly – are certainly possible, however. To find older examples, we should look first of all at the period before the Industrial Revolution.

The fact that in history there are not just times of progress but times of decline was actually the underlying principle of a text generally acknowledged as the foundation of art history, Giorgio Vasari's *Le vite de' più eccellenti pittori, scultori, e architettori* (*The Lives of the Most Excellent Painters, Sculptors, and Architects*, 1550–1568).[24] The timeline he lays down is well known. After flourishing in antiquity, art fell into decline until it was revived in fourteenth-century Florence and reached new heights with Michelangelo. This notion of a cyclical history has developed elsewhere as well: the Greek stoics believed in *ekpyrosis*, the periodic destruction of the world; Chinese history supposed that emperors succeeded each other according to a dynastic cycle; and according to Tunisian scholar Ibn Khaldun (1332–1406), cities developed only if they were destroyed now and then by nomads.[25]

The history of European global expansion includes obvious examples of clashes between a so-called 'modern' belief in progress on the part of the colonizer and the 'old-fashioned' cyclical temporal regime of the colonized. In his book about the Gulf of Bengal, Kenyan historian Sunil Amrith (b. 1979) observes, 'As the clocks and the cartography of modern Europe refigured time and space, coastal spiritual traditions offered a different understanding of history and geography: proximity was measured by spiritual intensity rather than by physical distance, and time was cyclical rather than linear.'[26] Now that we are facing profound climate disruption, it is becoming clear that the modernist notion of permanent progress is less capable of elucidating the course of history than other models. For heritage management too, a cyclical model may be of fresh significance, as we will see in the next chapter in relation to relics in East and South Asia.

An important marginal note needs to be placed here: in a time of climate crisis, we cannot be certain whether after a period of 'decline' another 'flourishing' will occur. Changes, after all, can accelerate exponentially and reach a tipping point that can never be reversed.

## THE GREAT ACCELERATION

If we want to reconsider, in the light of the Anthropocene, those forms of experience of time – linear and cyclical – that have traditionally been accepted, we need to pay attention to what is known as the 'Great Acceleration'. This is a reference to the dramatic, relentless increase on a global scale of a wide range of human activities, first observed in the mid-twentieth century and continuing unabated to this day. The increase was made possible by the use of fossil fuels, which caused labour, production, consumption and pollution to gain momentum. In the words of environmental historian John McNeill (b. 1954), 'The human population increased from 1.5 to 6 billions, the world's economy increased fifteen fold, energy use increased from thirteen to fourteen fold, freshwater use increased nine fold, and the irrigated areas by fivefold.'[27] The impact of human beings on the geology and ecosystems of the earth is a spectacular consequence of this; think of the famous hockey stick graphs that show an abrupt, worldwide rise in average temperatures (figure 24).

Since we are looking here at such a recent period, we may well wonder what the future will hold. McNeill argues that the Great Acceleration typifies the present era, and we can predict that it will eventually come to a standstill. Others have been unable to find evidence for this and assume that the acceleration will persist.[28] But it is clear that scenarios for the future will be far more chaotic than the schematic representation of the situation according to either the cyclical or the linear model.

Because climatological developments with all their economic, political and cultural consequences now succeed each other far more quickly than in the past, beliefs about the scale on which history is judged are changing. Both long and extremely short timescales will come into use. Those naturalists who in the eighteenth century first realized that the geological age of the earth goes far further back than the 6,000 years assumed from the Bible developed a concept of 'deep time'.[29] It was a term that reflected their impression of the unfathomable slowness of nature. What the twenty-first century will bring, by contrast, is an unprecedented acceleration, of the kind we experience when, for example, we see film of a thousand-year-old iceberg collapsing into the sea in mere seconds.

This acceleration can be such that it seems as if present and future are happening simultaneously. In his book *The Uninhabitable Earth* (2019), David Wallace-Wells (b. 1982) therefore suggests we should understand the climate crisis in terms of a concept of time that belongs to the Australian Aboriginals. They speak of 'dream time', or 'everywhen', a semi-mythical experience of a meeting in the present with both ancestors from a distant past and immortal heroes and gods.[30] Everywhen can provide an impetus that will enrich Huizinga's idea of the historical sensation for the twenty-first century. Our confrontation with the vulnerability of cultural heritage can bring about an experience in which a historical sensation prompts us to look forward in time, so that the present, the past and the future coincide.

## HUMAN AND NON-HUMAN TIME REGIMES

One characteristic of the Anthropocene is that anyone who continually follows the news is confronted with different, often highly tangible expectations of the future. Graphs regularly appear in the media showing estimates of increasing temperatures, the number of parts per million of $CO_2$ in the atmosphere, the melting of glaciers and ice caps, rising sea levels, the number of animal species facing extinction and so on, with timescales ranging from a few years to centuries or even millennia. Meanwhile, probably more people than ever are aware of developments in geological 'deep time', now that they can see with their own eyes how the weather is becoming more erratic and extreme, the winter seasons of ski resorts need to be adjusted, mountain routes are being diverted and vineyards are being established at higher latitudes. Of course, contemplation of these things does not prompt people to immediately let go of older convictions about the passage of time, whether on a small or a large scale, cyclical or linear. But the old certainties are starting to falter. I would therefore concur with an observation by Jilt Jorritsma (b. 1991), a novelist and historian, who writes that the Anthropocene is characterized by 'the coexistence of multiple temporalities and different temporal scales and rhythms that defy and challenge one another'.[31]

What does Jorritsma mean? This coexistence of different temporal regimes does not concern only the 'deep time' of geology versus the shorter timespan of a human life, or the recent period of the Great Acceleration. It also applies to the temporal regimes that exist outside Europe. Now that countries in the Global South – especially island states in the Pacific and Indian Oceans – are threatened most drastically of all by climate change, it is no longer possible to insist that the Western linear model is a serviceable export product that must replace local, non-Western temporal regimes. Jorritsma goes on to broaden his analysis further by pointing out that non-human actors too, such as animals, material objects and landscapes, can bring different temporal regimes with them. He sums up the outdated, Western-modernist concept of history by quoting Jacob Burckhardt, a famous historian of the Renaissance who believed that 'the awakening of consciousness' in European modernity was accompanied by a 'break with nature'.[32] Burckhardt saw this course of history, in which humans increasingly managed to uncouple their consciousness from the chaotic flow of the outside world, as a thoroughly positive development. But the detrimental consequences of that concept of time, which contributed to the industrial ravaging of the natural world, have since become clear. Because of climate change, we are confronted with the inescapable alternative temporal regimes that nature brings with it. Bearing in mind Chakrabarty's article, with which this chapter began, it has become clear in the Anthropocene that human history is limited by physical factors and can be understood only in close connection with nature.

Environmental historians Alessandro Antonello and Mark Carey have pointed to the importance in this regard of ice samples from a glacier or ice cliff that earth scientists use to gain information about climatological conditions in the past. In the Anthropocene these ice cores, some of which date back 800,000 years, have a decisive role to play in giving shape to conceptions of time:

> The practices involved in drilling, analyzing, discussing, and using ice cores . . . take part in constituting the temporalities of the global environment. . . . Ice core discourses have constituted and advanced specific textures and sensibilities of time in relation to Earth's past, the history of humans as both species and civilization, and certain apocalyptic and determined futures.[33]

Temporal regimes that are connected not to humans but to objects can therefore help to transform our consciousness of history. Icelandic-Danish artist Ólafur Elíasson (b. 1967) was attempting to interpret this scientific insight in ways understandable to the general public when he fished up fragments of icebergs in Greenland in order to exhibit them in the centres of London, Paris and Copenhagen, arranged in a circle like the face of a clock (2014–18). Rarely has the agency of objects in guiding emotions and ideas been so plainly represented in graphic form; for the duration of the melting of the ice, the public visiting those shopping streets were tangibly confronted with the consequences for the climate of our consumer society. But icebergs are not the only objects to which agency can be ascribed in light of the climate crisis. Humanmade landscapes too, such as the Dutch polders, Italy's Po Valley and the Mississippi Delta, presuppose a temporal regime of their own, because they demand constant upkeep. The same applies in fact to all material heritage.

## THE MULTIPLE TEMPORALITIES OF HERITAGE

Just like blocks of ice, material objects, including buildings, monuments and artworks, can bring a temporal regime of their own with them. Clearly heritage, which makes a claim on the continuation of a tradition, aims by its very nature to transcend the human scale. It is of course a platitude to say that much art refers to the past. To take just one example, Michelangelo's sculpture shows that he unashamedly drew inspiration from the Romans – as a tribute, not as a slavish imitation – who in turn imitated the Greeks. At the same time, artworks point to the future: their temporal regime is inseparably linked to the perishability of their construction methods and materials. Not without reason, Michelangelo often visited the marble quarries in Carrara in Tuscany, to inspect in person the quality of the stone in which he was to give his work, first modelled in clay, a durable form.

Another obvious example are the tombs, temples and pyramids of Egypt at the time of the pharaohs, which were built to last for eternity and managed to satisfy that demand remarkably well for millennia. Now, however, the Great Acceleration has caught up with them. They are being damaged by climate change, their once pink granite turning pale grey and their reliefs showing the effects of heat, damp and salt. (Some, as we shall see in chapter 7, have even been moved out of the way to make room for sources of green energy.) Less megalomanic artworks too presume a timeline that stretches far into the past and the future. Artists are often aware of this themselves and play with the timeline, for example by explicitly including in their works elements from older traditions. The eminent American art historians Alexander Nagel and Christopher Wood have suggested that in Italy, from the fourteenth century onwards, when in the sciences the origins were laid down for the linear Western temporal regime, art actually moved in the opposite direction and gave expression to 'a plural relationship to time'. By imitating the style and materials of older art, fourteenth-century painters attempted to make their works resemble early Christian mosaics or icons. Fragments (the technical term is spolia) of older architecture, classical temples for example, were integrated into new buildings in such a way that they were clearly recognizable. Nagel and Wood call it the 'plural temporality of the work of art'. With this 'anachronic Renaissance', art gained the capacity to 'bend time': 'the complex and layered temporalities of images offered a counterpoint to the linear chronologies that increasingly structured commerce, politics, travel, and everyday life in the fourteenth and fifteenth centuries'.[34]

Although Nagel and Wood focus mainly on Italy, it is not hard to see a comparable way of dealing with time in Netherlandish artworks from the sixteenth and seventeenth centuries, in which – again through the choice of materials, style and subject matter – reference is made to antiquity or to the more recent past, or indeed a claim is made on the future. Take Jan Gossaert (1478–1532), who probably taught the aforementioned Jan van Scorel. He painted the Madonna with her newborn child not in a stable in Bethlehem, in line with tradition, but in architecture that was clearly inspired by classical antiquity (figure 23). She is seated between two pillars and in front of a niche reminiscent of an imperial triumphal arch, part of what looks like a temple built in expensive stone. It is possible that Gossaert was alluding to the fact that the

Holy Land at the time of Jesus' birth was a Roman colony, but more important was a reference to Greco-Roman culture as the birthplace of the history of art.

By paying so much attention to the visual language of classical times, Gossaert was able to make clear that he could paint the Madonna just as well as the artist who created her very first portrait. According to tradition, Mary sat as a model for St Luke. In one of his other works, Gossaert places Luke in a building that, with its pilasters, capitals and geometric layout, recalls not Bethlehem but Greco-Roman antiquity (figure 25). The unusual architecture, paradoxically, was intended to contribute to an impression that the painting was true to life; Gossaert's depiction of the Madonna was close to the classical prototype, the portrait first created by Luke.

Another example is the aforementioned Amsterdam Town Hall. Its interior features eight life-sized sculptures of the gods of Olympus, carved in marble imported from Tuscany specially for the purpose, and in an idiom based on archaeological finds. As a result, the building stresses a physical continuity between the Netherlands and the world of classical antiquity. Moreover, above the sculptures of the gods are larger images that portray an event in local Dutch history, the revolt of the Batavians, a Germanic people, against the Romans (figure 26). Oil paint has been used to create these scenes, and here, too, the material is significant; it is said that the Batavians, who decorated their shields with warlike images, were associated with this medium from the start, as is made clear, the claim went, by the etymology of the Dutch term for painting, *schilderkunst*, a word supposedly derived from *schildenkunst*, or 'shield art'. The 'Golden Age' of deceptively lifelike oil paintings by Dutch artists was purportedly based on their genetic descent from the original Batavian shield artists. It was perhaps for that reason that Rembrandt, when asked to create a painting for the Town Hall depicting

Batavian leader Claudius Civilis and his warlike companions, used a strikingly loose and suggestive brushstroke that showed off his exceptional skill with oil paint as an artistic medium. (The burgomasters were less than happy with his painterly experiment, incidentally, and the canvas now hangs in Stockholm.[35])

While marble and oil paint refer back to the classical and the Batavian pasts respectively, the Town Hall also makes a claim on the future. Never before had natural stone, imported from Germany, France and Denmark, been used on such a scale to create a structure in the Netherlands, where brick is the traditional building material. The outer walls were constructed entirely of large blocks of sandstone from Bentheim and Obernkirchen. So whereas the brick facades of Amsterdam's canal-side houses need repointing from time to time, the Town Hall acquired a more durable character, reminiscent of the monuments of antiquity. Given the nature of the local peaty soil, the building needed to be supported, as we have seen, by 13,659 wooden piles. As poet Constantijn Huygens wrote, this was the 'eighth wonder of the world': 'Of so many stones above. On so much wood beneath.'[36] The new wonder of the world must be no less durable than its classical exemplars.

It has meanwhile become clear that the claim on the future made by the Amsterdam burgomasters involved a commitment on their part, namely an investment in upkeep. The durability of wooden piles is influenced by fluctuations in the groundwater, which are increasingly frequent now that climate change is bringing longer periods of drought. In a more abstract sense, the realization that the traditional temporal regimes of heritage are being overtaken by the Great Acceleration also applies to the paintings of the Italian and Dutch masters. As we saw in chapter 1, even famous collections such as those of the Uffizi in Florence, the Louvre in

Paris and the Getty Museum in Los Angeles have proven vulnerable to climate change. A linear development in which restorers, through growing expertise and more advanced techniques, are increasingly able to prevent paintings from deteriorating can no longer be taken for granted.

Climate change therefore forces us to hold up to the light the claim to historical permanence inherent in the term 'heritage', in other words the expectation that those things we inherit from our ancestors can in turn be left to our successors. With each monument or building, we need to ask ourselves to what extent the historical timeline can be extended into the future: how great is the likelihood that the object will continue to exist for at least as long as it has existed up to now? Of course heritage has always been exposed to a multiplicity of threats, from iconoclasts and urban renewal to war and natural disasters. New in the current situation, however, is that we have decades or even centuries to prepare for its coming demise, and in the process will be able to benefit from the knowledge of scientists as well as those who study the humanities.

## IN CONCLUSION

In the Anthropocene it is obvious that a linear temporal regime is no longer adequate, and that to supplement or replace it we need to consider alternatives that are less Eurocentric and anthropocentric, such as cyclical ideas of time, or the Australian Aboriginal 'everywhen', in which the historical sensation entails an immediate confrontation with the future. At the same time, the global scale of the crisis makes clear that individuals, organizations and institutions all over the world, independently of their experience of temporality, are in fact living in the same space and time. The $CO_2$

emissions of European museums can, after all, cause damage to museums in the Global South. In other words, thinking about the past, present and future of historical heritage in a time of climate change confronts us with the fact that different temporal regimes can exist alongside, or intertwined with, each other.

In the chapters that follow we will first investigate afresh, in the light of the climate crisis, the idea that the past can be brought back by the reconstruction of monuments. We will then look at alternatives to the claim of historical permanence, which has been an assumption of the Western ideology of heritage conservation for many years. Outside Europe more attention is paid to the cycle of deterioration and reconstruction, for example, or to flexible building methods. Digitization, moreover, has given a boost to the ideal of total recall.

# 5. Transformation

In the fourth century BCE, on the Adriatic coast of Croatia, at the site of the modern city of Split, the Roman emperor Diocletian, weakened by illness, built a palace so that he could withdraw and work in his vegetable garden. After the fall of the Roman Empire, new residents established themselves in the complex and adapted it. The imperial mausoleum became a cathedral dedicated to St Domnius, while the adjoining temple of Jupiter became the Church of John the Baptist.

It was not until the late nineteenth century that this situation sparked the interest of archaeologists schooled in the classics. In that period, Split was part of the Austro-Hungarian Empire, and the ruins were therefore the responsibility of a keeper of monuments in Vienna called Alois Riegl (1858–1905). When he inspected the city centre in about 1900, he was highly dissatisfied with the state of affairs. His colleagues were planning to demolish the more recent Christian architecture in order to expose the Roman remains. As a civil servant with responsibility for heritage, he refused to give permission for the work to go ahead. The beauty of the urban structure, which had grown over the centuries, must not be sacrificed, he believed, for the benefit of individual monuments.

Riegl's reluctance signified a change in the prevailing view that historical architecture must as far as possible be restored to how its creators originally intended it to be. He was campaigning against the historical sentiment that inspired so many of his contemporaries. Following in the footsteps of the influential German historian Leopold von Ranke (1795–1886), who had regarded it as his task to discover '*wie es eigentlich gewesen*' ('what actually happened'), writers, artists and architects all over Europe had enthusiastically produced historical novels, deceptively lifelike historical paintings and historicizing architectural styles. This had ultimately led to the 'supersaturation of an age in history', in the words of Friedrich Nietzsche (1844–1900). In his *Vom Nutzen und Nachteil der Historie für das Leben* (*On the Advantage and Disadvantage of History for Life*), the philosopher claimed that when the past holds sway over the present, history becomes a danger to life itself and it is better to refuse to look back.[1] Similarly, Riegl now expressed an aversion to historicism, the desire to reconstruct the past that had been a decisive factor in the conservation of monuments. In 1903 he published *Der moderne Denkmalkultus* 'The Modern Cult of Monuments', and from it flowed his 1905 bill for the protection of historical buildings.[2]

It was time, Riegl felt, to make a systematic distinction between different values that could be attributed to heritage. First of all, he contrasted *Gegenwartswerte* and *Erinnerungswerte*, or contemporary values and commemorative values. Contemporary values include, for example, practical value – such as the liturgical function of a church building – and artistic value – the aesthetic pleasure that users experience today. Commemorative values add to this a time dimension: the older the monument, the greater the role played by memory in the appreciation of it. Commemorative values, Riegl believed, can be further divided into two aspects: historical value and age value (*historischer Wert* and *Alterswert*).

Like Johan Huizinga, the Austrian keeper of monuments assumed that material heritage is tangible, perceptible evidence of the past, and therefore that it appeals to a basic need in human beings to look back in time. As with an ancient document, the better preserved a monument is, the more information can be gleaned from it. This Riegl called its historical value, which requires prior knowledge of the specific period associated with any given monument. This value demands the most comprehensive conservation possible and in theory even the removal of later additions. Distinct from historical value is age value, which Riegl found to be of greater importance, since it is accessible to everyone. Traces of the passage of time create an experience of threatened loss; this, like a religious emotion, is a feeling recognized by most people. Restorers must therefore not intervene, since they must avoid a single moment in time being artificially conserved.

By giving artefacts a 'voice' in this systematic manner, Riegl laid the groundwork for modern heritage studies, in which dozens of values have since been differentiated, including rarity value, for example, or 'visual value' (that which cannot be expressed in words about a work of art).[3] He first of all made clear that different heritage values can be valid at exactly the same time, or may even conflict. They are, after all, connected to specific historical, cultural and geographical contexts. Such a value system can help us to think about three strategies for dealing with historical heritage whose continued existence is threatened by the climate crisis: transformation (this chapter), digitization (chapter 6) and relocation and reconstruction (chapter 7). Riegl did not express an opinion on climate change, but his beloved Split is now one of those places on the Croatian coast that are vulnerable to storm surges and flooding, a growing risk as the sea level continues to rise.[4]

## AUTHENTICITY AND MATERIALS

Anyone who shares Riegl's belief in the importance of age value will want to make as few changes as possible to historical heritage. He argues that the most mature attitude is to accept that it is impossible to reconstruct an authentic past. It is illusory to think that objects, buildings and landscapes can be preserved unspoilt. In fact much of what we now regard as historical is the result of a centuries-long process of conservation, restoration and reconstruction. Take the little town of Bruges, which looks thoroughly mediaeval. It is in fact largely a nineteenth-century creation. Artworks, buildings and cultivated landscapes each have their own biography, and adaptation to the changing climatological situation will simply be the next chapter in their story. (As far as Bruges is concerned, an ecological factor was once responsible for its abiding mediaeval appearance; in the fifteenth century the delta of the Zwin silted up, so large ships could no longer reach the town and its development stagnated. Now the sea is lying in wait again, and the town finds itself in an area highly susceptible to flooding.)

Such a focus on the fluidity of heritage, and on the cultural memories connected to it as mental fabrications or invented traditions, was central to the thinking of those postmodernists who announced the 'end of history' (see chapter 4).[5] But from a practical point of view too, heritage specialists worldwide, mindful of Riegl and Nietzsche, have long since rejected the concept of 'restoring' and opted for the less ambitious 'conserving'. They start from the premise that heritage is always in flux and are aware that their own interventions may be deplored by future generations. It is therefore essential that those interventions can be undone. This is the reversibility principle: instead of fixing heritage in relation to a single historical period, conserving presumes that history is open-ended.

An even more important point requiring our attention is that the focus on the materiality of heritage – seeing the 'authenticity' of a building or object as a matter of the material from which it is made – is a typically European-American preference. The term fetish, in its psychoanalytical sense of pathological adherence to a detail, is undoubtedly applicable here. The centuries-old historical roots of this particular fetish have been investigated by Italian restoration historian Alessandro Pergoli Campanelli (b. 1968). He has studied the early centuries of the Christian era in the city of Rome, when a concept of heritage developed out of an interplay between Roman law and Christian doctrine. According to Roman law, the furnishing of proof must be based on original documents. The early Christians then became attached to relics, which is to say tangible traces of the life of the Messiah on earth, as unique markers on a timeline that ineluctably tracks the history of salvation. The combination of these two outlooks ensured that Europeans came to associate the authenticity of heritage with the ability to touch it.[6]

As a result of this 'material fetish', Riegl, who wanted to make the ravages of time visible, and his opponents, the Austrian archaeologists who aimed to restore the classical situation to its original glory, shared an essential belief. Both age value and historical value were, after all, expressed in terms of the material. Riegl stressed the patina that the passage of the centuries had given to the stone, while his opponents believed that old marble and granite should be cleaned and its cracks and holes filled. Afterwards this focus on the presumed authenticity of materials became characteristic of the European way of dealing with heritage, as set down by ICOMOS in the Venice Charter of 1964. Lowenthal has observed that this canonical charter leaves 'other cultures and traditions ill at ease, [for] *they* place more emphasis on spiritual values, on authenticity of thought, than on material symbols'.[7] Within UNESCO, too, the doctrine based on materials (as expressed in the Operational Guidelines for the Implementation of the World Heritage Convention) still prevails. But in 1994 ICOMOS formulated a new declaration that focused on cultural diversity, and therefore on the relativity of heritage values.[8] Its gathering was held in Nara, Japan, a location that was not chosen at random and that deserves to be explained.

## A CYCLICAL VIEW: BREAKING DOWN AND BUILDING UP

According to legend, the Ise Shrine, not far from Nara, is at least 2,000 years old. In the beginning, the divine princess Yamatohime-no-mikoto is said to have sought a permanent location for the worship of the sun goddess Amaterasu, and to have built a shrine to her in Ise. She left the Sacred Mirror there, one of the three Japanese crown jewels that to this day must be present at the coronation of a new emperor.

Although the shrine attracts millions of pilgrims each year, access to it is restricted in the extreme and the two central shrines, called Naikū and Gekū, are obscured from sight by fences. Nevertheless, the hallowed atmosphere is in itself reason enough for a visit. Pilgrims whisper as they approach the patch of ground, shaded by cypresses, from which they try to catch a glimpse of the gilding on the thatched roofs of the temples, bearing in mind the words of Princess Yamatohime: 'The province of Ise, of the divine wind, is the land whither repair the waves from the eternal world, the successive waves. It is a secluded and pleasant land. In this land I wish to dwell.'[9]

Naikū is completely rebuilt every twenty years. In a process known as *Shikinen Sengū*, a new shrine is always constructed beside the old, and the building process therefore alternates between those two spots. The idea is that since it was first built, the technique has changed hardly at all. Power tools are therefore banned; one of the objectives of the procedure is the handing down of traditional craftsmanship.

Furthermore, the reconstruction has ritual value. During the Okihiki Festival in the spring, local residents have the privilege of dragging the tree trunks to be used to build the structure through the streets of Ise to the shrine. A year later, carpenters begin to prepare the timber, and it is only in August of the year of completion that local people are briefly allowed to enter Naikū. Some pull a cart laden with white stones. Eventually, every participant receives two of the stones, wrapped in a white cloth, which they place in the area around the inner sanctum. In Ise the performative nature of heritage is obvious: this cyclical procedure is central, whereas the materials are entirely replaceable. As the Korean-German philosopher Byung-Chul Han (b. 1959) has written:

> For the Ise shrine . . . the technique of preservation resides in allowing the circle of life to begin anew over and over again, maintaining life not *against* death but *through and beyond death*. Death itself is built into the system of preservation. In this way, *being* gives way to the cyclical process that includes death and decay. In the unending cycle of life, there is no longer anything unique, original, singular or final. Only repetitions and reproductions exist. . . . Instead of creation there is decreation: not creation but iteration; not revolution but recurrence.[10]

Such a concept of heritage has practical application in a country like Japan, where earthquakes occur so frequently that stone was traditionally avoided in favour of wood, reeds, bark and paper (materials that are particularly fragile in a time of climate change).[11] Elsewhere in Asia too, we can see how communities, especially in areas close to the coast or to rivers, have adapted their heritage over centuries to suit changing natural conditions.

One example is the island of Majuli in the Brahmaputra River, in the Indian state of Assam. The local denomination of Hinduism on the island, Vaishnavism, has a monastic culture. Since the fifteenth century, disciples of the local saint, Srimanta Sankardeva, have built monasteries or *sattras* here. They form the core of society, regulating all aspects of social and religious life, and attract pilgrims from far and wide. In this respect the religious culture of Assam seems closer to traditional Catholicism than to Hindu denominations elsewhere. On Majuli there are still twenty-two of these *sattras*.

The bed of the Brahmaputra is not stable, however. In fact the river has been called the 'moving ocean' because of its huge body of water, flowing out of the Himalayas, which brings large amounts of sediment with it. Every year, the course of the river changes, resulting in floods and erosion. Over the centuries, therefore, the inhabitants of Majuli have developed portable, modular building techniques for which they can use local materials. Architecture can be relocated, rebuilt elsewhere or, as in the case of the traditional *chang ghar* dwellings, erected on tall bamboo stilts. So the movements of the river have become part of daily life on Majuli and an aspect of the worldview of the residents, who are said to believe that when a stretch of land floods, the river will give it back to them a few years later at another place. The *sattras* too are subject to this movement, and some have been relocated five times over the past three centuries. The monastery buildings and the traditions attached to them have therefore developed to become portable heritage, able to adjust in a landscape that continually changes its shape.[12]

In fact much of Dutch World Heritage is a recognition of a comparable symbiotic relationship between humans and water. One example is Schokland, a former island in the Zuider Zee that flooded from time to time and only later became part of the polder landscape. It would be logical if, when the time comes for a decision to give up some of the current dykes, this heritage was also adapted so that it can move with the sea. But as the 1996 report by the World Wide Fund for Nature that we looked at earlier (in chapter 1) indicates, the Netherlands has become yet more vulnerable to climate change precisely because it has done its best to stabilize its coastline and rivers by building dykes.

While that report clearly explains the consequences of allowing water into the natural landscape, the consequences for cultural heritage are less obvious. Should Europeans study Asian traditions in order to be able to adjust to the climate in other ways, and perhaps value heritage even more in its fluid and changeable state?

## LOOK ON MY WORKS, YE MIGHTY, AND DESPAIR!

A flexible disposition towards the conservation of heritage might also mean that objects that cannot possibly be moved are valued in their eroded state. This has been happening for decades in the case of Lake Reschen in northern Italy. Shortly after the Second World War, the lake was greatly enlarged by the building of a hydroelectric power station. The village of Graun had to be abandoned, but the fourteenth-century church steeple was retained. It still sticks out of the water like an admonishing finger and from time to time it is repaired to prevent further decay (figure 27). Thailand has a comparable monument in the sunken temples of Mueang Badan, which were partially flooded in the 1970s for the construction of a reservoir. Both locations have since become crowd-pullers. Tourists can take organized boat trips on Lake Reschen, and in winter they can cross the ice to look at the iconic steeple close up. (Recently it even served as a location for a Netflix horror series.)

It is not hard to imagine that Venice, Hội An and Miami will become particularly attractive tourist destinations during the period when flooding is in progress, visited by people in a state of dark euphoria, as the futurist writer Bruce Sterling (b. 1954) puts it.[13] After that, each of these cities will be transformed into a diver's paradise. Here too we can point to older examples. For years it has been possible to book underwater excursions to the ruins of Baia, a Roman resort close to Naples that was once frequented by the super-rich, including emperors Nero and Caligula, but which is now under water.

A good deal more impressive still is 'Lion City', or Shi Cheng, built during the Eastern Han dynasty (25–220 CE). In the 1950s the Chinese government decided a new hydroelectric power station was needed to provide power to the growing metropolis of Hangzhou. It resulted in the creation of the Thousand Island Lake, for which dozens of towns and more than a thousand villages were flooded. The authorities had no interest in the local heritage. It was not until 2001 that a civil servant responsible for tourism, Qiu Feng, in the process of investigating whether the lake could provide amusement for a diving club from Beijing, found Lion City, 30 metres down, practically untouched. The motionless fresh water, the constant temperature and the absence of vegetation meant that the structures, made of stone and wood, had been excellently preserved. Within the sixteenth-century city walls, hundreds of gates and facades are still intact, richly decorated with lions, dragons, phoenixes and calligraphy.

Since then, various plans have been drawn up to make Shi Cheng accessible to tourists. The idea of a submarine specially made for the purpose was rejected because the displacement of water it would cause was certain to damage the ruins. Another plan involved an Archimedes bridge, meaning a submerged floating bridge. A Chinese–Italian consortium is working on a feasibility study, along with Norway, Switzerland and the US. It would be the first Archimedes bridge to be built anywhere in the world.[14]

The attraction of the 'Chinese Atlantis' to European partners is not hard to explain. The aesthetic of ghost towns and monumental ruins is at least as old as the Romantics, especially the English and German poets of the nineteenth century. The iconic portrait that Joseph Severn (1793–1879) made of his friend Percy Bysshe Shelley (1792–1822) expresses the sentiment well (figure 28). The poet, a book on his knee and a meaningful gaze fixed on the viewer, is seated in a relaxed pose against a background of crumbling, overgrown Roman ruins. In one of Shelley's most famous poems, 'Ozymandias', fragments of a once colossal statue are accompanied by an exhortation to the great of the earth: 'Look on my works, ye Mighty, and despair!'

Shelley's German contemporaries spoke of *Ruinenempfindsamkeit* (ruin sensibility) and *Ruinenlust* (pleasure in ruins). In a book entitled *Pleasure of Ruins*, Rose Macaulay (1881–1958), an adventurous historian who travelled across the Middle East in the 1950s by camel, attempted to explain why Europeans feel attracted to buildings of which only ruins remain. It might, for example, be out of admiration for the architecture as it must once have looked, or appreciation of heritage in the state in which it now finds itself. It might also be a matter of interest in the historical and literary associations of heritage, morbid enjoyment at the sight of decay, self-satisfied appreciation of retribution, or a mystical experience of the destruction of all things mortal as set against divine eternity.[15]

In the twentieth century, various attempts were made to conserve monuments in their ruined state. In Berlin, for example, the decision was taken to leave traces of the Second World War visible, as in the famous 'Hollow Tooth', the half-collapsed Kaiser-Wilhelm-Gedächtniskirche. At the entrance to the Neues Museum, bullet holes have not been plastered over but instead preserved as relics, incorporated into the new architecture. The Germans even have a special term, *Mahnmal*, to refer to a monument that serves as a warning. In fact they have a remarkable history where this attitude is concerned. Hitler tasked his architect Albert Speer (1905–81) with constructing prestigious buildings of the Third Reich in such a way that after centuries of decay, they would look at least as splendid as the ruins that feature in Shelley's portrait. They were to have solid walls and as little reinforced concrete as possible, since that would eventually result in unsightly rust. Speer – who seems to have extended Riegl's theory of heritage value into the future – spoke in this connection of *Ruinenwert* (ruin value), the potential of architecture to decay into an impressive ruin.

The appreciation of ruins chimes neatly with the linear experience of time that, as indicated in chapter 4, has been in the ascendant in the West since early Christendom, such that looking back at the past is mainly a matter of nostalgia: time takes a progressive course and the past does not repeat itself. Yet this attitude to ruins is not confined to Europe. As the eminent art historian Wu Hung (b. 1945) has shown, appreciation of ruins in China is different from but still comparable to Europe's *Ruinenlust*.[16] In classical Chinese culture, some painters addressed the effects of the ravages of time, including collapsed buildings and withered trees, and admired the patina on antiquities. But because Chinese architecture is traditionally constructed in wood, it does not make such a strong claim to permanence as Westerners are used to. So it is far from surprising that the most famous Chinese ruin is the Yuanmingyuan or Old Summer Palace in Beijing, built with the help of an Italian missionary and destroyed in the nineteenth century by British and French soldiers. Although the rebuilding of the palace has been contemplated on several occasions (and there is a life-sized reconstruction in a theme park in the southern Chinese city of Zhuhai), its significance as a *Mahnmal* has proven decisive. As a ruin, the palace nowadays confronts visitors with the historical suffering inflicted on China by the West.

One of the most famous of all monuments that serve as a warning is in Japan. In the Hiroshima Peace Memorial Park, all that remains of the Genbaku Dome is its metal skeleton. The dome has never been either rebuilt or demolished, in order to demonstrate all the more convincingly the destructive power of the only atomic bombs ever to be deployed as weapons of war.

## ABANDONING HERITAGE

The climate crisis might have such consequences that it becomes difficult or impossible to preserve heritage even in a damaged state. From the perspective of 'deep time', the polder landscape created by human hand in the Netherlands may never have been a viable project, and Dutch hydraulic engineers may eventually, with a sigh of relief, give their land back to the sea. That would be a more radical decision than simply drowning cities like Shi Cheng, where in the fresh water even woodwork survives. In the North Sea, abandoned locations would be exposed to salt water and powerful tides. Yet we can find examples even in this part of the world, such as the archaeological sites called Holme, on the coast of Norfolk in Britain. 'Holme I' and 'Holme II' were prehistoric oak-timber enclosures built on the edge of 'Doggerland', which now lies under the North Sea but once connected Holland

and England before disappearing from 6500 BCE onwards as sea levels rose. They were preserved on the seabed, covered in sand.

Holme I, which by analogy with Stonehenge is sometimes called 'Seahenge', consisted of a circle of wooden pillars with at its centre a tree trunk placed upside down, its roots sticking upwards (figure 29). The site was discovered in 1998 when the sea washed away parts of the beach. At low tide the landscapes of thousands of years ago were exposed. In the wet peatland (over which a layer of sand had formed), the timber structure had survived for millennia, but exposure to the air meant it would now rot and disappear.

When a year later the remains were removed for conservation treatment and then housed in a museum in nearby King's Lynn, there was an outcry from the public. Surely their removal meant in reality the destruction of the site. Local residents felt they should have been given a say, and that heritage had been taken from them. Some neopagans (who adhere to the beliefs of the druids) even voiced religious objections. Large groups visited the site to protest, which brought with it further risks to the monument's fragile location. When 100 metres to the east another timber enclosure was found, and named Holme II, the decision was therefore made to leave the monument in situ, exposed to the tides. Since then, the site has become a breeding ground for birds and hardly anything is now visible of the archaeological remains. Events surrounding Holme I and Holme II make clear that public appreciation of heritage, and beliefs about its authenticity, are closely bound up with location and accessibility, suggesting there may be good reasons for abandoning heritage rather than musealizing it. (We will look further at this 'sense of place' in chapter 7.)

The conscious decision to allow heritage to be lost can sometimes be marked with a ritual. As far as I am aware, this has not happened at Holme, nor with other historical heritage that has been abandoned. But a relevant example comes from Iceland. In 2019, after the hottest July ever recorded, a 'funeral' took place for the Okjökull glacier. From its original size of 16 square kilometres (as measured in 1890), the glacier had shrunk by 2012 to just half a square kilometre. Now it had officially disappeared. The authorities unveiled a bronze plaque with a text by poet Andri Snær Magnason (1973): 'Ok[jökull] is the first Icelandic glacier to lose its status as a glacier. In the next 200 years, all our glaciers are expected to follow the same path. This monument is to acknowledge that we know what is happening and what needs to be done. Only you know if we did it.' At the bottom is the number 415, the number of parts per million (ppm) of $CO_2$ in the atmosphere at that moment (a peak has since been reached of 430 ppm).

The placing of this plaque might serve as a model for comparable rituals to be established in the future for lost heritage. It goes without saying that such a definitive conclusion – the abandoning of monuments to the ecology, so that as a result of climate change they become unrecognizable or disappear altogether – goes further than the conviction of the postmodernists that heritage (as, in their vision, a mental construct and invented tradition) is fluid. Because of the climate crisis, not just preservation in the long term but even the possibility of handing heritage on to the next generation seems impossible. Archaeologists, conservators and other specialists see themselves as forced to accept that monuments and artworks are becoming fundamentally precarious because of climate change. What is more, in their plans for the future, they will need to take into account the loss of part of this heritage. On the basis of arguments of the kind developed by Alois Riegl and subsequent scholars, they will have to weigh up against each other the different values – historical, aesthetic, spiritual and so on – attached to the remaining objects and sites. They will have to prepare themselves for the need to make firm decisions about what must be abandoned. This may sound like a radical psychological reversal, but it will be accelerated by the multiplicity of other choices with regard to nature, society and the economy that the climate crisis will force upon us over the coming decades. As far back as 1996, the Dutch branch of the World Wide Fund for Nature wrote in strikingly diplomatic terms in its report *Meegroeien met de zee* (Grow along with the sea), 'As a society we will have to get used to the idea that a dynamic relationship with the sea offers us better prospects than a hard confrontation.'[17]

In this connection, it is important to be aware that the ideal of conserving heritage in a completely controlled way is less and less realistic. Climate change disturbs the carefully calibrated atmospheric conditions, such as temperature and humidity, that are needed for the preservation of old paintings and sculptures. This became clear during the heatwaves of 2017 and 2022, when the Uffizi and the British Museum had to close their doors. Maintaining a suitable museum climate will be increasingly costly and $CO_2$-intensive. Already today, large museums in Europe and the US use as much energy as small villages. They feel a growing unease about their ecological footprint, since it can have a detrimental effect on the condition of collections in the Global South, where the consequences of climate change – certainly in relation to heat – are felt more strongly. (In light of this it is all the more problematic when museums, like the Louvre, accept subsidies from oil companies.)

In short, over the coming decades more and more conservation bodies, curators and other heritage professionals will notice that they are standing in the shoes of General Kesselring, who felt forced to blow several bridges in Florence but left the Ponte Vecchio intact.

# 6. Digitization

The previous chapter began with Alois Riegl's distinction between the historical value and the age value of heritage. If we find the former more important than the latter, and therefore want to fix and document heritage in time, then digitization is one obvious option. The same goes of course for heritage that cannot be preserved in any physical way. In 2022, Tuvalu, an island state in the Pacific Ocean whose future survival is threatened by rising sea levels, announced that it wanted to make a backup of everything – houses, trees, beaches – so that at least a Digital Nation would be preserved for its 11,000 inhabitants.[1]

Migration to the virtual domain is without doubt a relatively cheap and accessible solution for heritage in a time of climate crisis. In archaeology and the history of architecture, various methods have now become accepted as ways of scanning or digitally modelling objects in three dimensions (back in 2009, in London, an ethical charter was set down that is still recognized).[2] Such reconstructions can easily be enriched by interactive references to historical archive material, relevant images and other data. Moreover, artificial intelligence can help with the addition of missing elements and the prediction of future chemical and physical changes to the materials.[3]

In 2020 an initiative by Google called 'Heritage on the Edge' selected seven heritage locations that are threatened by climate change, from Bangladesh to Rapa Nui (Easter Island), for the making of high-resolution digital replicas.[4] Although Google presents these reconstructions as an aid to conservation, they appear to serve a dual purpose, since they test the route towards a convincing 3-D experience. With the help of virtual reality goggles, and the accompanying sensors for movement and the sense of touch, these experiences can be further perfected, so that users will find themselves in the suggested space. It is more than possible that Google's efforts are part of a strategy for persuading us that the reality outside our smartphones is less urgent and meaningful than the worlds offered to us digitally. Wallace-Wells has suggested that our tendency to become addicted to screens is in fact a harbinger of the way the next generation will successfully adjust to climatic extremes by increasingly living in the digital world.[5] Wearing a headset, we will be able to immerse ourselves in a pleasant (cooled and guaranteed tourist-free) Virtual Venice Experience, avoiding the sweltering temperatures outside. How ideal. At last we as travellers will be free from the hell that is other people.

Migration from the real to the digital world is indeed a cultural tendency that is hard to ignore, and not limited to academics and gamers. Cloud services have already largely taken the place of physical bearers of data such as memory sticks and hard discs, and, rather remarkably, they are often regarded as more dependable. Science fiction plays with the idea that ultimately even human consciousness can be copied and uploaded to a virtual environment, the suggestion being that this virtual experience is no longer inferior to life in the real world.[6] But how realistic are these expectations, and can material heritage indeed be replaced by a digital reproduction?

## THE REAL AND THE VIRTUAL

Debates about the value of copies of artworks are as old as classical theories about artistic imitation. The Romans wrote extensively on the subject; their marble statues were, after all, based on Greek bronzes. 'Originality' is a relatively new value within art history. Until the seventeenth century, the making of copies was standard practice in the big artists' studios of Italy and the Netherlands. Furthermore, in cultivating their fame, artists were largely dependent on engravers who reproduced their work in the form of prints. It was only when the notion of artistic genius became dominant in the eighteenth century that originality came to be valued more highly than artistic skill.[7]

Nevertheless, as German philosopher Walter Benjamin (1892–1940) argued, with the mechanization of reproductive techniques in the twentieth century, a significant change took place. He wrote his famous 1935 essay 'Das Kunstwerk im Zeitalter seiner technischen Reproduzierbarkeit' ('The Work of Art in the Age of its Technological Reproducibility') at a time when Nazi propaganda was making productive use of photography and film. He observed that the new media would bring with them a different appreciation of art. We would no longer see it as coupled to the materiality of the original, and broader availability might lead to the democratization of heritage. But in the process, he believed, something would be lost that he called the 'aura' of the original. 'Aura' relates to uniqueness and authenticity:

> In even the most perfect reproduction, one thing is lacking: the here and now of the work of art – its unique existence in a particular place. It is this unique existence – and nothing else – that bears the mark of the history to which the work has been subject. This history includes changes to the physical

> structure of the work over time, together with any changes in ownership. Traces of the former can be detected only by chemical or physical analyses (which cannot be performed on a reproduction), while changes of ownership are part of a tradition which can be traced only from the standpoint of the original in its present location.[8]

The mechanical copy clearly changes the physical and cultural context in which the work was originally placed. Furthermore, Benjamin argued, the ways in which new media such as photography and film can bring us closer to the art object actually devalue the aesthetic experience. One of the core values of the original is a certain distance between the viewer and the object of perception. Aura, according to Benjamin, means the 'unique apparition of a distance, however near it may be'. This paradoxical (and rather puzzling) formulation is reminiscent of Huizinga's notion of historical sensation, which is the greater when a more distant past suddenly seems close to us. (For Huizinga, too, our 'contact with the past' was accompanied by 'an utter conviction of genuineness and truth'.[9]) A photographic close-up, Benjamin writes, reduces the intensity of the sensation that a mental distance is being bridged:

> First, technological reproduction . . . in photography . . . can bring out aspects of the original that are accessible only to the lens (which is adjustable and can easily change viewpoint) but not to the human eye; or it can use certain processes, such as enlargement or slow motion, to record images which escape natural optics altogether. . . . Second, technological reproduction can place the copy of the original in situations which the original itself cannot attain. Above all, it enables the original to meet the recipient halfway. . . . The cathedral leaves its site to be received in the studio of an art lover.[10]

For Benjamin, all these tricks in fact lead to an entirely new creation: zooming in does not so much make more clearly visible 'what we see indistinctly "in any case," but brings to light entirely new structures of matter'.[11] Although the philosopher was referring to photography and film, his analysis is of course also relevant to the digital world, in which standpoints and focus points can just as easily be manipulated in relation to the original, analogue experience. But some of Benjamin's objections do not apply to a good 3-D digital reconstruction inside which users can move around as they choose. They are not delivered to a fixed point of view, as with a camera, but can determine their distance from the object for themselves and decide on their own viewing journey. Sometimes digital reproduction even makes possible entirely new and more effective spatial pathways, allowing us to move through objects, buildings and cities, or to get a bird's-eye view of them.

In virtual reality, 'the sky's the limit', as the saying goes. The graphic resolution of reproductions on the screen or in 3-D goggles is increasing all the time; we move through the virtual landscape in a more natural way; and it may not be long before we can also experience solidity, weight and temperature in the digital world. But despite these technological promises, it is hard to negate Benjamin's underlying idea about the aesthetic authority of the original.

Within aesthetics there is now a particular school of thought, called phenomenology, that investigates how the viewer relates to the object of their experience, such as an artwork or a landscape. Factors like the format of the object in relation to our own bodies and the trajectory that the viewer takes towards it (or through it) have an important part to play. Other acts too, such as feeling and smelling – for which a virtual version, guided by the digital world, is far from unthinkable – can be part of the aesthetic experience.

Phenomenology assumes that this experience consists of more than just a confrontation between the viewer and the object of interest; in fact something like an interaction takes place. Since we have bodies as well as minds, we share essential characteristics with the artwork. Canadian poet Lisa Robertson (b. 1961) describes, for example, how the chemical elements of which her body is composed, including iron, copper and calcium, create a sensation of 'mineral sympathy' with artworks in which those same materials have been used, such as limewash for the base coat and copper for the green pigment of an oil painting: 'Mineral affinities act within and across bodies and across times. We are paintings.'[12]

Analytic philosophers who focus on mental processes (in what is known as the philosophy of mind) have also proposed that the experience of being somewhere can never be replaced by a representation of the surroundings, however precise. According to a well-known thought experiment developed by Frank Jackson (b. 1943), a scholar called Mary has applied herself to the scientific aspects of colours, but she studies them on a monochrome screen and lives in a black-and-white room. She has collected all the scientific information about what happens when, for example, we see a bunch of roses: which wavelengths stimulate the retina and what contractions of the vocal cords result in the speaking of the word 'red'. When Mary leaves her room and sees a rose for the first time, does she learn anything new? According to Jackson she does. If you gather all the physical and scientific data about something, that does not mean you have all the information at your disposal.[13] There is a fundamental part of the experience that cannot be described; it can only be experienced. This has everything to do with the viewpoint from which we experience things. Easter-Island-from-your-living-room provides a different experience from Easter Island itself. What is missing from the armchair adventure is this specific experience of being somewhere. In short, the experience of historical heritage cannot be replaced by a virtual-reality reconstruction, even if all the senses are addressed in the digital world.

For anyone who taught or received education during the Covid-19 pandemic, this insight will not come as a surprise, incidentally, especially in relation to art history. Excursions to museums and historical sites are always the highpoint of such degree courses, classes or study trips, and this has to do with the unique experience of being able to develop your thoughts in the presence of the artwork, which is irreplaceable even by means of the most advanced photographic or digital reproduction. An experience at a screen can never replace the 'encounter' with the work. There is a fundamental difference between knowing all the relevant data about an object and actually seeing that object – for this insight we do not really need Benjamin's 'aura'.

## THE UBIQUITY AND EPHEMERALITY OF THE DIGITAL WORLD

Elaborating on Benjamin's ideas about industrial reproduction, in 2014 the German-American literary theorist Hans Gumbrecht (b. 1948) pointed to the risks presented by the ever-growing number of digitally accessible images. Amid this abundance, he believes, people in the West have lost the capacity to evaluate information. The billions of photographs and countless hours of film material available online carry the promise within them of 'total recall'. In their superabundance they signify the end of meaningful historical retrospection. There is no longer any way to distinguish between essentials and side issues. Anyone who has ever tried to remove traces of a broken relationship from social media will know that it can actually be enormously difficult to dispose of your digital memories, since information about us on the internet is interwoven with that of countless other people.

Gumbrecht claims that the combination of, on the one hand, a future that is 'closed off' by threats such as climate change and, on the other, an 'ever-available past' leads to an 'ever-broadening present of simultaneities'.[14] The overfilled digital systems for storing knowledge have led to 'presentism', an inability to relate meaningfully to the past or the future: 'Between a threatening future and an overwhelming past, the present expands as a temporal milieu characterized by simultaneity, stasis, and stagnation.'[15] This conclusion actually confirms the postmodern belief that each person creates their own reality. Because of the growth in the amount of information available to us online, we are each forced to construct our own past; in this cacophony of opinions, it is no longer possible to produce Grand Narratives. One consequence is that essential issues, such as the global and cross-generational problem of climate change, are becoming harder to address.

Meanwhile (and already ten years have passed) Gumbrecht's promise of total recall seems to testify to an unbearable lightness of intellect – in common with other postmodern ideas – and even misplaced optimism. The climate crisis confronts us with the volatility of digital media in the long term. Digitized objects are in essence no more stable than physical objects, since the preservation of electronic files is complex and costly. In contrast to much of our material heritage, digital images are protected by copyright and their accessibility is therefore limited. Changes in hardware and software are practically impossible to predict on the timescale applied to historical heritage, which is calibrated in centuries rather than decades. Servers on which files are kept can crash, and hackers or authoritarian regimes can wipe digital archives with one click of a mouse. Even large-scale media for digital storage, such as the servers that host cloud services, are vulnerable to increasing heat and to flooding. What does the sustainability of digital data amount to, if the community responsible for preserving it is forced to move elsewhere?

It is therefore ironic that data centres belonging to several of the world's biggest tech companies are located in Dutch polders that are fated not to last very long. Microsoft has a data centre in the Wieringermeer, for example, not far from the polder once imagined by Jan van Scorel (see pp. 55–7). In 2021 it became clear that this and similar data centres in North Holland use so much water to cool their equipment that they might cause a shortage of water for households and nature. Furthermore, chemicals are added to the cooling water that end up in the environment. The building of a data centre by Meta (Facebook's parent company) in Flevoland (not far from Richard Serra's artwork *Sea Level*), was stopped after much public debate because it would require such huge quantities of scarce renewable energy. This makes it obvious that the cloud is also in essence extremely vulnerable to climate change.

## DIGITIZATION AS A TOOL

We need not lapse into either Gumbrecht's pessimism or a utopian expectation of the non-perishability of the digital world. It is more realistic to regard digitization as one of the tools to be used in a holistic treatment of material heritage. The widespread availability of digital photographs, 3-D scans and reconstructions presents us with new opportunities for using and experiencing heritage.

One good example is presented by the Bamyan Valley in Afghanistan. The largest Buddha statues in the world once stood here, carved into a cliff in the sixth century. A rare artistic synthesis of Indian, classical Greek, Persian and Byzantine elements, the statues survived the coming of Islam and of the armies of Genghis Khan. But for orthodox Muslims they were for years seen as an affront, and in 2001 they were blown up by the Taliban using grenades and dynamite. Because of the size of the statues (more than 50 metres tall), the only successful attempt so far to replace the lost originals has been digital in nature. In 2015 a holographic reproduction was projected at full scale on the original location, at the close of a ceremony ('A Night with Buddha') to commemorate their destruction.

Of a more ambitious order are the attempts to keep memories of the destroyed heritage of Syria alive and, in the long term, to reconstruct it. Climate change probably played a role in the outbreak of the Syrian civil war in 2011, since persistent drought drove 1.5 million people from the countryside to the cities, where unemployment and poor social security provision caused rising tensions.[16] In the chaos that followed, Islamic State (IS) was able to seize power. In 2015 IS started deliberately destroying remains from the Roman period in Palmyra, a place they associated both with heathen idolatry and with the secular Syrian nation state. Moreover, members of IS took the opportunity to sell antiquities on the international art market. In the ancient amphitheatre, they beheaded the famous archaeologist Khaled al-Asaad (1932–2015), whose efforts had ensured that in 1980 Palmyra was added to the list of World Heritage. He had refused to say where valuable artefacts were hidden.

Even while fleeing for their lives, Syrian artists in a refugee camp in Jordan attempted to make models in miniature of their 'City of a Thousand Pillars'. Then researchers, united in the 'New Palmyra Project', systematically collected images of the destruction to chart its scope and make reconstructions possible. From those photographs, the Institute for Digital Archaeology in Oxford was able to create a digital model of a triumphal arch from 200 CE, which originally stood at the entrance to the Temple of Bel. The model was then replicated in Egyptian marble, at two thirds its original size. In a tour of Europe and the United States, it was triumphantly shown to the general public.

Russia took the lead in a more extensive reconstruction plan. President Putin's military support for the Syrian leader Bashar al-Assad had catastrophic results for the civilian population, but one of its consequences was that Russian researchers got hold of extremely detailed information about Palmyra's monuments. In 2020 the Syrian Directorate-General of Antiquities and Museums agreed with the Russian Association of Stone Industry that they would rebuild the triumphal arch at its original location and at its original size. The University of St Petersburg set up a digital geo-information system called 'Palmyra in Time and Space', to bring together all the scientific data about the city. In 2020 a freely accessible online 3-D reconstruction of the city was completed, based on 55,000 aerial photographs. Syrians and Russians then asked UNESCO to facilitate an investigative commission that would look at the possible 'reconstruction and rebirth' of Palmyra.[17]

The example of Palmyra illustrates that digitization does not have to be an endpoint; rather it can be a helpful tool for physical reconstruction. The complete rebuilding of threatened and lost heritage is, however, a subject enmeshed in protracted controversies, as will become clear in the next chapter.

# 7. Reconstruction

Pharaoh Ramses II (*c.* 1303–1213 BCE) earned himself the epithet 'the Great'. He expanded the Egyptian Empire far into Nubia and the Levant. In 1244 BCE he had two temples known as Abu Simbel hacked out of a mountainside close to the Nile, to immortalize himself on his war chariot, arrows aimed at the enemy Hittites. At the entrance to the larger of the temples he placed four identical statues of himself, hands on his knees, his pupil-less eyes staring far over the heads of mortals. Every year, on 22 October and 22 February, the dates of his coronation and of his birth, a ray of sunlight reaches into the inner sanctuary to illuminate another sculpture with the face of the pharaoh.

The temples were abandoned for centuries, colossuses covered with desert sand. But in 1817 an Italian circus muscleman, Giovanni Belzoni (1778–1823), exposed the entrance, and curious travellers and scholars began to visit. Hundreds of tourists now come every day. This is not such a natural course of events as it might seem, since if heritage policy had developed only slightly differently, the temples would now be under tens of metres of water in Lake Nasser.

Abu Simbel is one of the earliest examples of heritage threatened by the increasing use of energy, in this case green energy produced by a hydroelectric power station. In 1960 the Egyptian president, Gamal Nasser, decided to construct one of the biggest dams in the world, to generate electricity for the whole of the Nile Valley. He compared his Aswan High Dam to the monuments built by his pharaoh forebears. After all, it required as much rock as the building of twenty-six pyramids. But his Ministry of Information also stressed the modernity of the project. While the pyramids were 'monstrous architectural conceptions', which sacrificed raw materials and slave labour to the memory of a handful of despots, the Aswan Dam was a new kind of monument, 'larger and more human', because, in the service of all Egyptians, it would provide energy 'in hydrological perpetuity'.[1]

The only brake on this modernization project was the fact that for millennia the Aswan Valley had been scattered with countless, still largely unmapped, relics of the Nubian, Egyptian and Roman civilizations. Within a few years, the rising waters of the Nile would destroy all of that.

This was the moment for UNESCO – for the first time since its founding in 1945 – to spring into action. The most obvious solution was to move the temples. But several of its own experts dug in their heels immediately. In May 1963 a group of specialists wrote that they were 'immensely repulsed at the thought of recommending a project that leads to the cutting or fragmenting of these precious monuments in any way possible, even if they can be reconstituted in another site'.[2] The alternative was to conserve the site under water. A young British engineer, Ted Happold (1930–96), called in several architects who had worked with Le Corbusier on radically modernist projects in Chandigarh, India. They invented a system of transparent tunnels in which visitors could descend to the drowned temples of Abu Simbel. Their design drawings show tourists comfortably walking in casual clothing through the underwater environment.

Happold's plan was seen as unrealistic, and in November a group of hydraulic engineers, architects and archaeologists set about relocating both temples. More than 7,000 blocks of stone were sawn by hand, numbered, moved and reconstituted on a plateau 60 metres higher. The complex was aligned with the sun, so that the face of Ramses II would continue to catch the light twice a year. According to UNESCO rhetoric, 'the world' had made it possible; fifty countries contributed money or expertise. The project, completed in 1968, has become famous as one of the greatest challenges ever undertaken by archaeologists, tackled in the desert, far from the inhabited world in uniquely demanding conditions. (Fascinating film material of the whole operation – the saw blades eating away at hieroglyph-covered sandstone, the mutilated face of the pharaoh being hoisted up – is available in abundance on the internet [figure 30].) For UNESCO this was the perfect opportunity to demonstrate the reason for its existence and the value of collaboration between its members.

As an expression of thanks, Egypt donated several of the monuments that would have been flooded by the Aswan Dam to countries that had contributed. The Metropolitan Museum in New York acquired the stately Temple of Dendur, while the modest Temple of Taffeh was relocated to Leiden in the Netherlands. The Temple of Ellesiya ended up in Turin and the Temple of Debod in a park in Madrid. For each of these places, the gift represented a major addition to their archaeological collection. In New York and Leiden especially, the temples became a highlight, for many people a reason to visit the museum. They are the oldest buildings not only in the Low Countries but in the entire Western Hemisphere.

Although all this took place within the framework of development aid and collaboration, it was in fact consistent with a custom of hauling Egyptian monuments from place to place that dates back to the time of the Roman emperor Augustus. To this day there are more pharaonic obelisks in Rome than in all of Egypt, and others can be found adorning the streets of London and Paris. So UNESCO could be reproached for perpetuating colonial politics with its prestigious Aswan operation. Western countries found themselves in a position to demonstrate their superiority to modern Egypt, a place unworthy of its own past. At the same time, the ancient world of the pharaohs was claimed as part of Western heritage. Although these activities (in the words of one historian) were 'couched in the language of global cooperation, in practice they were a one-way flow of expertise and standards-setting, from Western powers to developing countries'.[3] The Nubian population was not consulted on decisions about the dam, and 100,000 people were forced to move. They received hardly any compensation with which to build new homes. UNESCO claimed to be operating from a position of political neutrality and scientific objectivity, but there was obviously collateral damage. Was not the unspoken objective of the whole operation actually the attraction of foreign tourists, and was the wellbeing of the local population not sacrificed to that economic imperative?

Criticism came from the heritage field, too. To make it possible for the temples and statues to be sawn and the blocks moved without further damage, the naturally porous sandstone was filled with prodigious amounts of epoxy resin. This caused the monuments to change colour, including the face of Ramses II, giving it a dark, shiny film that in fact obscures the original stone.

The fierce debates about the Aswan operation acted as a catalyst for the theory and practice of World Heritage. In 1959 – a year before the decision was made to construct the dam – UNESCO compiled a priority list in which temples in the Aswan Valley were labelled as of primary or secondary importance. There was also a residual category of monuments that were abandoned. New locations for the heritage had to be chosen, and when it came to the gifts to Europe and the US, a different cultural and climatological context needed to be anticipated. For all of this, the organization had to invent a brand-new legal, ethical and bureaucratic framework. Various heritage values could remain in place (such as the authenticity of the material, since beneath the epoxy resin the original sandstone remains), but others were violated (such as the authenticity of place).

This framework from the 1960s can serve as a starting point for contemplation of the relocation and reconstruction of heritage in a time of climate crisis – especially of monuments in coastal regions, which are threatened by rising sea levels. However controversial it may be, moving them to higher ground is in many cases preferable to abandoning them (although there is room for debate here too, as we see from the example of Holme II, discussed in chapter 5). One difference is of course that much of the heritage threatened by climate change, unlike the Abu Simbel temples, does not belong to a complex abandoned for centuries, far from the inhabited world, but is enmeshed in a living social fabric. St Mark's Basilica in Venice, the fifteenth-century Cathedral of St James in Šibenik (Croatia) and the early-Christian churches of Ravenna, which will be threatened if sea levels rise by 1 metre, are still in use as places of Christian worship.

Drawing upon more recent examples, we can give further consideration to climate-related reconstructions. Two success stories come from America and Europe, where heritage at isolated locations needed to be moved because of a shifting coastline. The third example is from China, where heritage was wrenched out of its context of traditional use and therefore became the subject of considerably more discontent.

## A RECEDING COASTLINE: THE CAPE HATTERAS LIGHTHOUSE AND CLAVELL TOWER

Cape Hatteras in North Carolina is in a climatologically interesting place. Currents along the Atlantic coast speed up shipping, but sometimes the nearby Gulf Stream, coming from the Caribbean, collides with the colder Labrador Stream, which originates in Baffin Bay, resulting in ocean storms and tidal surges. Because of the many ships that ran aground on the moving sandbanks, the area became known as the 'Graveyard of the Atlantic', until one of the American founding fathers, Alexander Hamilton (1755–1804), decided to place a beacon there. In 1871 the largest brick lighthouse in the world, at 64 metres high, was built on Cape Hatteras. By the late twentieth century, however, the coast was eroding. Although the lighthouse had already lost its function by then, in 1999 it was regarded as essential American heritage. It would not be demolished but moved further inland in its entirety, remaining upright throughout.

The International Chimney Corporation of Buffalo, New York, was charged with the task of sawing it free of its wooden foundations and hoisting the 5,000-ton structure onto specially laid rails. It could then be slowly moved by means of hydraulic pistons; in the space of three weeks it covered a distance south-westwards of almost a kilometre. Its relocation, celebrated as 'The Move of the Millennium', ultimately contributed to the popularity of Cape Hatteras as a tourist destination. Yet in 1999 nobody was prepared for the speed at which the climate crisis would unfold. The sea has now come inland far further than anticipated, and the lighthouse is once again in jeopardy. Meanwhile the engineers have been deployed to another, more important task: the relocation of the Statue of Liberty in New York to a spot less susceptible to flooding.

The situation in North Carolina was rare in that the lighthouse could be moved along an entirely level track. The alternative is far less interesting to engineers, but the only option when a difference in altitude must be overcome: to dismantle and build anew elsewhere. One example related to rising sea levels is Clavell Tower. This monument once looked out over the sea from a cliff that is part of the Jurassic Coast in the south of England, a landscape recognized as World Heritage, where coastal erosion has exposed 185 million years of geological history on the cliffs. The area was once desert and tropical swamp, as documented in the fossil remains of creatures that once lived here. So that visitors could observe the landscape, a tower was built on one of the cliffs in 1830, ornamented with a ring of slim Tuscan pillars. Novelist Thomas Hardy (1840–1928) often took his first love, Eliza Nicholls, there to gaze out over the dramatic panorama. But the coast has been eroded to such an extent that in 2006 the decision was made to demolish the tower. All 16,272 stones were numbered and photographed, and the tower was reconstructed further inland.

It was not a completely faithful reconstruction: the interior was adapted and part of the tower was built in new stone. This aroused little controversy, perhaps because the folly, a curiosity for enthusiasts, had never been intended as high culture. The curators seem to have shared the sentiment of aesthete John Ruskin (1819–1900), who famously remarked that restoration is by definition 'the most total destruction which a building can suffer'.[4] In short, heritage is always in motion, the British believed. For an example of relocated heritage that certainly did cause much dissatisfaction, we need to look to China.

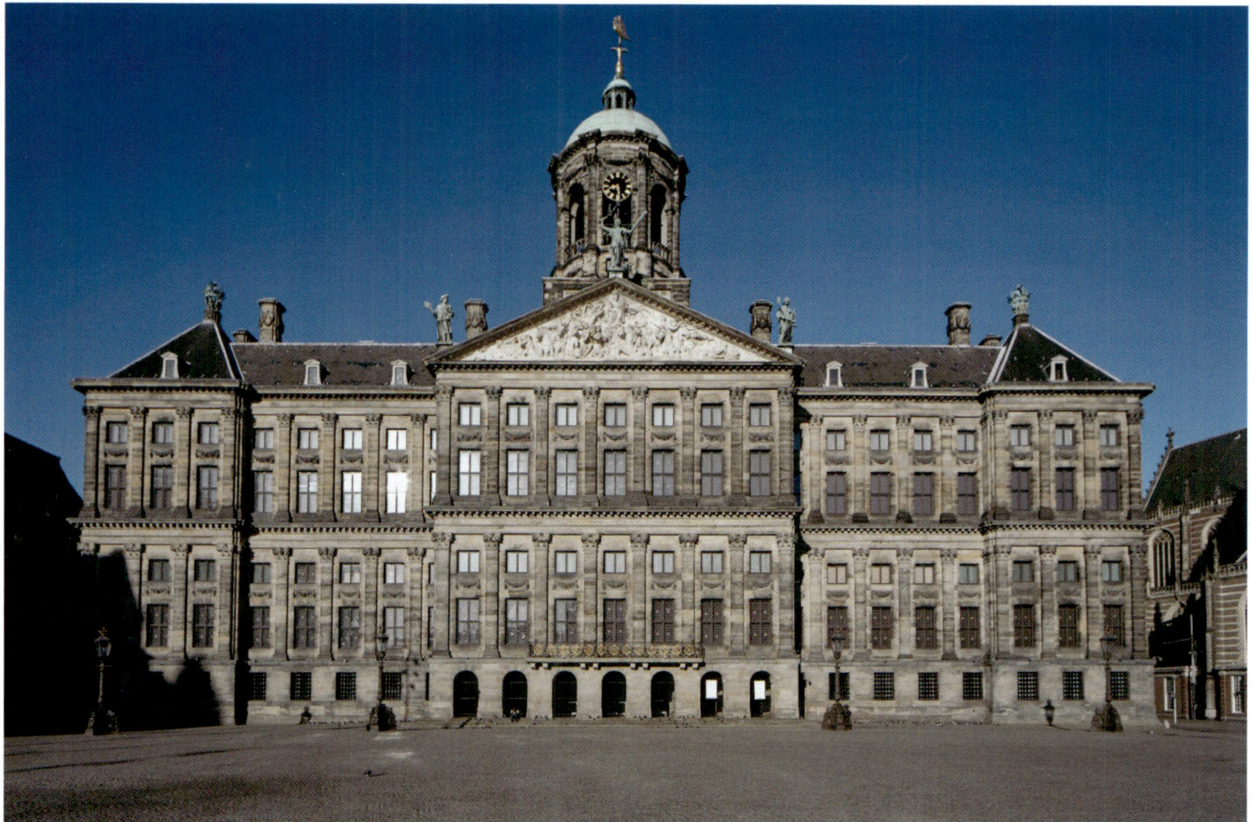

Figure 1. Jacob van Campen, Amsterdam Town Hall (now Royal Palace), 1648–65.

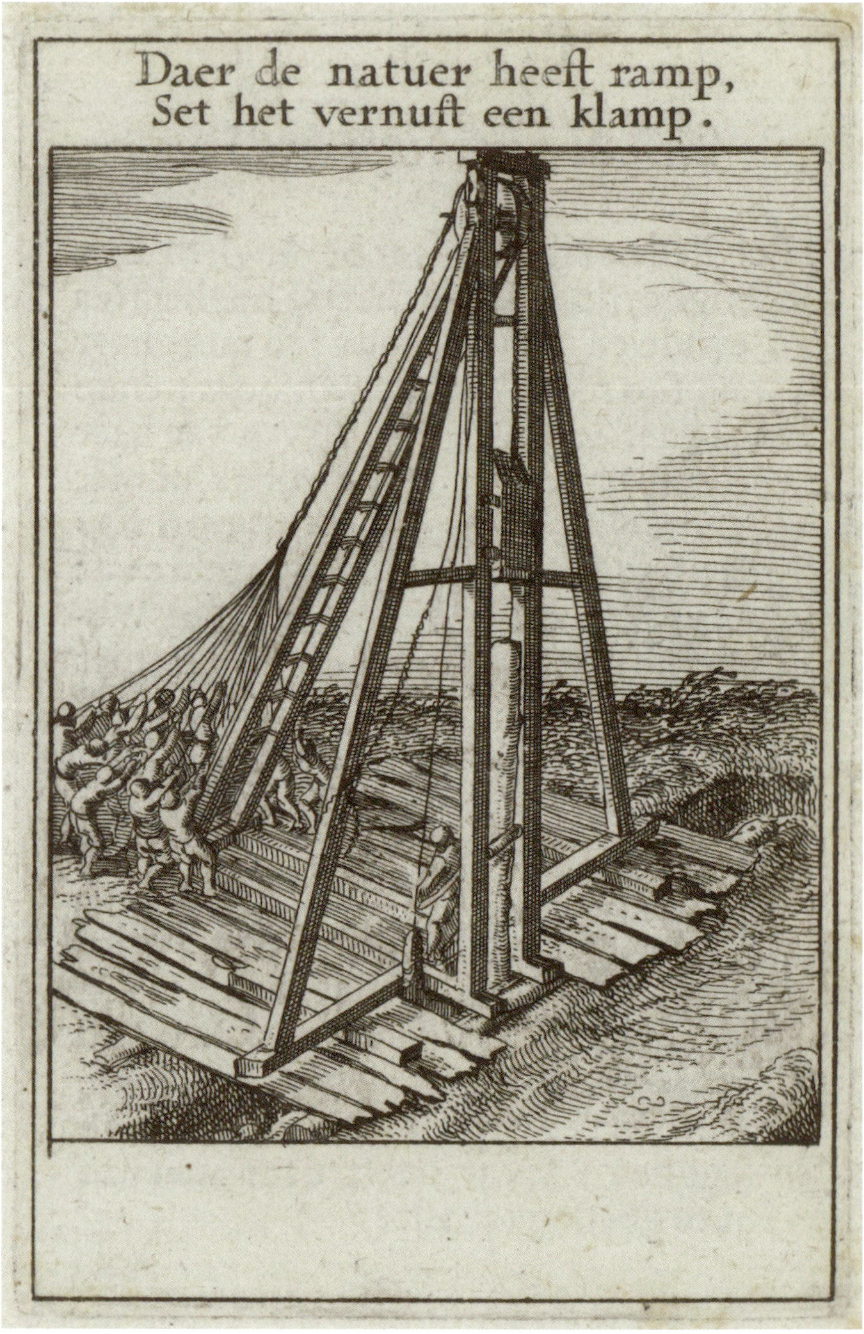


Figure 2. Claes Janszoon Visscher, emblem in Roemer Visscher, *Sinnepoppen*, 1614.

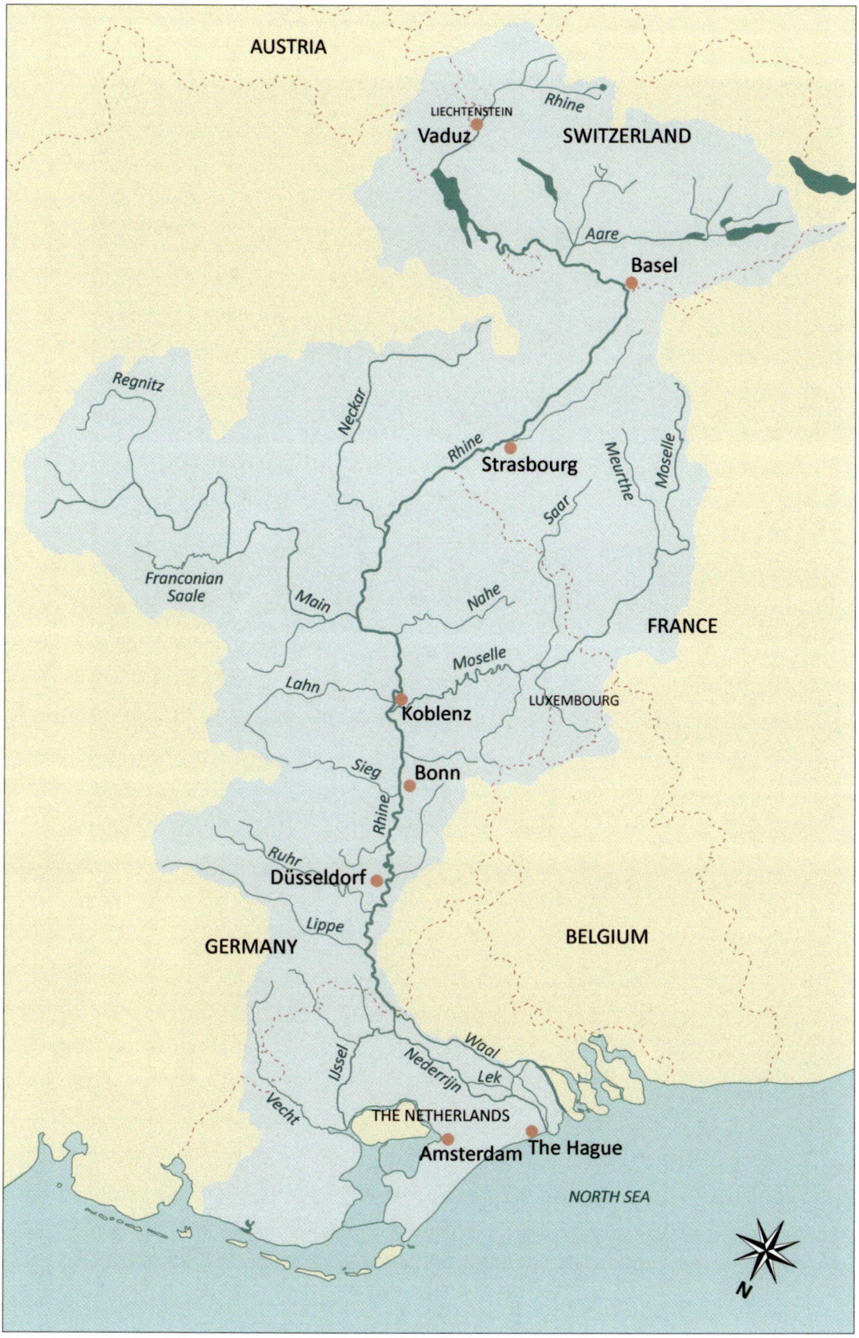


Figure 3. The River Rhine.

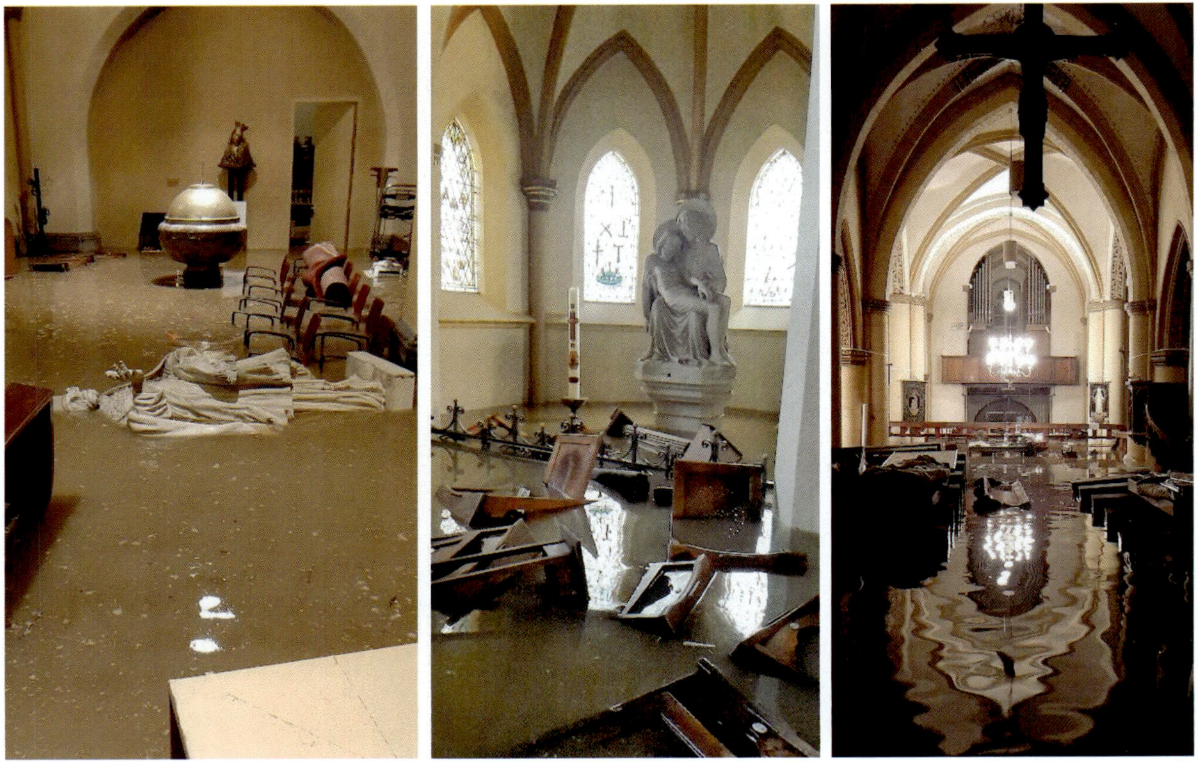

Figure 4. The flooded church of St Nicholas and St Barbara in Valkenburg, 14 July 2021.

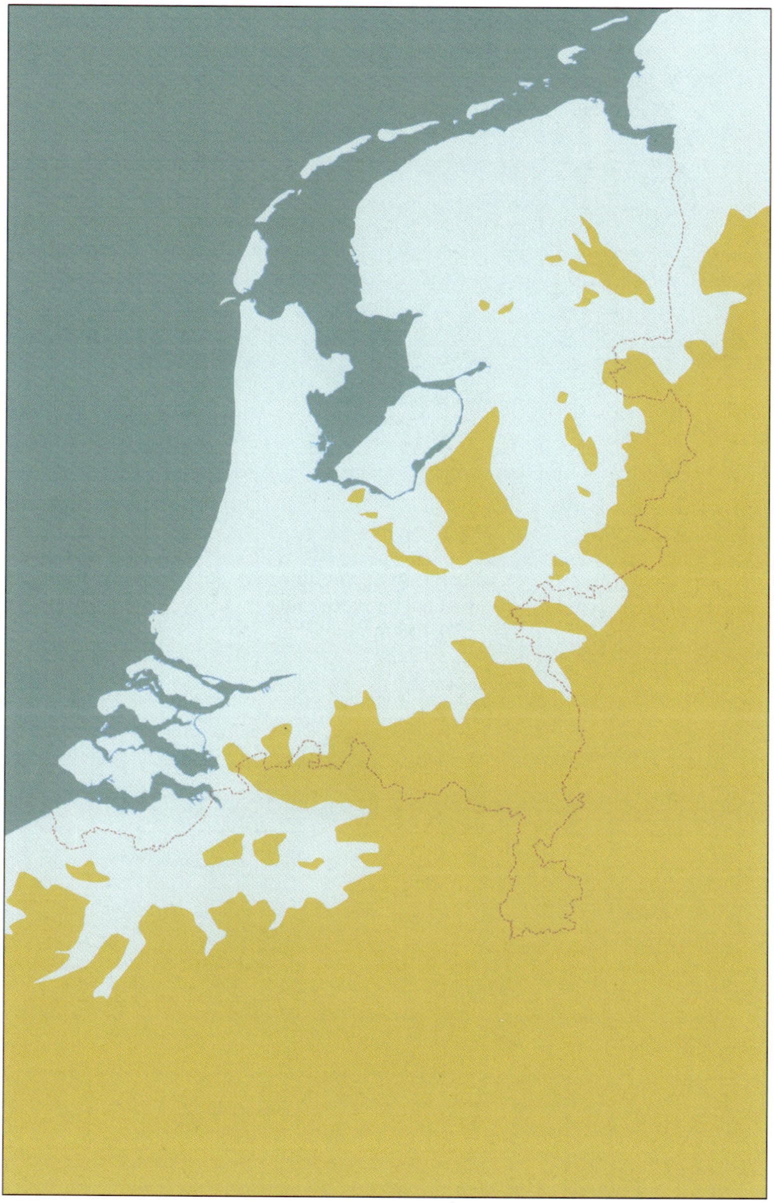

Figure 5. The Netherlands in the year 2300 (based on Schuttenhelm, 'In Face of Rising Sea Levels the Netherlands Must Consider Controlled Withdrawal', 2019).

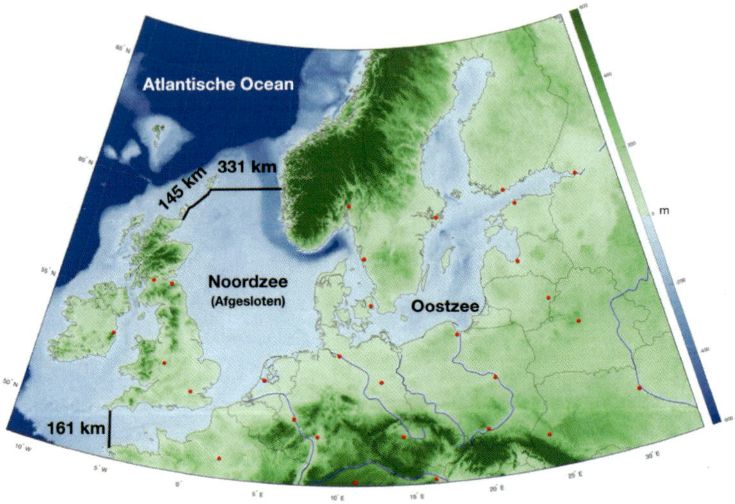


Figure 6. The Northern European Enclosure Dam (NEED).

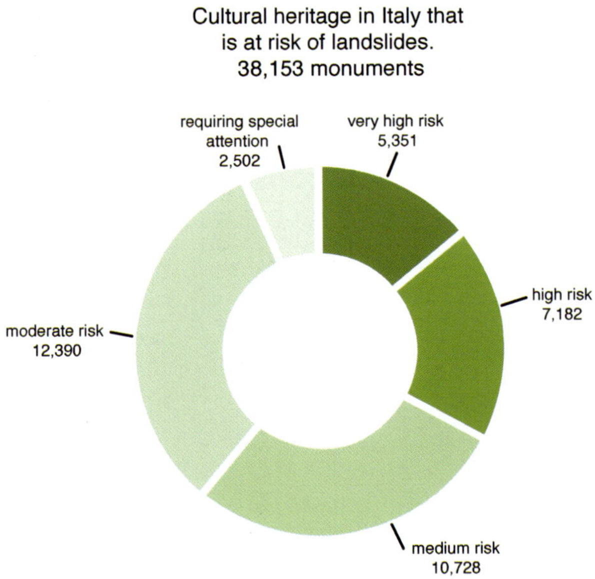


Figure 7. Heritage threatened by landslides in Italy.

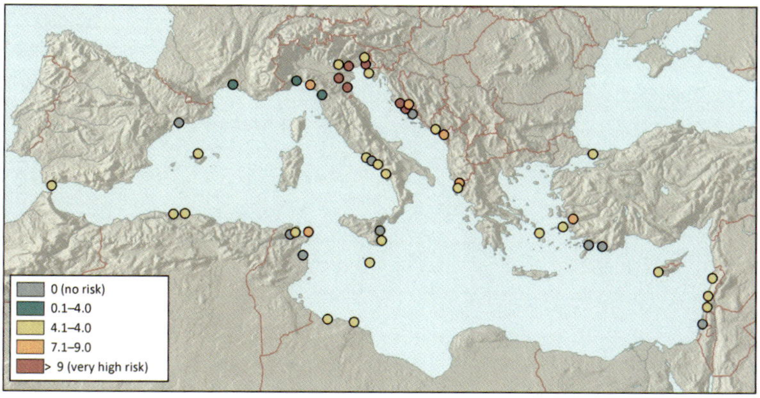


Figure 8. Flood risk of World Heritage Sites in 2100.

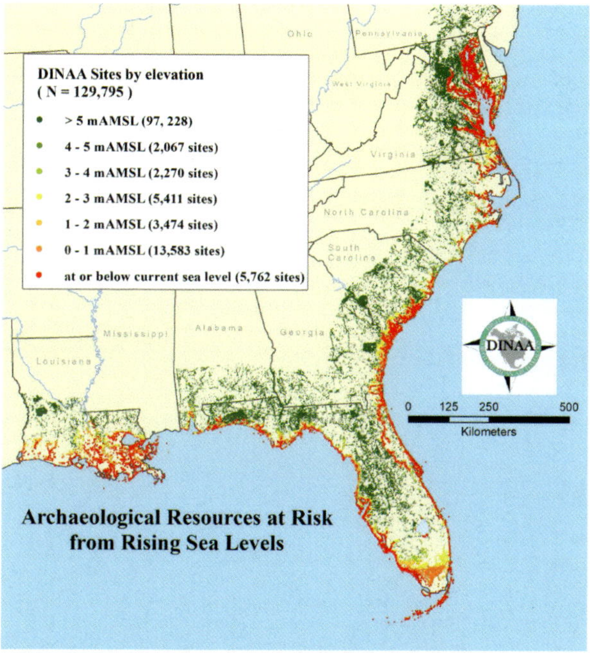


Figure 9. Archaeological sites at risk from rising sea levels in the south-eastern United States.

(Overleaf) Figure 10. Floods near the Wat Mahathat Temple, Ayutthaya, 2011.

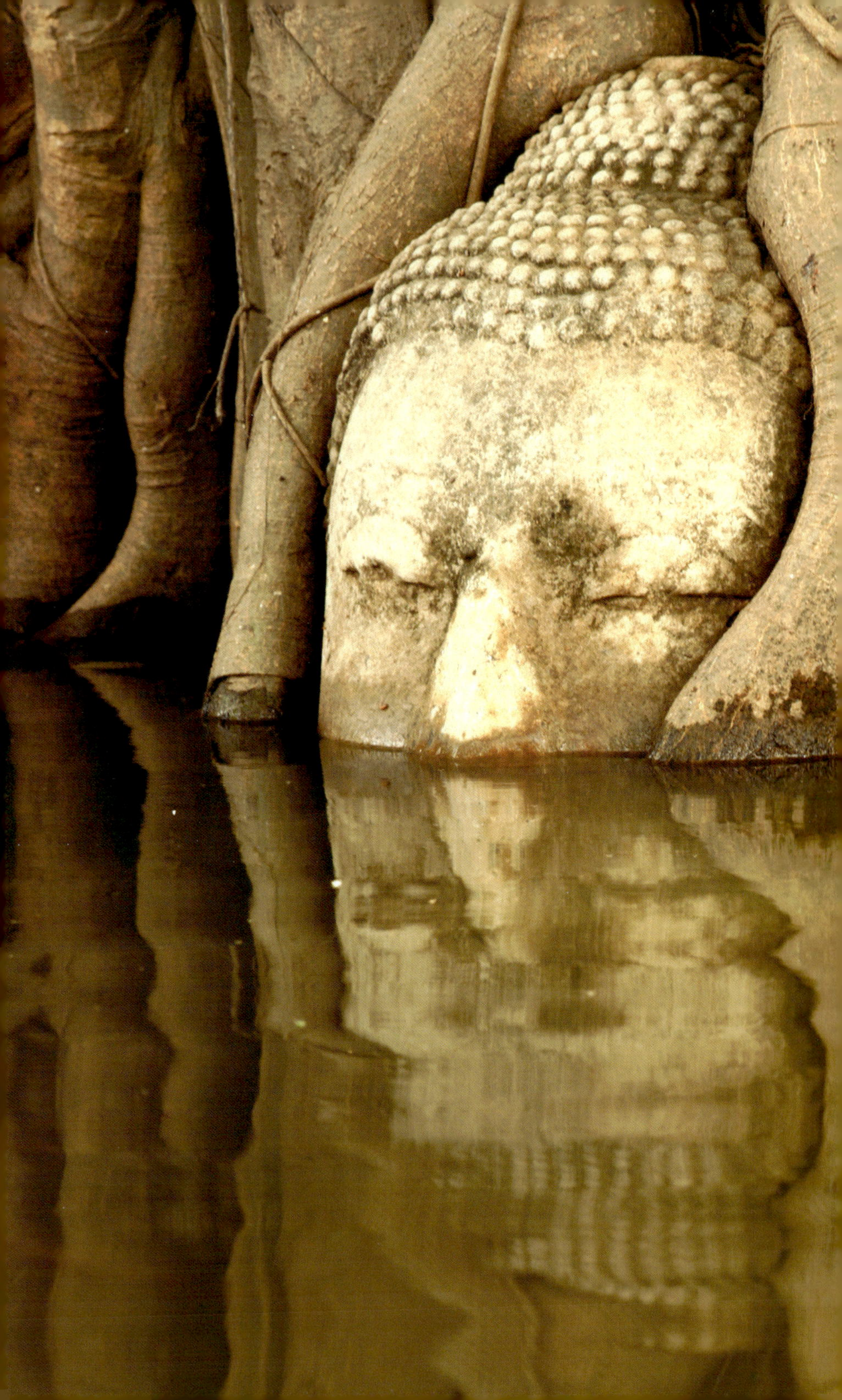

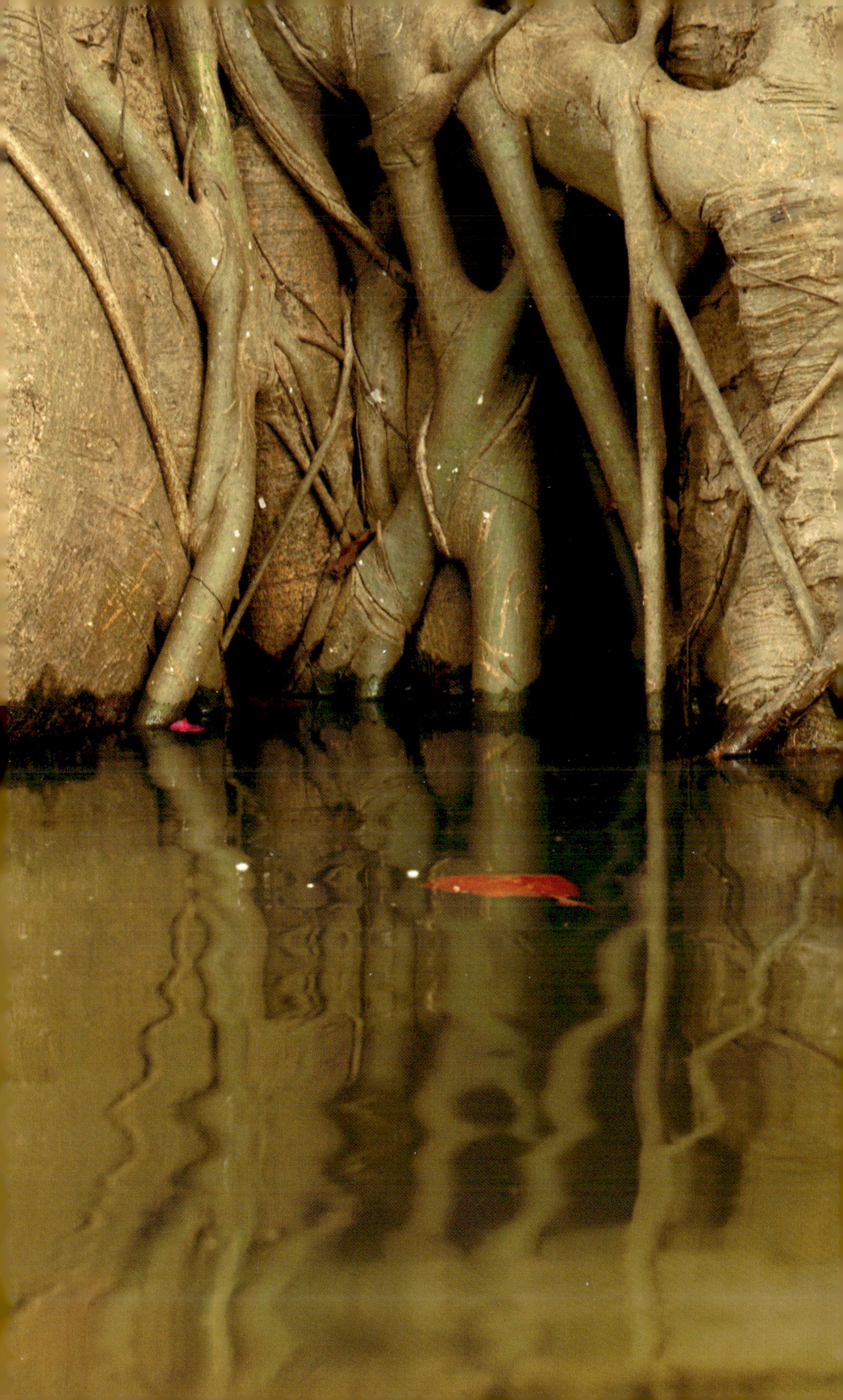

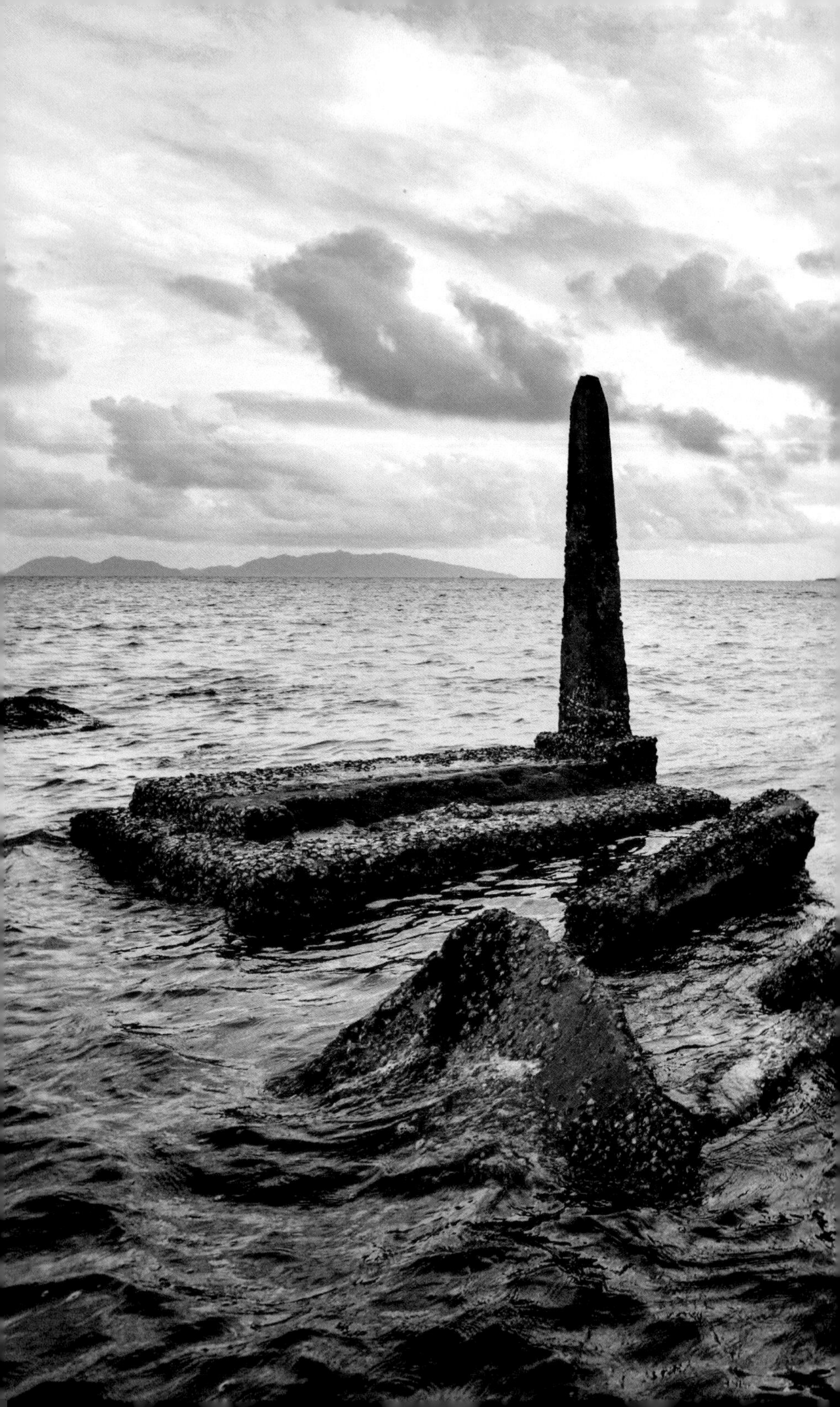

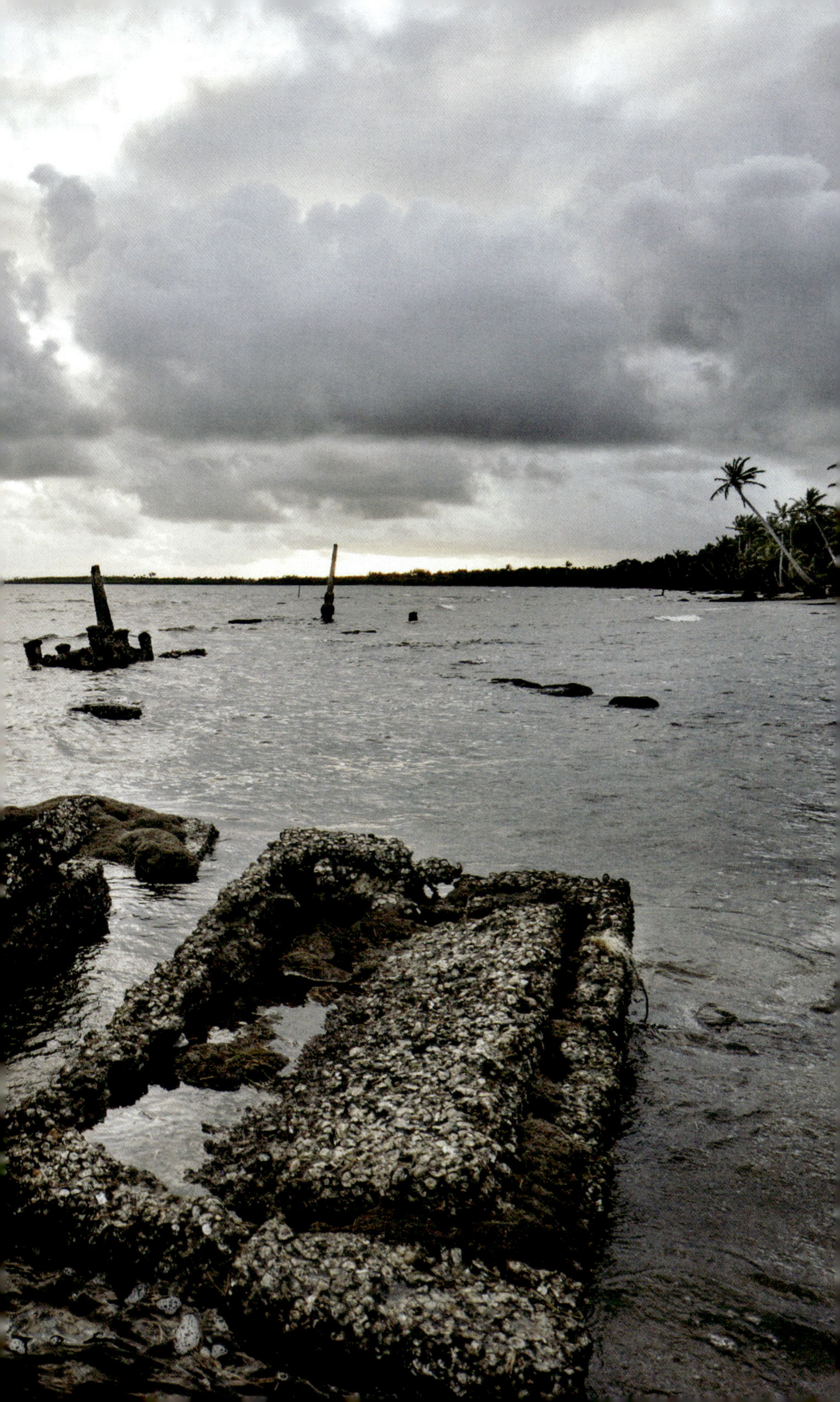

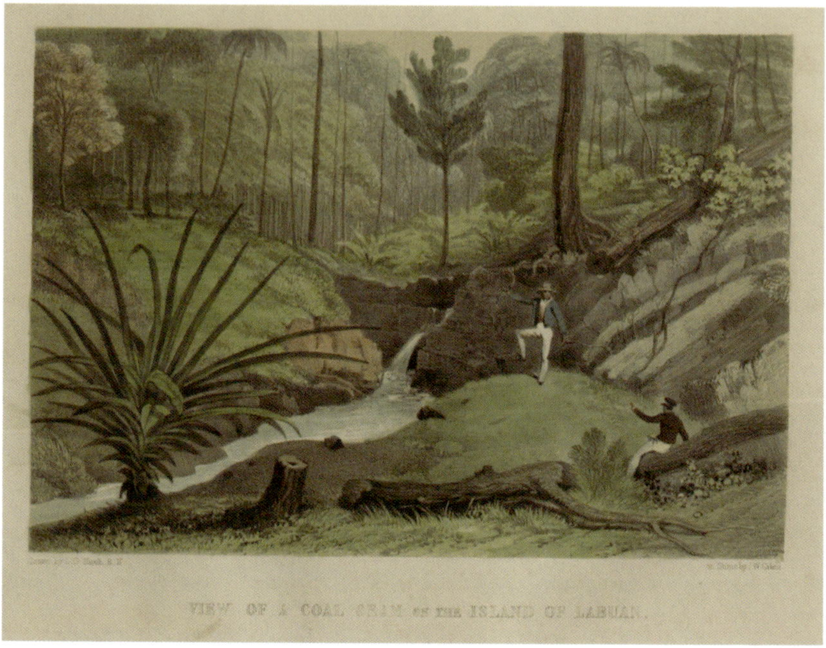

Figure 12. Leopold George Heath,
*View of a Coal Seam on the Island of Labuan*, 1847

(Previous) Figure 11. The cemetery at Togoru (published 2021).

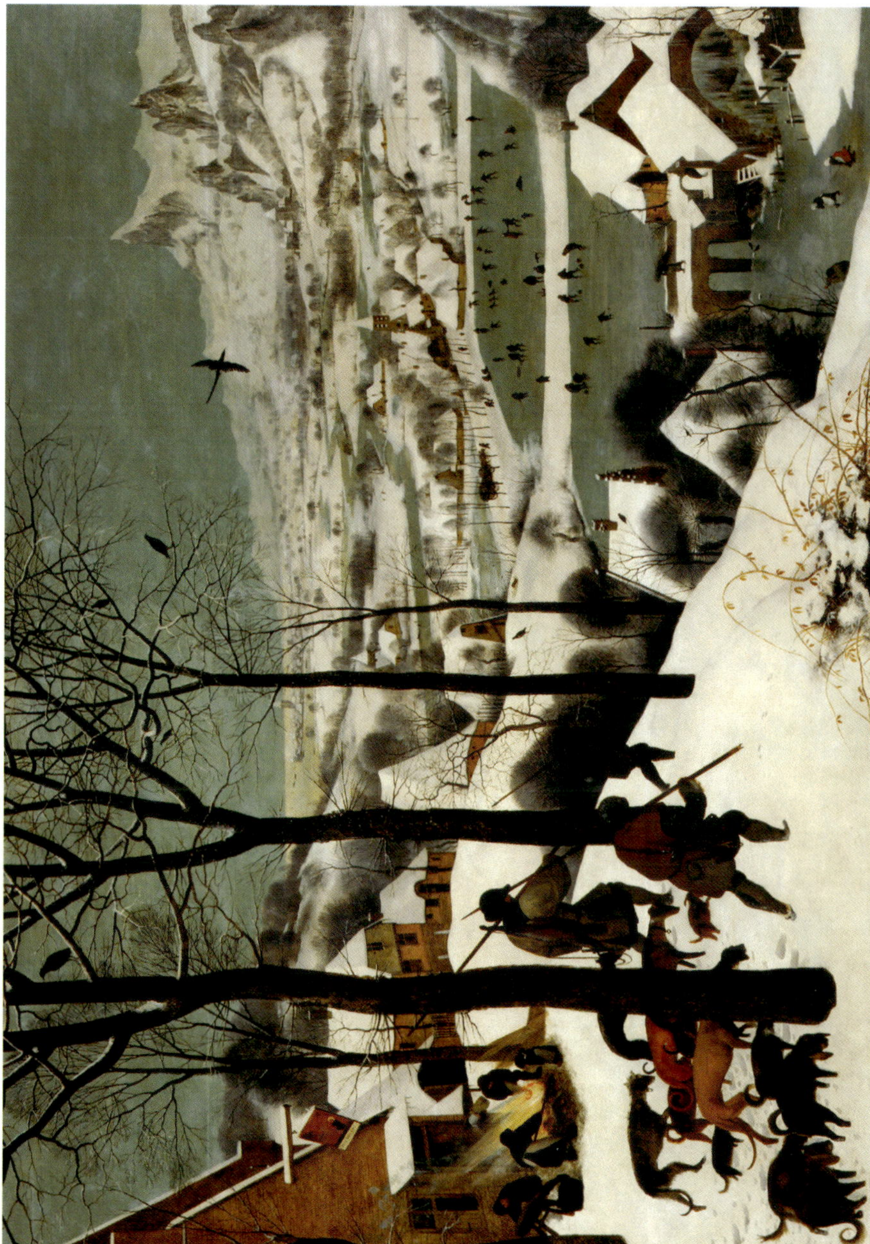

Figure 13. Pieter Bruegel, *Hunters in the Snow*, 1565.

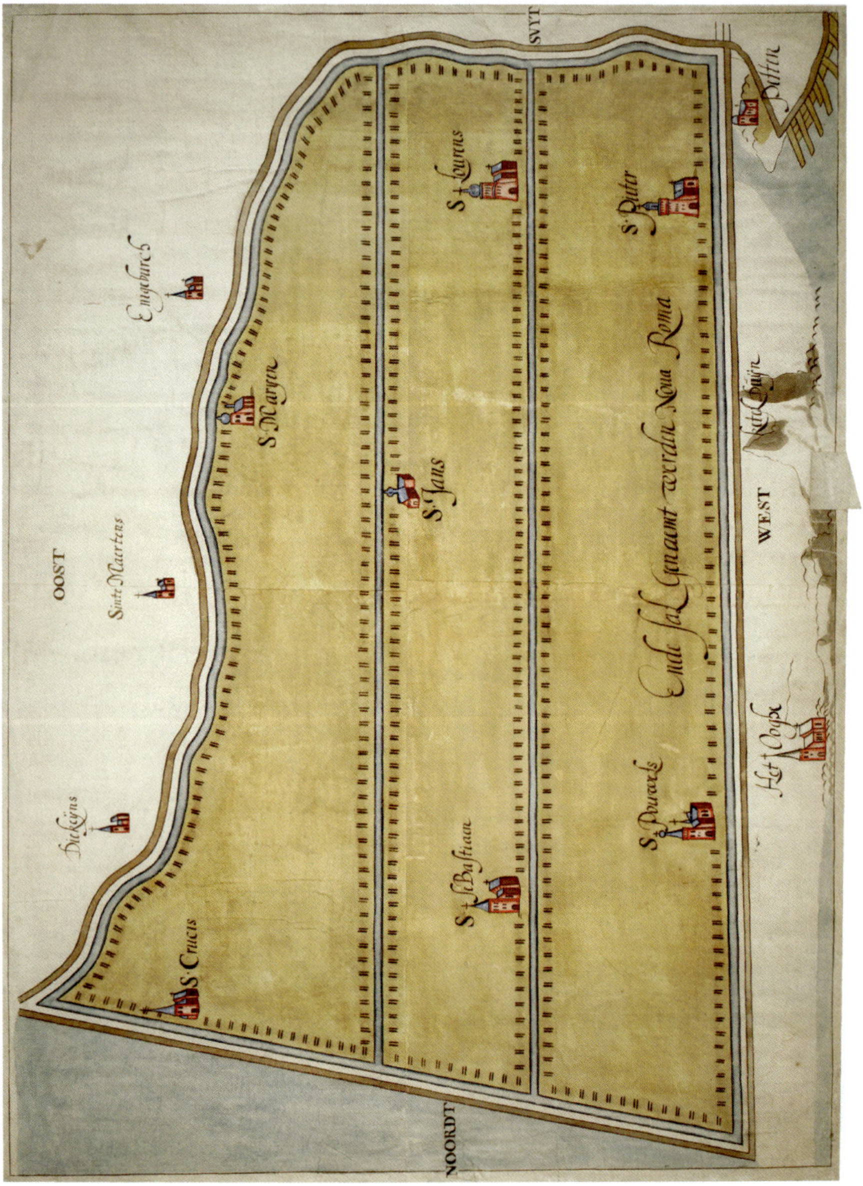


Figure 14. Jan van Scorel, *Nova Roma*, manuscript map, *c*. 1550.

(Right) Figure 15. Jan van Goyen, *Polder landscape*, *c*. 1550.

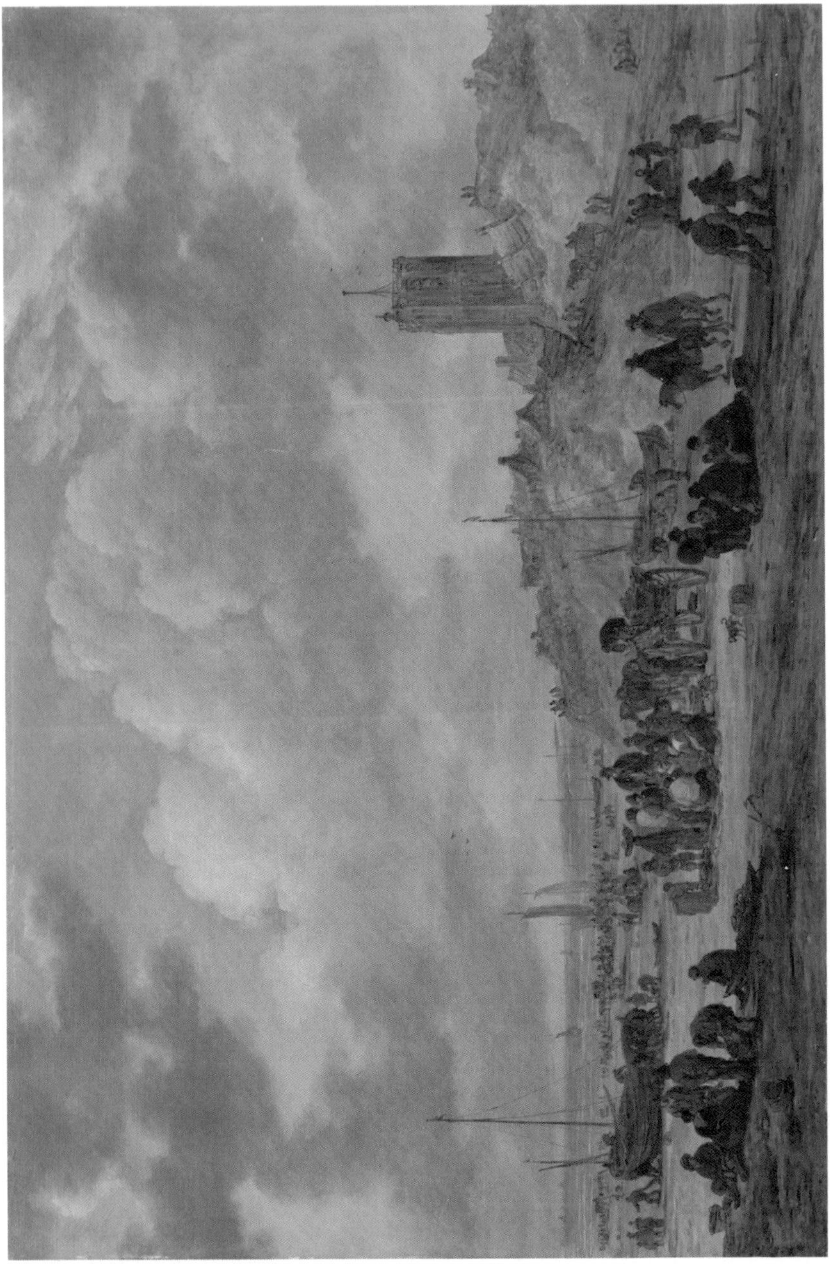

Figure 16. Jan van Goyen, *The Beach at Egmond aan Zee*, 1653.

(Right) Figure 17. Salomon van Ruysdael, *River Landscape with Ferry*, 1649.

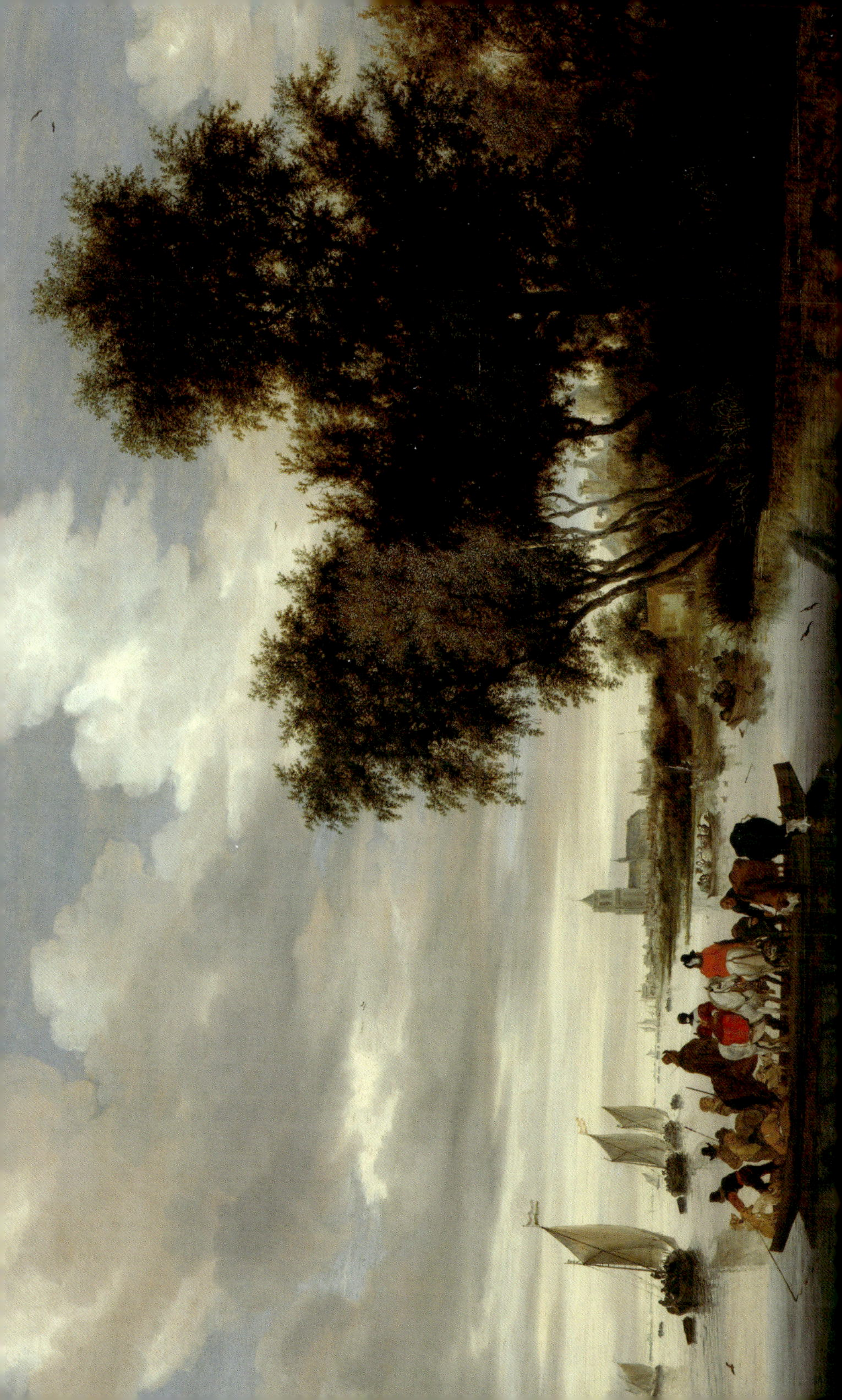

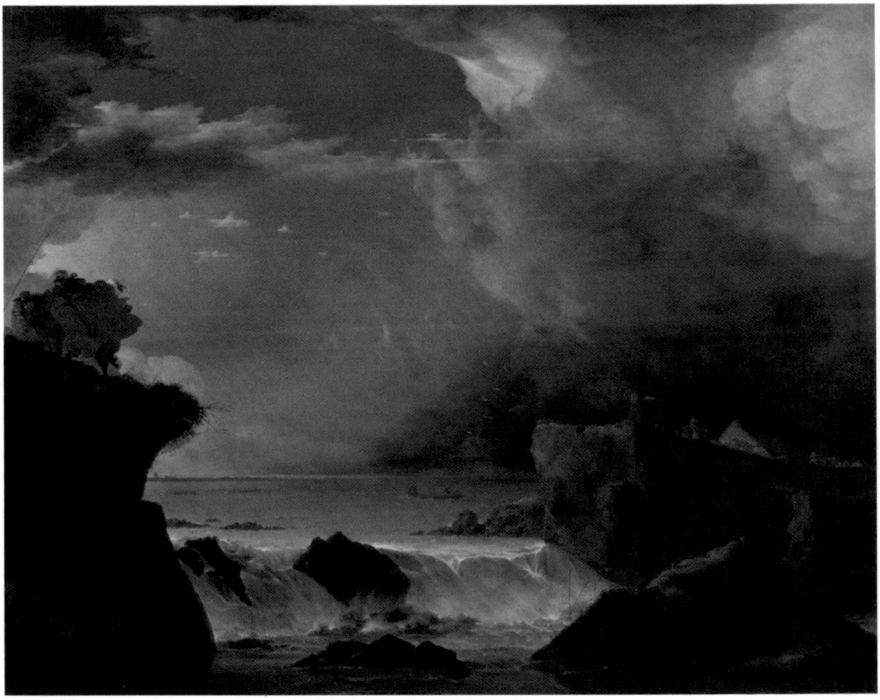

Figure 18. Jan Asselijn, *The Breaching of St Anthony's Dyke at Houtewael in 1651.*

(Right) Figure 19. Matthias Withoos, *Reparation of the Zuiderzeedijk at Schardam after the All Saints Flood*, 1676.

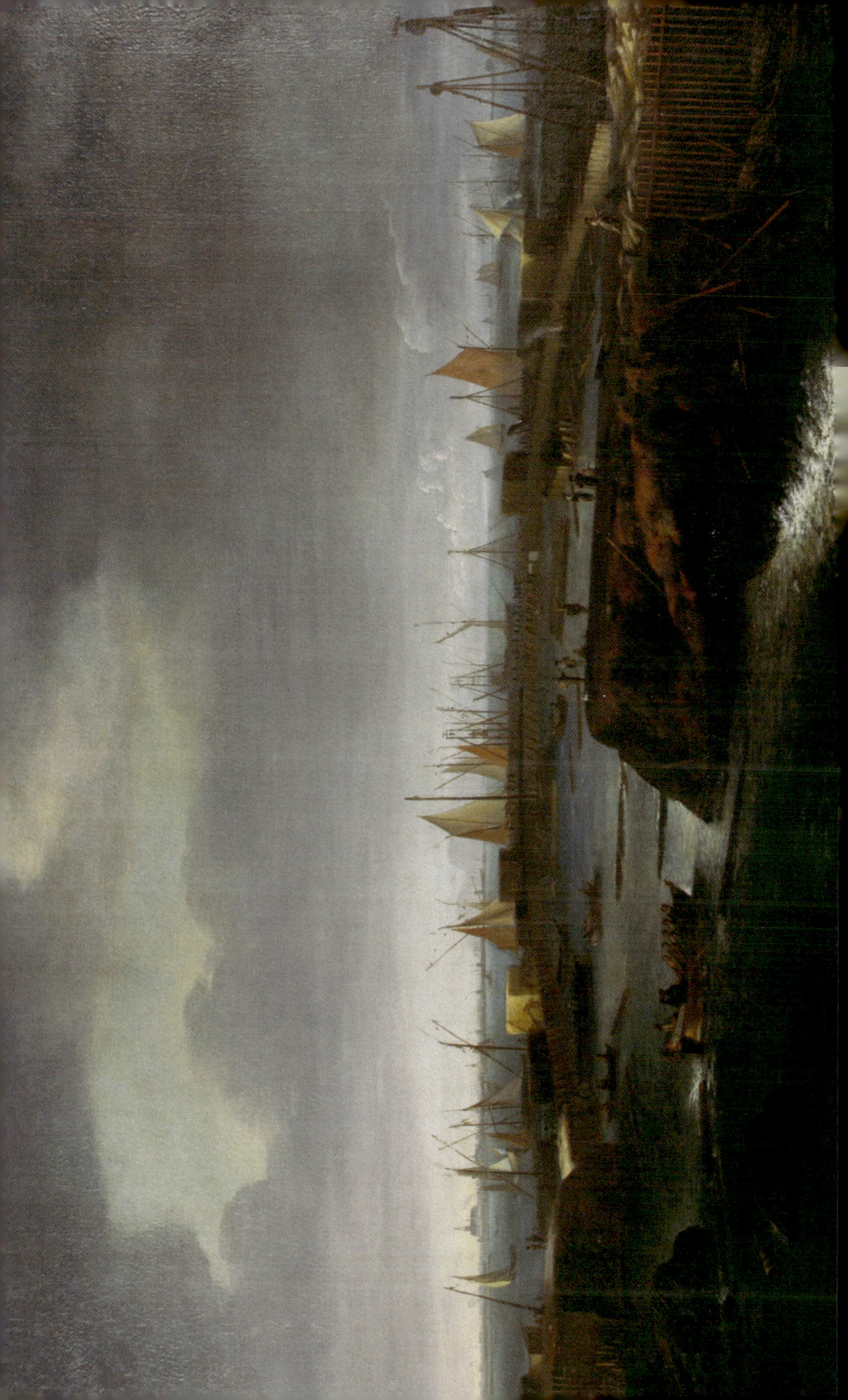

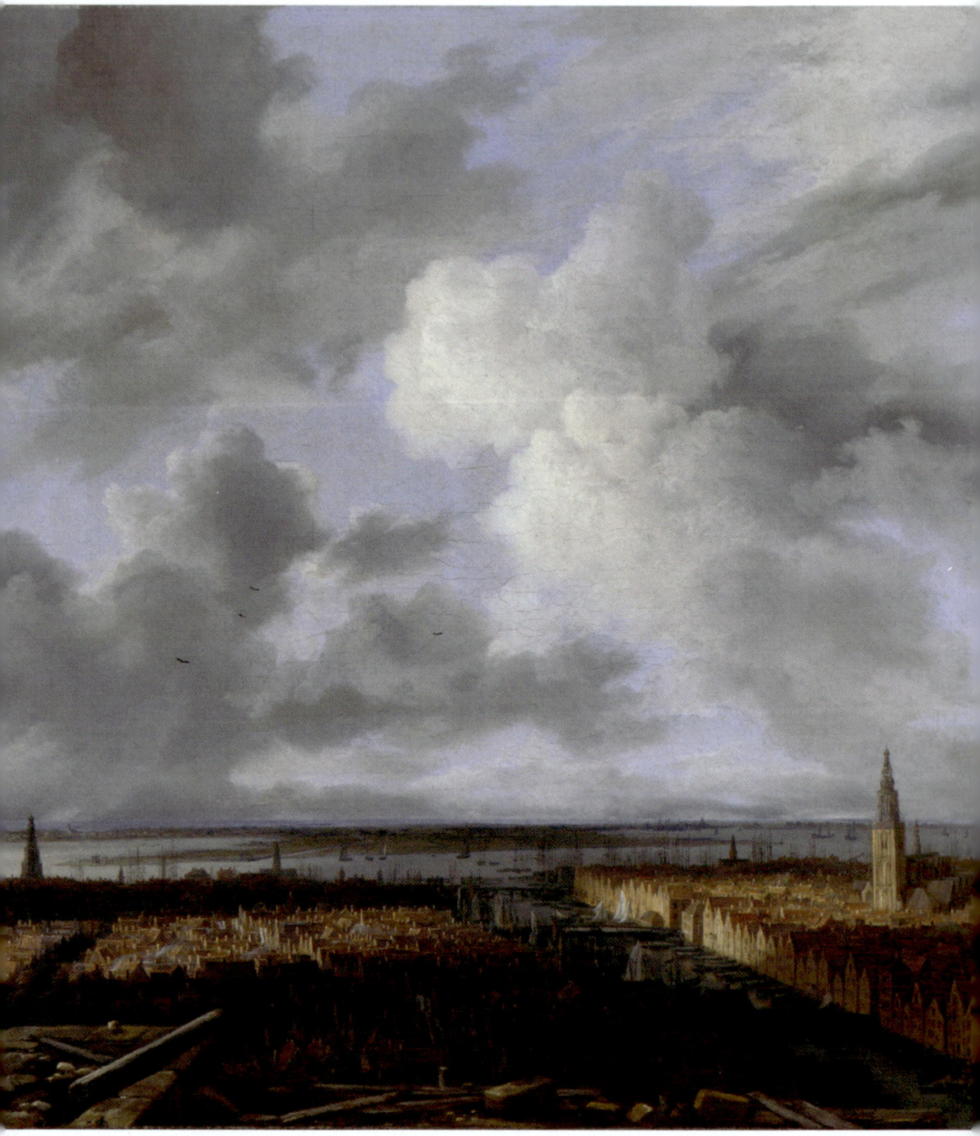

Figure 20. Jacob van Ruisdael, *A Panoramic View of Amsterdam*, *c*. 1670.

(Right) Figure 21. Pieter and François Hemony, Atlas on the west facade of the Amsterdam  own Hall (now Royal Palace).

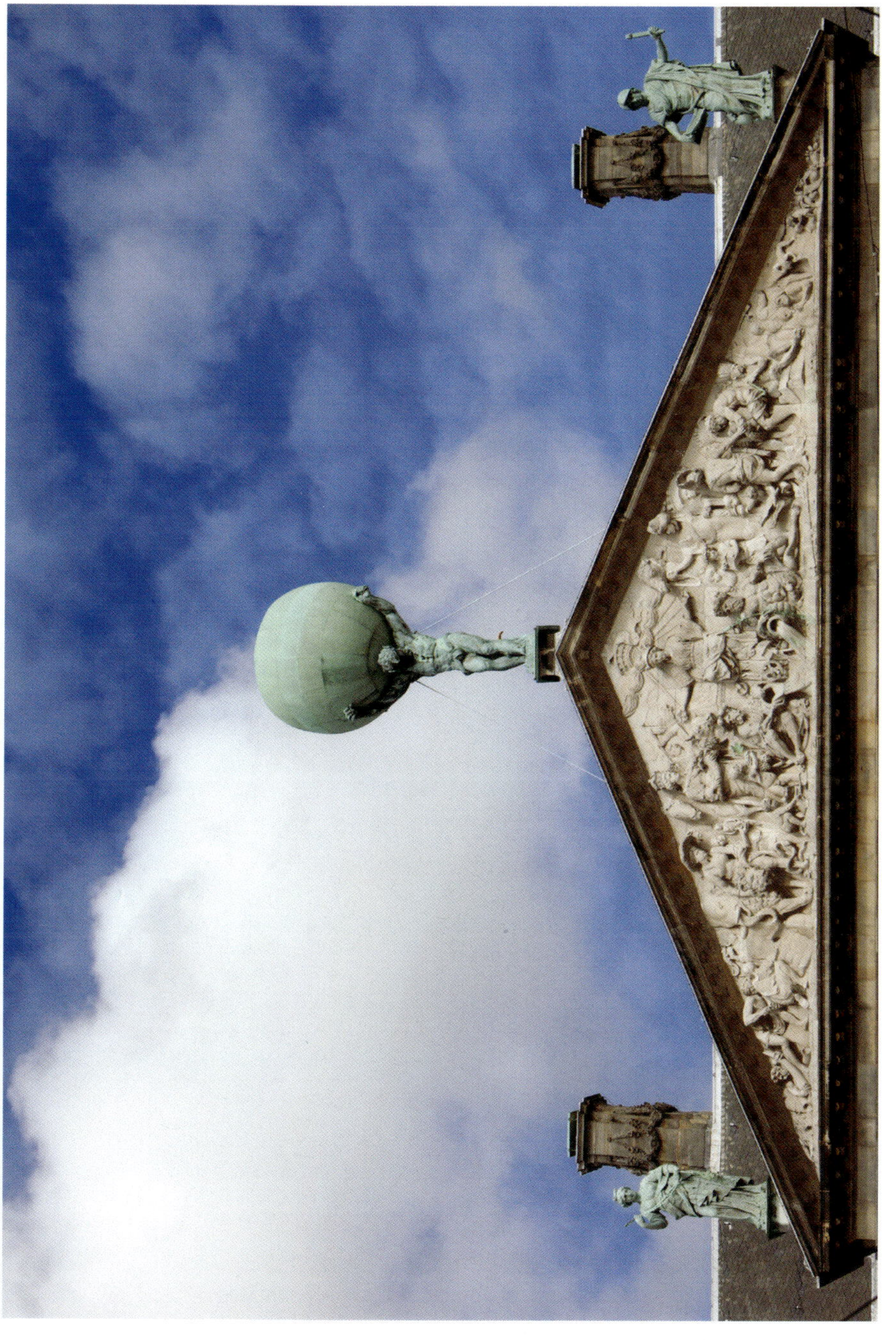

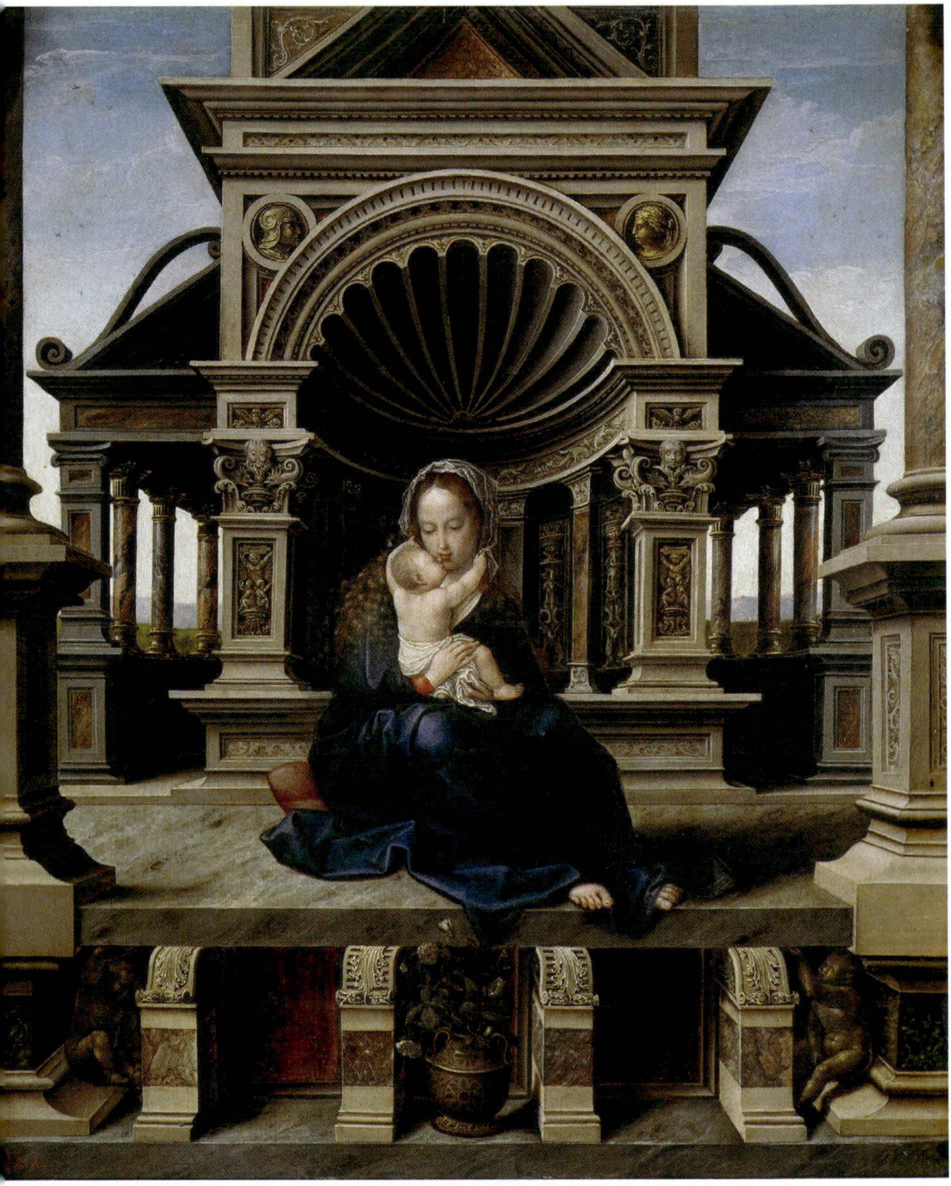

Figure 22. Wim T. Schippers, *The Steeple of Drienerlo*, 1979.

(Right) Figure 23. Jan Gossaert (attributed.), *Madonna van Leuven*, *c.* 1516.

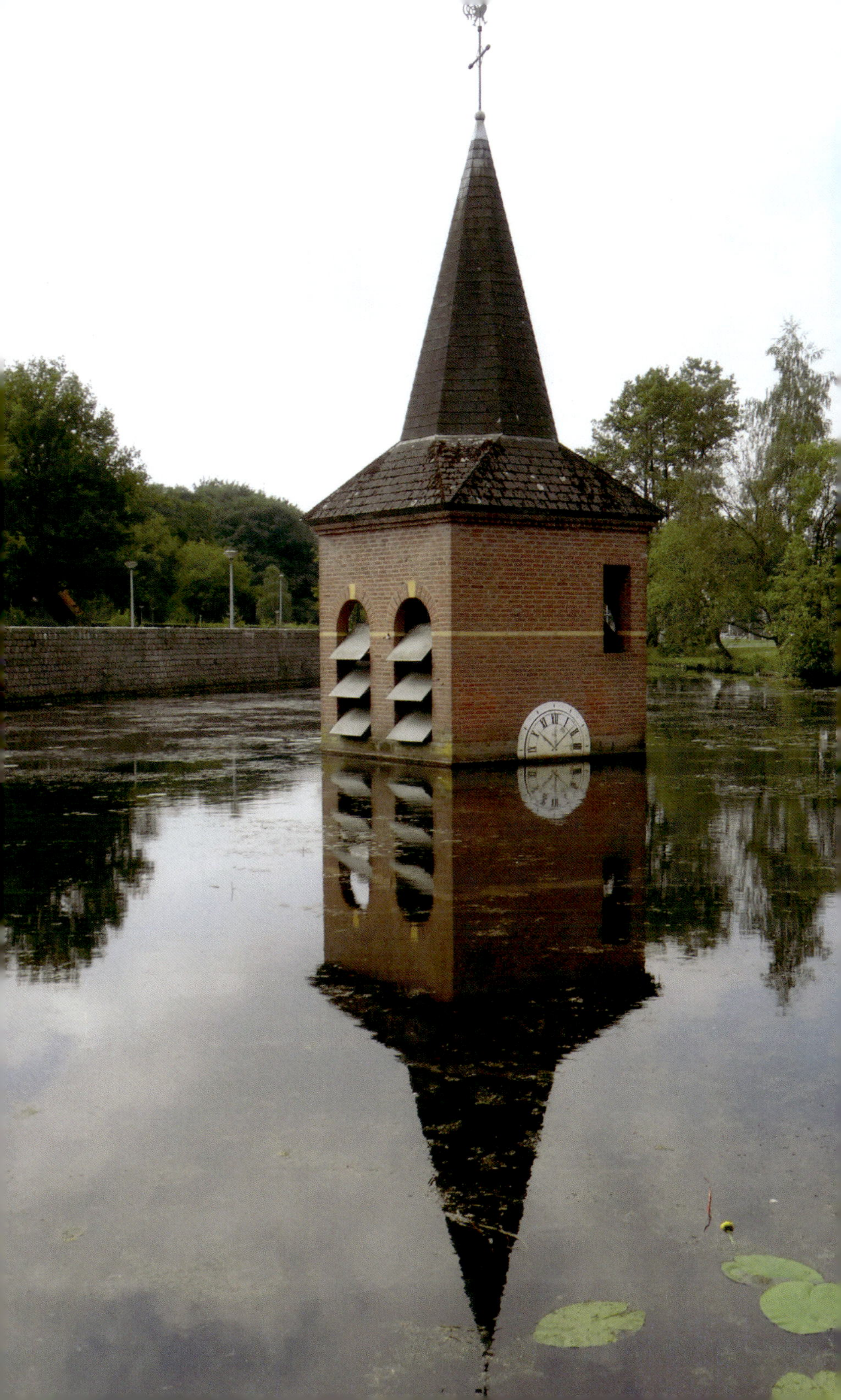

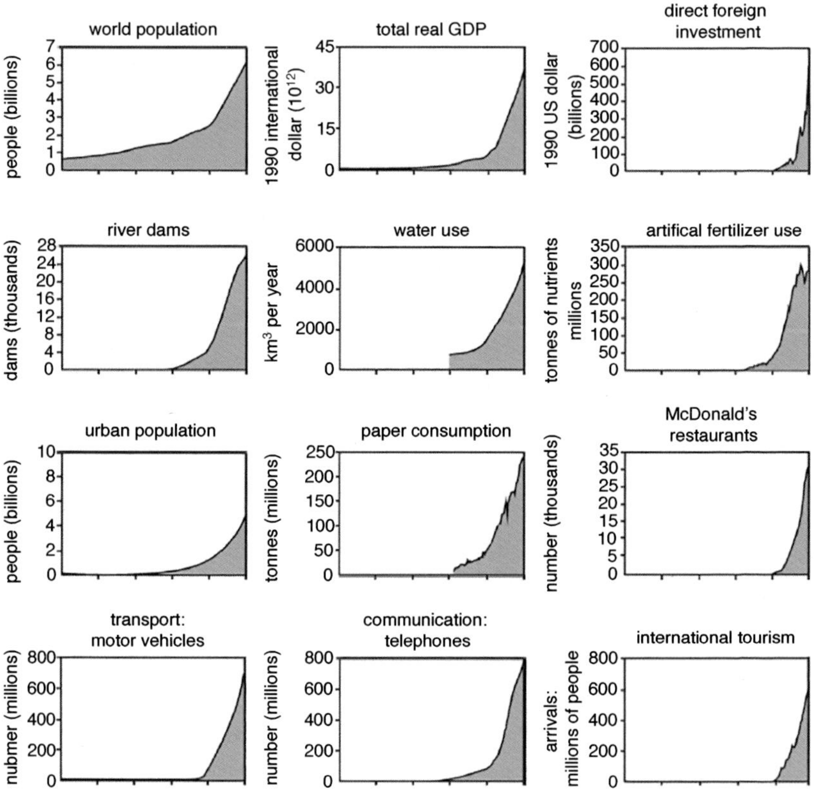


Figure 24. The Great Acceleration.

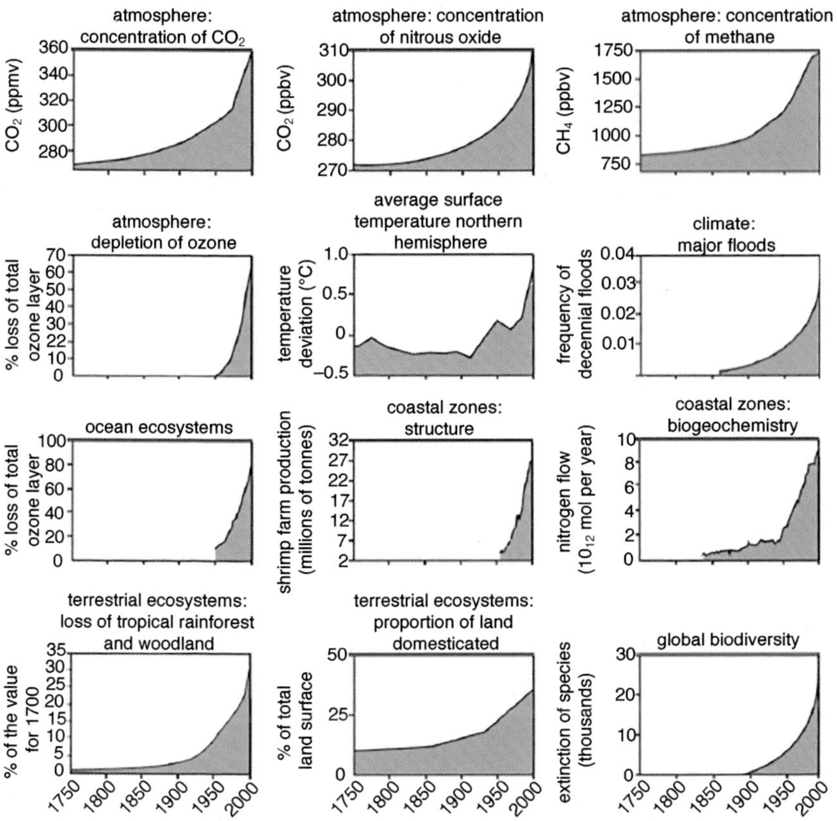

atmosphere: concentration of $CO_2$
$CO_2$ (ppmv)
360
340
320
300
280
atmosphere: concentration of nitrous oxide
$CO_2$ (ppbv)
310
300
290
280
270
atmosphere: concentration of methane
$CH_4$ (ppbv)
1750
1500
1250
1000
750
atmosphere: depletion of ozone
% loss of total ozone layer
70
60
50
40
30
22
10
0
average surface temperature northern hemisphere
temperature deviation (°C)
1.0
0.5
0
–0.5
climate: major floods
frequency of decennial floods
0.04
0.03
0.02
0.01
ocean ecosystems
% loss of total ozone layer
100
80
60
40
20
0
coastal zones: structure
shrimp farm production (millions of tonnes)
32
27
22
17
12
7
2
coastal zones: biogeochemistry
nitrogen flow ($10_{12}$ mol per year)
10
8
6
4
2
0
terrestrial ecosystems: loss of tropical rainforest and woodland
% of the value for 1700
35
30
25
20
15
10
5
0
terrestrial ecosystems: proportion of land domesticated
% of total land surface
50
25
0
global biodiversity
extinction of species (thousands)
30
20
10
0
1750
1800
1850
1900
1950
2000

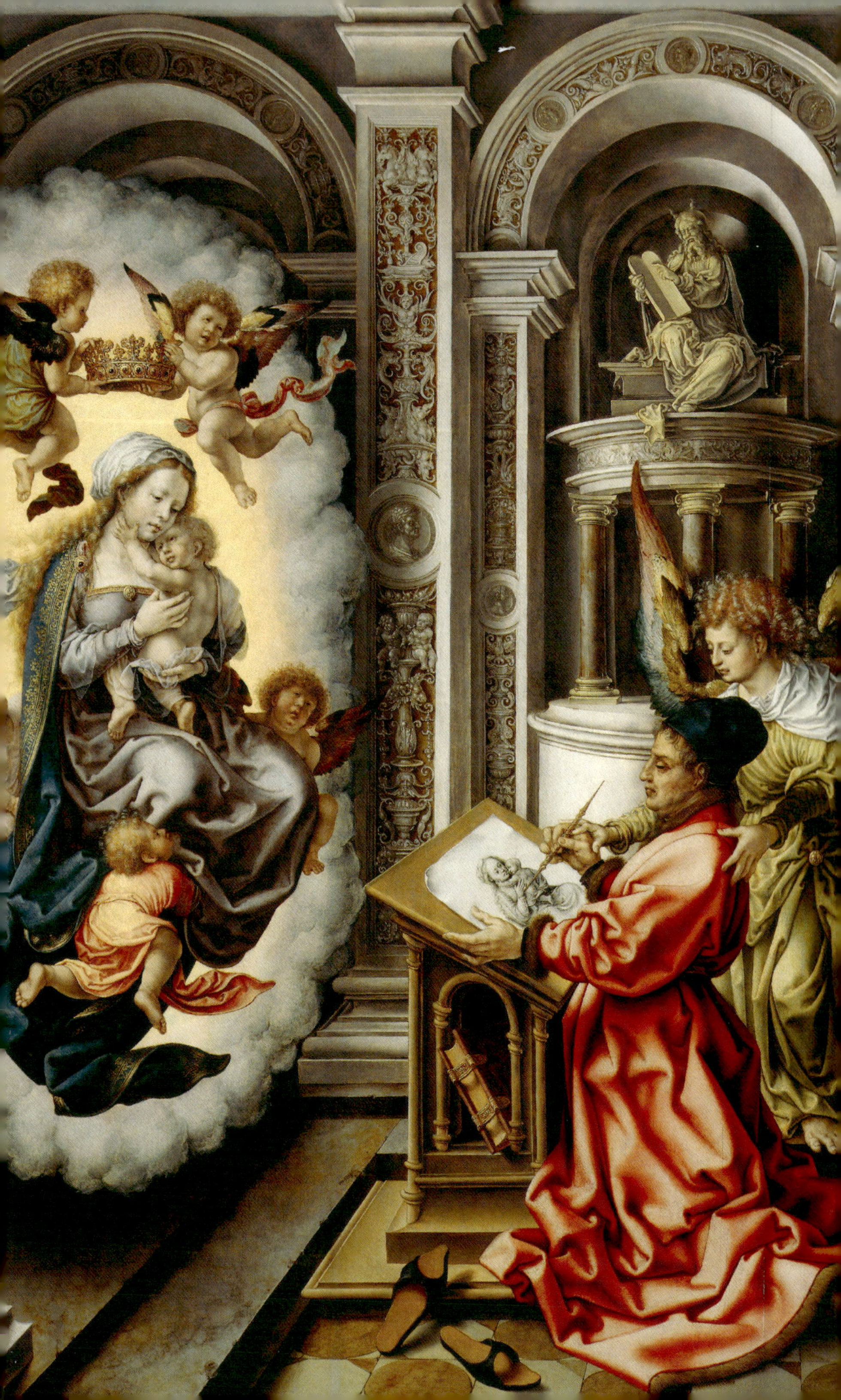

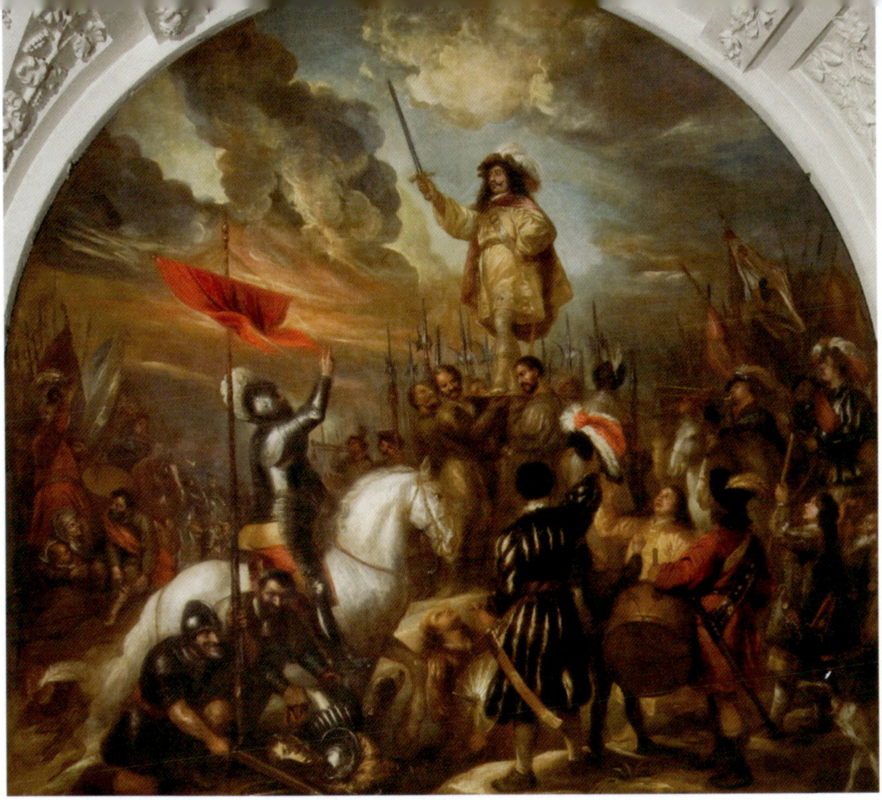

Figure 26. Jan Lievens, *Brinio, Raised on a Shield*, 1661.

(Left) Figure 25. Jan Gossaert, *St Luke Painting the Madonna*, *c.* 1520.

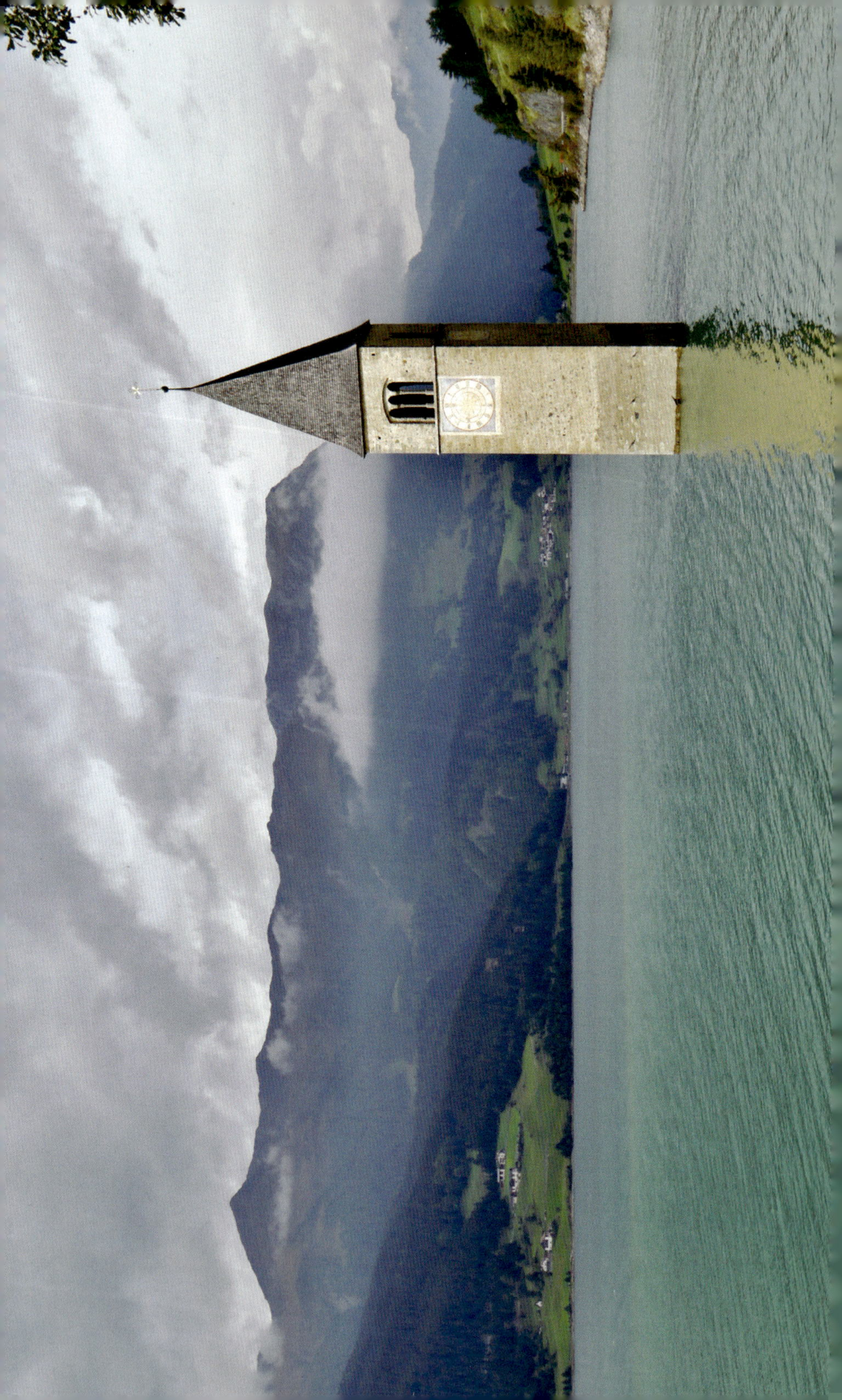

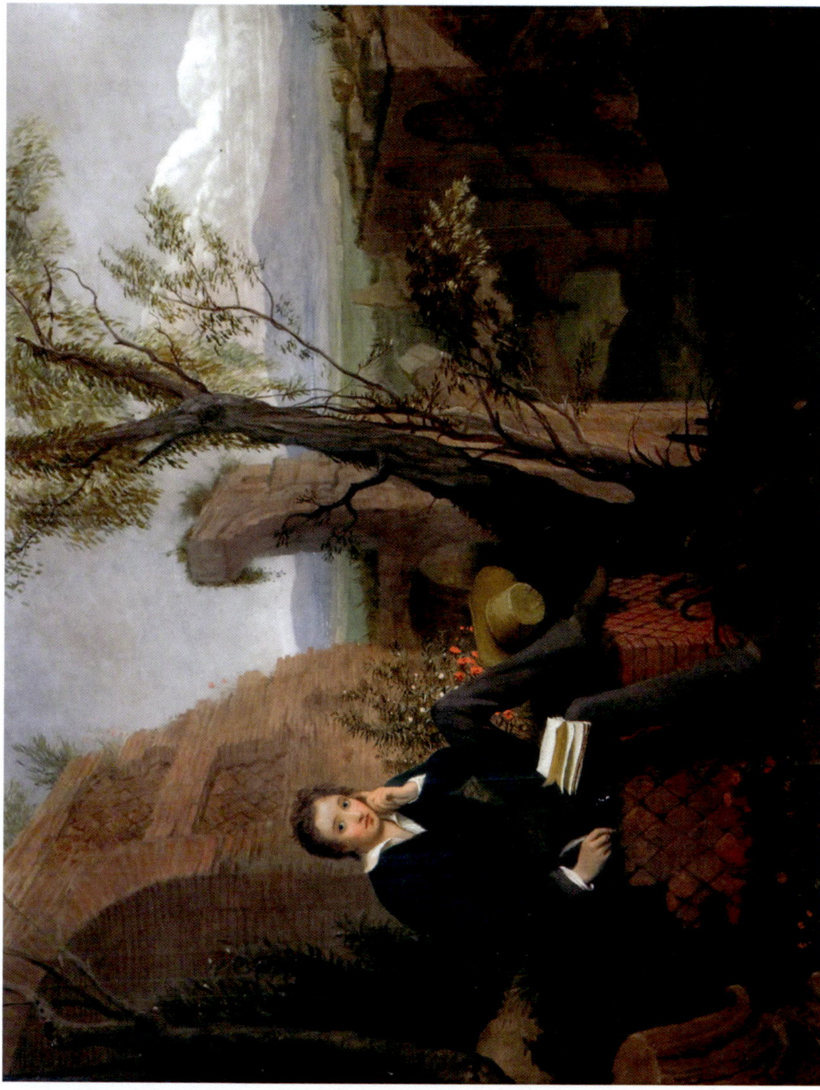

Figure 28. Joseph Severn, *Posthumous Portrait of Percy Bysshe Shelley Writing Prometheus Unbound*, 1845.

(Left) Figure 27. Reschen Lake.

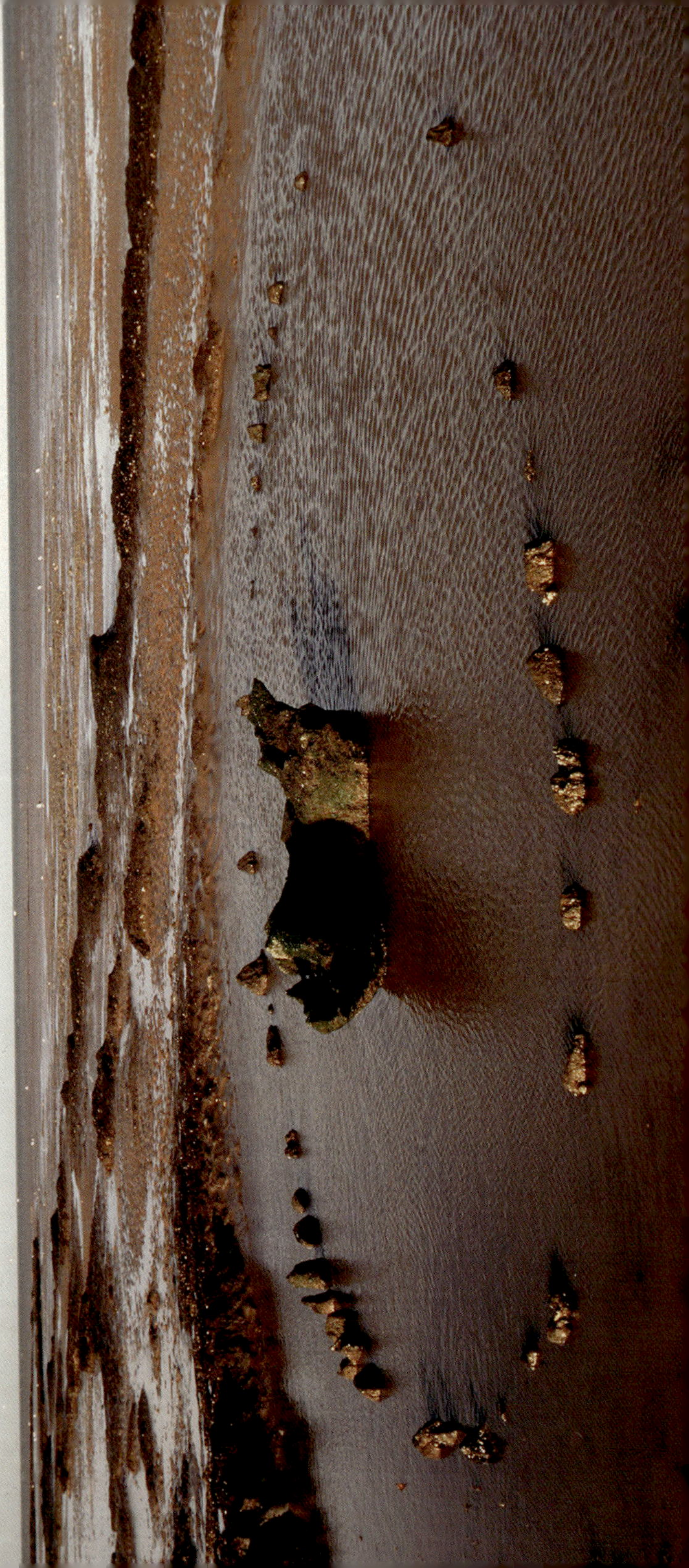

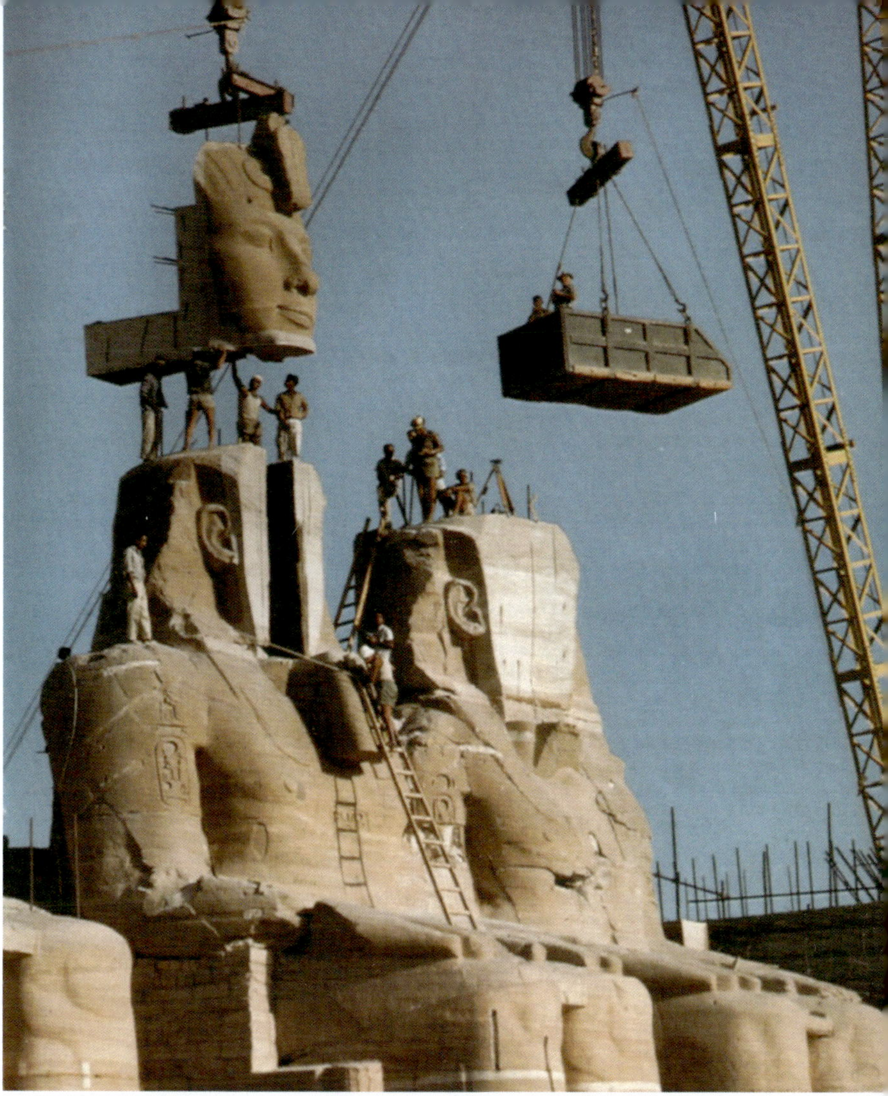

Figure 30. The Reconstruction of the Abu Simbel Temple, 1968.

(Left) Figure 29. Seahenge/Holme I, Norfolk, 1998.

(Overleaf) Figure 31. Cosquer Cave, Marseille, 2005.

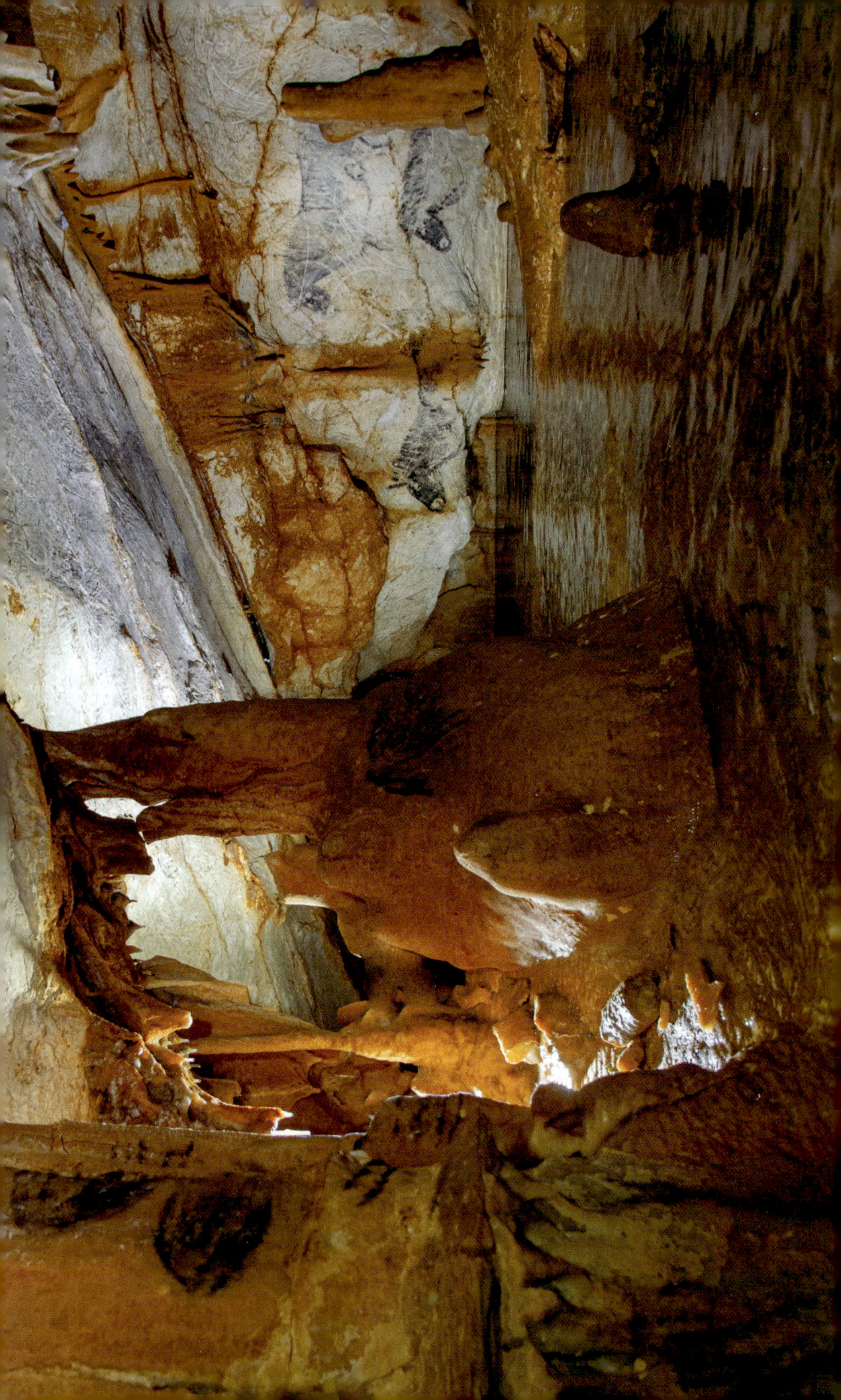

## THE TEMPLE OF ZHANG FEI

Hubei, a mountainous province cut in two by the mighty Yangtze River, is seen as the cradle of Chinese civilization. In the Three Gorges region, human artefacts have been found that date back to the Palaeolithic, 100,000 years ago. Later, a mysterious collection of clans, known as the Ba (*c.* 2000–220 BCE), left behind some refined bronze objects. The ceramics found in this region are more varied in form and decoration than those produced elsewhere in China in roughly the same period.

Today, however, this renowned region is covered by a dam reservoir. The building of the Three Gorges Dam (Sanxia Daba, 1994–2006), with its hydroelectric power station, caused the most far-reaching destruction of historical heritage in the world since the Second World War. Thirteen major cities, 140 towns and over 1,000 villages were flooded, including immovable heritage such as temples, shrines and cemeteries. Chinese curators of monuments tried to save what they could. The temple of Baidicheng became an island, for example. Likewise located on a hilltop, the Shibaozhai pavilion, built during the Ming dynasty (1368–1644) and famous as the most complex wooden building in the world, was protected by a dyke. Elsewhere, visitors can go down into a tunnel to the underwater museum of White Crane Ridge and admire inscriptions that record the changes in water level of the Yangtze over a period of 1,000 years. The picturesque ancient town of Dachang was partially preserved too: thirty of its characteristic houses with their blue rooftiles and curved ornamental woodwork were demolished and rebuilt 5 kilometres away.[5]

The most complex operation, however, involved the 1,700-year-old temple of Zhang Fei, majestically located on the forested north bank of the river, close to the ancient town of Yunyang. General Zhang Fei was a legendary warlord of the Three Kingdoms period (220–280 CE), who plays a leading role in the fourteenth-century classic *The Romance of the Three Kingdoms*. For centuries, fishers prayed to Zhang as their patron, and every year hundreds of thousands of visitors came to pay their respects. The temple dedicated to him consisted of a compound with elegant courtyards, shade-giving trees and pavilions. It housed hundreds of statues, as well as stelae (stones with writing on them) and calligraphy. According to the rules of feng shui, a Chinese form of geomancy, the location of temples and cemeteries is of spiritual significance. Zhang Fei himself is said to have chosen the Hill of the Flying Phoenix as the site for his temple, looking out on the Yangtze and with a verdant cypress forest nearby as well as a cool spring, both of which are seen as symbols of life. Four large Chinese characters were carved into the foundations of his temple, reading *jiang shang feng qing*: 'cool breeze blowing over the river'.

When planning to build the dam, the authorities understood the great religious and cultural value of the temple, so they decided to have it dismantled in its entirety. Stones, wooden pillars and rooftiles were photographed, numbered, packaged and, along with decorative rocks from the courtyards, moved 30 kilometres upstream. At the new location (Bangshang Yuanzi in the village of Long'an) the landscape was reasonably similar to the original surroundings. More than a hundred trees were relocated as well. The intention was to follow the original technique as precisely as possible during reconstruction. Metal nails were avoided, for example, and materials were reused. We may wonder to what extent this ambition was met: the most important ritual object in the temple, the terracotta statue of Zhang Fei himself in the central hall, proved so fragile that it could not be moved. A new version in bronze took its place.

An even more drastic discontinuity was the fact that the relocation meant the loss of the favourable geomantic characteristics of the temple. While the original building was accessed directly from the river, in its new location it must be visited by road, via a huge ramp. For a deity that protected fishers, this is a striking change. Fieldwork by French ethnologist Katiana Le Mentec shows that the local people are unhappy with the new situation, saying it 'no longer really looks like a temple'.[6] Visitors are also dissatisfied with the time they spend there, claiming the temple is less 'effective' because the auspicious surroundings are missing, as is the comfortable access from the river and the opportunity to burn your own incense at the foot of the statue of the god. In the countryside there are rumours that Zhang Fei is angry and has refused to be moved. As a result, local residents have decided to build a small shrine close to the old location, where several centuries-old traditions are perpetuated and activities pursued that are forbidden in the new temple. Local spiritual mediums (called *huopusa*) are said to conduct rituals there at Chinese New Year and on Zhang Fei's birthday. The presence of a new stone statue has even given rise to a new legend about the effectiveness of the god.

Comparable expressions of discontent can be heard regarding other solutions for the heritage of the Three Gorges Dam. The thirty houses of the village of Dachang that were moved have become a kind of soulless theme park, and nobody lives in them. As Tang Yuyang, an engineer at the Beijing Institute of Civil Engineering and Architecture, which assisted with the relocation, has claimed, 'The people of the Three Gorges no longer exist. What I mean is that the environment, the local customs, the feeling is gone. Before, locals carried things in baskets on their back, climbing steep stairways up the hillsides to get to the towns; now it's all highways.'[7]

The American and British relocations we have looked at dealt with structures that were already quite divorced from any social context. The Chinese examples show how much more complicated the situation becomes when heritage is part of living cultural and religious practices. Even when its material authenticity is largely preserved, the feeling that the original has been violated can come to predominate. In the previous chapter we came upon the limitations of the focus on material that is typical of UNESCO's original concept of heritage, which adheres to the European model. In Japan, as in the case of the shrine buildings of Ise, the performative element, which is to say the religious traditions connected with the heritage, can be more important than the physical material (with the result that the Ise Shrine, at the time of writing, does not have World Heritage status). For the Chinese, in turn, the specific geomantic characteristics of a location (according to the philosophy of feng shui) can have great emotional value.

## UNESCO'S VIEWS ON RECONSTRUCTION

In Europe, beliefs about the reconstruction of heritage have fluctuated wildly. In the nineteenth century, curators of monuments, adhering to the ideals of historical scholarship, assumed that it was possible to summon up the past. Missing or ruined elements of architecture were completed or repaired 'as the original builders intended' and of course additions or removals were necessary to accomplish this. Architect Eugène Viollet-le-Duc (1814–79) applied a great deal of imagination to the reconstruction of the walls of the fortified mediaeval city of Carcassonne, and his disciple Louis Delacenserie (1838–1909) was given the task of similarly restoring the city of Bruges in all its historical glory. As well as stripping the architecture of all its later white stucco and classical elements, Delacenserie made additions in neo-gothic style and even added entire buildings. This mediaeval makeover was intended to give an economic and touristic boost to Bruges, which had fallen into poverty (an operation that can only be described as outstandingly successful, given the millions of visitors who come each year).

In chapter 5 we discussed Riegl's criticism of such historicism in the heritage profession, and his preference for age value – leaving the ageing process visible – above historical value. In the first half of the twentieth century, his views came to predominate, and historicism was increasingly regarded as a puerile error. Towards the end of the Second World War, it became clear that not only monuments, such as the abbey of Monte Cassino, but entire city centres had been all but flattened. With Riegl's ideas in mind, many European cities, including Berlin, Cologne and Rotterdam, took advantage of the situation to implement large-scale urban renewal, retaining only a select few historical buildings. Until the end of the century, the Venice Charter (1964), which took Riegl's idea as its starting point, was of decisive importance. The World Heritage Committee was therefore extremely cautious when it came to reconstruction. But there was one crucial counter-example: Warsaw.

During the Warsaw Rising in 1944, the Polish resistance inflicted considerable harm on the occupying forces. In revenge, the Nazis decided to burn down the historical centre of the city. While elsewhere the devastation was a side-effect of acts of war, Warsaw was deliberately destroyed only after the battle ended. As early as 1945, Stalin, who wanted to keep control of Poland and negotiated with the US and Britain on the issue at the Yalta Conference, believed that the Polish capital must be rebuilt.

The execution of that task can be credited mainly to architectural historian Jan Zachwatowicz (1900–1983) of the Office for the Reconstruction of the Capital (Biuro Odbudowy Stolicy). He managed to persuade the authorities to enable the city to be completely rebuilt. Nobody had ever attempted to reconstruct monuments on such a scale, but Zachwatowicz believed that the Polish identity had been uniquely expressed in the old architecture of Warsaw. Many residents of the city voluntarily lent him a hand. Furthermore, the twenty-two virtuoso cityscapes, or *vedute*, by Venetian painter Canaletto (1697–1768) had survived the war and could form the point of departure for a precise reconstruction.[8]

Most of the work was completed by 1955, and eventually Warsaw was added to the UNESCO list of World Heritage. Interestingly, the reconstruction work itself was crucial in making it possible to talk of the 'exceptional universal value' of the new old city. This reconstruction, after all, had amounted to 'a major contribution to the changes in the doctrines related to urbanisation and conservation of cities in most of the European countries' after the destruction of the Second World War.[9] In chapter 2 we looked at the first five criteria used by UNESCO that determine which 'masterpieces of human creative genius' deserve World Heritage status. But in Warsaw, where the masterpiece had been destroyed, a sixth criterion was applied: heritage is also valuable if it is 'directly or tangibly associated with events or living traditions, with ideas, or with beliefs, with artistic and literary works of outstanding universal significance', in this case the exceptional experiences of the Polish nation.[10] The fact that in reality not the historical architecture but the work of Zachwatowicz was awarded World Heritage status was emphasized once again in 2011, when UNESCO added all the architect's documents to the Memory of the World Register.

As far as the activities of UNESCO are concerned, it is obvious that over the past two decades Zachwatowicz's ideas have increasingly prevailed over those of Riegl. Civil servants and conservators are now more positive about reconstruction, in light of the increasing damage suffered by heritage as a result of human and natural factors. In the current version of UNESCO's Operational Guidelines, the Venice Charter still resonates: 'In relation to authenticity, the reconstruction of archaeological remains or historic buildings or districts is justifiable only in exceptional circumstances. Reconstruction is acceptable only on the basis of complete and detailed documentation and to no extent on conjecture.'[11] Yet in practice there is clearly a shift from material to immaterial elements, which can furnish a good reason for reconstruction. As early as 2005, the rebuilding of the Stari Most in Bosnia was justified, as we saw in chapter 2, by reference to the bridge's cultural significance, which is to say to an immaterial dimension that legitimized reconstruction even though the material dimension had been lost.

A striking role in these shifts has been played by Islamic fundamentalism and the war on terror. We looked in the previous chapter at the destruction of the Buddha statues of Bamyan by the Taliban and the devastation of Palmyra and Aleppo by Islamic State. No less traumatic was the destruction in 2013 of fourteen Sufi mausolea in Timbuktu, by an Islamic group called Ansar Dine, which has links to Al-Qaeda. Appeals from the director-general of UNESCO and from the World Heritage Committee, which actually took the matter to the International Court of Justice, only inspired the extremists to use more violence. They associated material heritage with idolatry and so even desecrated a local mosque. After the Islamists left, UNESCO nevertheless immediately took upon itself the reconstruction of the mausolea and completed it in record time, within two years. The organization indicated that reconstruction was the preferable option if it meant a cultural practice could be maintained, and complete documentation was available. The Exceptional Universal

Values that UNESCO had attributed to the mausolea initially related to their significance for Timbuktu's past, without any mention being made of social factors or traditional construction skills. Only after the tombs were destroyed was the emphasis placed on these immaterial values.

Along with the risk from terrorism, there is a growing awareness of the vulnerability of heritage to natural disasters. In the case of the architecture of Timbuktu, including the famous Sankoré Mosque, built largely of clay, the climate crisis is causing considerable damage, since it results in both more rainfall and desertification. In 2010 a fire destroyed the tombs of the Buganda kings in Kasubi, part of Uganda's World Heritage. In 2015 an earthquake hit another UNESCO location, the Kathmandu Valley in Nepal, where hundreds of buildings were reduced to heaps of bricks and timber beams; at the time of writing, very little restoration has taken place. Meanwhile we are becoming aware of climate-related risks worldwide, as described in chapter 1, threatening not just ancient shrines in Mali and coastal towns in Vietnam but European institutions such as the Louvre and the Uffizi. As we have seen, the World Heritage Committee touched on this back in 2005, writing that 'the impacts of climate change are affecting many and are likely to affect many more World Heritage properties, both natural and cultural in the years to come'. This produced a succession of recommendations, working groups and committees in which the impact of climate change was further explored.[12]

Both the increasing risks and a growing interest in immaterial aspects have therefore opened the door to reconstruction, while concerns about the authenticity of the material can be dismissed as an old-fashioned Western 'fetish'. As in Warsaw and Timbuktu, in Kasubi UNESCO gave its approval to complete reconstruction, as long as it was based on extensive documentation and original building techniques. The traditional use of the royal tombs must also be perpetuated.

Now that materials and locations are becoming more precarious because of climate-related risks, we can expect that reconstruction will increasingly be advocated. The most recent example is the Cosquer Cave near Marseille, which during the Upper Paleolithic, 19,000 years ago, was decorated with virtuoso depictions of animals, ranging from bison and horses to great auks, not to mention a man with the head of a seal (figure 31). The cave, which is open to the Mediterranean, is slowly flooding; the water level is currently rising by 3 millimetres per year. Laser scans and cameras have therefore been used to make as accurate a three-dimensional copy as possible, and since 2022 the resulting replica has been on view in a nearby museum. The original paintings will disappear under water at some point in the foreseeable future.

## PLACE, IDENTITY AND THE 'GLOBAL COMMONS'

One of the seemingly inevitable climate-related threats to heritage, a changing coastline (see chapter 1), will lead to more debate, not just about the authenticity of materials, but about the authenticity of a new location. Material has been much discussed since Alois Riegl, but location has received far less attention, even though relocation will be an increasingly obvious solution in light of rising sea levels.

For local communities, relocation is generally the least attractive option. People tend to remain in place as long as possible, adapting to changing circumstances.[13] Psychologists speak of 'place attachment' or a 'sense of place'. An even loftier term is 'topophilia', from the Greek *topos* (place) and *philia* (love). It was first used by poet W.H. Auden (1907–73). In Auden's vision, topophilia has little to do with love of nature and far more to do with the historical associations a place evokes.[14] Locations that lack a sense of place, which therefore might just as well be practically anywhere, are experienced as artificial. This applies not just to shopping centres and airports but to historical sites that have to a great degree been given over to commercial tourism.[15] Think for example of the aforementioned Chinese village of Dachang, which after its relocation turned into a theme park about which one of the engineers complained (see p. 143): 'The people of the Three Gorges no longer exist. . . . The environment, the local customs, the feeling is gone.'

The history of monument preservation likewise suggests that the appreciation of heritage is strongly connected with its original location. Sentiments of national or local identity have been decisive. One of the most prized possessions of the Victoria and Albert Museum in London is still the seventeenth-century marble rood loft from St John's Cathedral in 's-Hertogenbosch, the Netherlands. It was purchased in 1866, legitimately, by a British art dealer called Murray Marks, who had it shipped to London. This sparked for the first time a broadly shared awareness of the importance of heritage among people in the Netherlands. The sale inspired politician Victor de Stuers (1843–1916) to write his essay 'Holland op zijn smalst' ('Holland at its narrowest', 1873), which laid the foundations for both the Cultural Heritage Agency of the Netherlands and the world-famous Rijksmuseum. In Britain itself, the alarm was raised when Americans were about to dismantle parts of the fifteenth-century Tattershall Castle in Lincolnshire and take it with them. It led to the first British law aimed at protecting built heritage, in 1913. The Spanish erupted with comparable fury when American financier John Pierpont Morgan (1837–1913) – responsible for, among other things, General Electric and other automobile and railway companies – bought a staircase that came from Casa de Miranda, a Renaissance palace in Burgos.[16]

Such moves can be complicated immensely by colonial or neocolonial relationships. In recent years, former colonies have tried to reclaim heritage that was hauled off to the European metropolises many decades ago. It took until 2005, for example, for a huge fourth-century Ethiopian obelisk, erected in triumph in Rome by the dictator Mussolini, to be taken back to its country of origin. In 2018 French president Emmanuel Macron compiled a recommendation regarding research into the origins of colonial heritage, with a view to eventually returning it to African museums.[17] That example was followed elsewhere in Europe, with Belgium going so far as to invite claims from today's Democratic Republic of Congo regarding the heritage once taken from the Belgian Congo. But the British Museum, for example, remains so stubborn that some have labelled it the '*Brutish* Museum'. One issue, out of many, concerns the return of the Elgin Marbles to Greece. Among the solutions now proposed is for the museum to make accurate 3-D-printed copies, so that the original sculptures can be sent back to the place they came from, the Acropolis in Athens. It is conceivable that eventually the Egyptians will demand that the temples donated to New York, Leiden, Madrid and Turin when the Aswan Dam was built be returned.

Even when completely new copies are involved, the relationship between Europe and its former colonies is complicated. The reconstruction made in Oxford of the destroyed arch at the Temple of Bel in Palmyra, which we looked at in chapter 6, was exhibited in cities including New York, Washington, London, Florence, Bern and Luxembourg, but at the time of writing it has not yet reached Syria itself. Some believe that this is a matter, once again, of neocolonial appropriation of Syrian heritage by Western countries.[18]

This brings us to a paradox that is inherent in the notion of World Heritage. On the one hand, it belongs to all of humanity, as 'global commons', and therefore should find a home in museums anywhere in the world. On the other hand, when it comes to heritage values, increasing attention is paid to the degree to which monuments are integrated into characteristic locations, and into living customs and traditions. It is somewhat ironic that, as a consequence, people who are not part of those traditions – for example, wealthy inhabitants of Western countries that have become estranged from indigenous crafts and rituals – may no longer wish to identify with such locally rooted heritage. Future discussions about climate-related relocation and the reconstruction of heritage will have to manoeuvre between those two extremes.

Now that it is becoming increasingly clear that a collective, supranational approach to the atmosphere, oceans and polar areas is required – the $CO_2$ emissions of one country can after all lead to flooding in another – ideas about World Heritage as global commons may receive a boost. When in 1965 Buckminster Fuller compared cultural heritage to a fossil resource that the whole world must learn to share (see chapter 2), there were high hopes for the ideal of international collaboration. In the context of postwar optimism about reconstruction and development aid, the saving of heritage was merely a means to a higher end, namely to expedite world peace and toleration. According to the first UNESCO charter in 1945, 'a peace based exclusively upon the political and economic arrangements of governments would not be a peace which could secure the unanimous, lasting and sincere support of the peoples of the world, and that the peace must therefore be founded, if it is not to fail, upon the intellectual and moral solidarity of mankind'.[19]

This ideology underpinned the drastic decision to relocate several of the Egyptian temples of Abu Simbel in their entirety to the US and Europe. But such international optimism proved short-lived, and since that time no operation on a comparable scale has taken place. In the recent past, the opposite, if anything, has happened, and the ideal of the solidarity of humankind has waned. The large-scale destruction of built heritage in Kathmandu in 2015 did not lead to campaigns for its salvation, or even to sizeable financial support from other countries. It is more than possible that climate change will merely encourage a self-serving mentality. With its border controls, 'Fortress Europe' is increasingly shutting out migrants for whom the climate crisis, if they come from Bangladesh or Syria for example, was one of the factors that made them leave their home countries. Some of those who joined what became known as the 'migrant caravan' that gathered at the US border with Mexico in 2019 were climate refugees. Even with regard to a country's overseas territories, the dividing lines are firming up. When in 2017 Hurricane Irma hit the island of Sint Maarten, part of the Kingdom of the Netherlands, and left it largely in ruins, columnist Marianne Zwagerman (b. 1969) expressed a widely shared sentiment: 'You don't *have* to live on an island where a hurricane destroys everything every few years.'[20] An even better example is the inadequacy of President Trump's response to hurricane damage in Puerto Rico (a territory of the United States) that same year, which caused severe damage to cultural heritage.

When, after the horrors of the Second World War, thoughts turned to a new world order based on cooperation, philosopher Hannah Arendt (1906–75) claimed that the ideal of a unified humanity could arise only through 'negative solidarity', namely when the species was threatened with extinction.[21] But, for the time being, a future in which countries facing the climate crisis shut themselves off from each other like gated communities seems a more realistic prospect.

As far as world politics goes, we are on course for a repeat of moves from colonial history (or a new 'climate coloniality'), in which rich countries in the Global North manage to shift the burden of climatological damage onto their former colonies.[22] At the very least we are seeing an obvious asymmetry. When in 2022 Pakistan was hit by devastating monsoon rains – which not only made 8 million people homeless but also damaged the 4,500-year-old ruins of Mohenjo Daro – it pointed out that in its entire industrial history it has caused roughly the same amount of $CO_2$ emissions as the United States produces now in just one year.

A relevant thought experiment concerns the Three Gorges Dam, whose story has not yet ended. There are doubts as to whether the mammoth project is capable of withstanding climate change. Increasing rainfall means that its reservoir collects more water than it was designed to hold. In 2020 this led to dramatic images attracting attention around the world. Upstream from the dam, in the province of Sichuan, volunteers made huge efforts to protect the Giant Buddha of Leshan from floods. More than 70 metres tall, the statue, which dates from the Tang dynasty (around the year 800 CE), had its toes in the water. That had not happened since 1949. In fact it remains to be seen whether the Three Gorges Dam will be able to hold out against the increasing water pressure. Should it give way, to what extent will China be able to count on 'the intellectual and moral solidarity of mankind' if it calls for help to rescue its heritage?

# Epilogue: Looking the beast in the eye

*The old world is dying,*
*and the new world struggles to be born:*
*now is the time of monsters.*
Antonio Gramsci

When in 2013 seawater washed away the cliffs on the English coast at Happisburgh, it exposed the oldest human footprints ever found outside Africa. They were made by a family (possibly of the human species *Homo antecessor*) that walked across the land bridge that then existed between the British Isles and the European mainland 800,000 years ago. Melting glaciers worldwide, from Norway to Argentina, have since relinquished historical remains, including Roman coins and sacrificed Inca children. At the same time, persistent drought has made ancient traces of human activity in the landscape of Western Europe visible: fields, houses and even castles whose existence was all but forgotten. In the 1960s and 1970s many places worldwide were flooded by the building of dams, but in 2019 the 7,000-year-old Dolmen of Guadalperal, known as the Spanish Stonehenge, emerged from the waters. When Iraqi Kurdistan was hit by drought in 2018, the reservoir of a dam in the Tigris lost so much water that the ruins of a Bronze Age palace reemerged. Archaeologists linked it to the Mittani Empire of the fifteenth to fourteenth centuries BCE. Other examples of drowned settlements that have become visible again are the Mormon village of St Thomas in Nevada, the town of Igaratá in Brazil and Potosí in Venezuela.

It is clear as day that climate change can prompt excitement among historians and heritage experts. How many new articles, books and careers might be possible now? But their enthusiasm is bittersweet. Archaeological finds in melting glaciers, for example, have been preserved under exceptional circumstances. Once exposed to oxygen and higher temperatures, the time within which they can be found and saved is extremely short. Many will be lost over coming decades, or never noticed at all.[1]

Similarly, the writing of this book was for me rife with ambiguities. Over the past few years I have listened and spoken to many colleagues about the challenges of the climate crisis. Many previously unthinkable phenomena exert a huge power of attraction on meteorologists, geologists and physicists, who eagerly throw themselves upon happenings that suggest a new relevance for their disciplines – from the unprecedented speed at which levels of $CO_2$ in the atmosphere are rising to the disappearance of glaciers and the shifting of climate zones. In the newly established Centre for Environmental Humanities at my university, a great deal of fresh energy was released, comparable to the buzz brought about a decade earlier by the digital humanities. Academics, including art historians, are only human. I too have felt flurries of enthusiasm of a comparable kind as I worked on this book, even when I was forced to leave my home in Amsterdam while the wooden foundations it stood on were replaced with concrete. It took a long time for the penny to drop, incidentally; only after quite some time had gone by did I realize that I had become part of a larger scenario in which wooden piles are rotting as a result of climate change.

Here and there I spoke about my ideas on heritage and the climate crisis, and in 2021 I published an article on the subject in the popular-science periodical *Aeon*.[2] It provoked considerable debate. Many people were shocked by my suggestion that the Royal Palace in Amsterdam should be relocated, stone by stone, to a part of the country close to the German border that is several metres above sea level. But in most of the reactions, the prevailing impulse was to step on the brake, for example by observing that the Global South will be far less resilient to climate damage than Europe – so what was I making such a fuss about? My articles created two kinds of unrest. Some people accused me of climate alarmism, unbecoming in an academic. Others were angry that I dared to pay attention to the loss of historical heritage when nature was destined to suffer far greater damage.

One remarkable reaction came from my immediate colleagues, scholars in the humanities. They tended to point out to me the intrinsic fluidity and fleeting nature of heritage. The insight that we cannot in fact conserve the past would, they felt, lead to the logical conclusion that it does not matter if bits of it are lost every now and then. My editor at *Aeon* even read an implicit radical plea in my manuscript, as if I were actually wholeheartedly opposed to the 'musealization' of Europe's city centres. The rigidity of heritage conservation and the gentrification in which it often results can be at odds with urban dynamism and social justice. Perhaps, she suggested, I could make a more audacious but poetic point in my manuscript, namely that life itself is fleeting, and even the most beautiful and wealthy cities do not last.

I had thought of a title for my article: 'The future of historical heritage'. My editor came up with a more philosophical suggestion: 'Heritage at Sea: Must We Simply Accept the Loss of Beloved Buildings and Cities to the Floods and Rising Seas of the Climate Crisis?' The new title suggested I had decided from the start that nothing can be done about the problem. In fact it expressed, like my colleagues who instinctively pointed out the fluidity of heritage, a form of defeatism. I regard this as a pernicious outgrowth of the postmodern idea that truth does not exist. Such defeatism is a good illustration of the degree to which the humanities have themselves contributed to imputations of their social irrelevance. But my article in fact presented solutions (transformation, digitization and reconstruction) that I have examined in more detail in this book.

Since 2021, when my article appeared in *Aeon*, much has happened. The sixth climate report by the IPCC, produced in 2021–2, the most comprehensive pooling of scientific knowledge about climate change thus far, turned out to be far more radical in its predictions than expected, especially in relation to rising sea levels. In 2021, Shell was ordered by the Dutch courts to limit its $CO_2$ emissions. This inspired a multiplicity of climate court cases elsewhere in the world, as well as increasing calls for rights to be given to nature. Particularly successful were Extinction Rebellion's protests in the Netherlands. For months, tens of thousands of people regularly blocked a motorway in The Hague, to draw attention to government subsidies for fossil fuel companies. They included me and twenty of my colleagues, dressed in the gowns and caps of our universities. Sweating all day under a thick layer of black velvet, seated on the tarmac in expectation of water cannon fired by the military police – I will not quickly forget it. (The government of the time promised to improve its act but was then replaced by a more right-wing coalition.) Supporters and opponents have since dug themselves more firmly into their trenches. In 2024 Shell was acquitted on appeal, whereas Phoebe Plummer and Anna Holland of Just Stop Oil, who had thrown soup over Van Gogh's *Sunflowers*, were sentenced to long jail terms. The re-election of Donald Trump in that same year marked a settling of accounts with progressive Democrat climate policy.

I saw in my classroom, too, just how quickly reversals of mentality can occur. In front of my eyes I am witnessing the rapid advance of 'shifting baseline syndrome': every generation accepts its own situation as a benchmark and therefore does not take into consideration in its own contemplation of climate change what has already been lost. (Think of the number of insects squashed on car windscreens, to the great annoyance of motorists until the 1990s; it rarely inconveniences us today.) The term 'shifting baseline syndrome' (or the similar 'generational amnesia') is directly applicable to historical heritage. I initially came upon disbelief among my colleagues when I shared with them my concern that Venice will not last for ever, but the current generation of students has completely internalized that insight.

All the same, I do not think, despite growing attention to the climate crisis, that anything fundamental has changed in the concepts that I first addressed in 2021. 'Ambiguous loss' is still the determining factor of the human condition in light of what awaits us. It is possible that the IPCC reports are too cautious, that temperatures are rising more quickly than expected and we are heading for warming not of 3°C by the end of the century but of 4.8° (as NASA director James Hansen has claimed). If climate change has one obvious consequence, then it is mounting uncertainty about the development of weather phenomena and related disasters, as these all too often turn out to diverge from the models. It is possible, although far from certain, that the huge Thwaites glacier at the South Pole will collapse even before 2030. The impact such an event would have on sea levels worldwide would not be much less dramatic than that of a meteor strike.

## HERITAGE CONTRIBUTES TO BETTER UNDERSTANDING

In the last few chapters I have proposed three solutions for heritage during a climate crisis: transformation, digitization and reconstruction. But the most important reason not to succumb to defeatism is of a different order altogether. It is precisely attention to the future of historical heritage, and therefore a switching of the focus from nature to humankind when it comes to climate change, that can lead to a new understanding and a new readiness to act. Every year, more than 200,000 scientific articles are published with the word 'climate' in the title. But the vast majority deal with the influence of climate change on the natural environment and on animals (or 'non-human animals', as the environmental humanities would put it). Although more and more social scientists and scholars of the arts and humanities are addressing climate change, Wallace-Wells makes an acute observation:

> Until now, it seems to have been easier for us to empathize with the climate plight of other species than our own, perhaps because we have such a hard time acknowledging or understanding our own responsibility and complicity in the changes now unfolding, and such an easier time evaluating the morally simpler calculus of pure victimhood.[3]

If we take into account the loss of cultural heritage, it becomes clearer to what extent humans and their environment are interwoven. Both culture and nature will suffer under the climate crisis; solutions to that crisis will have to consider cultural and natural factors in combination.

Furthermore, a focus on historical heritage might lead to greater commitment. When the Taliban smashed the Buddha statues in Bamyan and IS bombed Palmyra, there was a far greater international outcry than there had been in response to much of the human suffering, which remained invisible. By the same token, the realization that the building blocks of their own civilization are threatened might mobilize people for whom the loss of tropical coral reefs remains an abstraction, far removed from their immediate concerns. People who derive their identity in part from cultural heritage will perhaps make more climate-friendly political choices. As Israeli historian Yuval Noah Harari (b. 1976) has remarked, in his country the slightest corrosion of the Wailing Wall in Jerusalem causes more outrage than the demise of the Amazon region, which literally supports life on earth.[4]

In this respect, the Low Countries present another interesting practical example. American literary theorist Simon Richter has been trying for some time to understand the Dutch situation with the help of Freud (and he points out that Freud himself compared psychoanalysis, which is intended to expose the unconscious, to the draining of polders[5]). Richter is amazed at the blinkers the Dutch wear with regard to their own situation. (Questionnaires make clear that of all the nationalities of the EU the Dutch are the least likely to think they might have to move house because of climate change.[6]) He sees this narrowing of vision as a psychological deviation; the Dutch are repressing, in the Freudian sense, the seriousness of the climate crisis. It is not as if information fails to reach them, but they refuse to associate it with their own situation. Richter uses the psychoanalytical term 'taboo', which has its origins in the culture of Polynesia. There it referred to a religious ban on certain places, objects, people or acts (according to Freud, incest and patricide were the main taboos in Europe). As variations on this theme, Richter identifies 'seven adaptation taboos', behaviours that should be the focus of attention in the Netherlands at the moment:

1. Don't question our peerless water management prowess, at home or abroad.
2. Don't cause panic.
3. Don't carry on about the severity of climate change.
4. Don't endanger our Moody's AAA rating.
5. Don't notice our poor greenhouse gas mitigation record.
6. Don't get in the way of spatial planning.
7. Don't mention [eastward] retreat.[7]

The first and last points especially go to the heart of the matter. First of all, successful water management is such a powerful element of their identity that it simply does not occur to the Dutch to question its capabilities; that would undermine their self-image too radically. An even greater taboo is withdrawal eastwards, which would make enormous demands of the Germans – precisely the neighbours who, ever since the Second World War, have been seen as the greatest rivals and traditional enemies of the Dutch. Richter expresses hope, however, for a new 'Peace of Münster'. He is referring to the year 1648, at the end of the Dutch Revolt and the Thirty Years' War, when for the first time the Dutch nation was formed within a framework designed to guarantee peace in Europe. To celebrate the peace, Amsterdam decided to build its monumental Town Hall (now the Royal Palace), on the roof of which a bronze personification of Peace waves an olive branch. Before very long, Richter believes, comparable negotiations with Germany and Belgium will be needed to create a region straddling the borders. There the Dutch population will be able to settle after agreements have been reached about living space, transport, land use and energy. Eventually this peace treaty must become a model for a new culture of welcome, the starting point for flourishing communities in the Anthropocene all over the world.

Richter's taboos make clear the extent to which landscape and geography can play a part in the construction of a national self-image. But identity is also strongly associated with historical heritage – see the first few chapters of this book – and we therefore ought to add another subject to the list. The climate crisis endangers our patrimony, our inheritance from our ancestors. Richter's last taboo might give rise to an interesting thought experiment: when is The Hague going to ask the Gemäldegalerie in Berlin to make space on its walls for Vermeer's *Girl with a Pearl Earring*? To say the least, this idea will grate for many Dutch people. Similar sensitivities of identity are in play worldwide, as we have seen, from the graves of the Dunn dynasty on the island of Togoru to the Moai statues on Easter Island and the Statue of Liberty in New York.

## CATHEDRAL THINKING

In her far-sighted 2011 study *Living in Denial: Climate Change, Emotions, and Everyday Life*, American sociologist Kari Norgaard pointed out that confrontation with more and more scientific data, such as are produced daily by climatologists, actually makes the public less prepared to take action. Since then, her position has been elaborated upon, with observations about 'shifting baseline syndrome', about 'plant blindness' – the human inability to value biodiversity at its true worth – and about the 'doomerism' of the latest generation of young people, who are growing up with the climate crisis and do not feel responsible for it. Even more cynical are those billionaires who no longer deny that climate change is happening but assume they can protect themselves and their children from its consequences. As Norgaard concludes, the only thing that can help is if people are affected at a deep emotional, psychological and spiritual level.[8] 'Rational scientific data can lose against a compelling emotional story that speaks to people's core values.'[9]

In this compelling emotional story, heritage may have an essential part to play. History teaches us that people have quite literally thrown themselves into battle for their patrimony and put their lives and those of their children on the line for it. There is no reason to think that this sacred flame has since been extinguished. In chapter 2 we saw, moreover, that the intermediary level to which heritage appeals, in between micro and macro (heritage transcends generations by definition, but it never becomes an unmanageable 'hyperobject'), offers a clear framework for action with regard to the climate crisis.

Bearing in mind the words of Giambattista Vico, referenced earlier, we see that there is a fundamental distinction to be made between nature and historical heritage. Our own species created heritage, and so by definition we are in a position to save it. The same does not apply to coral reefs, for example, despite all the heroic efforts now being made to preserve them (from feeding by hand to genetic manipulation). This explains why Greta Thunberg used the metaphor of a cathedral to urge government leaders to take action on the climate.

Over the coming years, during which we will have to set to work literally rather than metaphorically to save heritage, we must first of all make a careful selection. Heritage professionals are faced with the task of dusting off and updating Alois Riegl's system of heritage values (think for example of historical, visual and spiritual values, and rarity value) and on that basis engage in cultural triage, with an eye to disasters in both the short and the long term. What are we going to preserve, relocate, transform, document, digitize or abandon? And will we mark abandonment with a ritual, like the one staged for the Okjökull glacier? They will furthermore need to supplement the traditional, predominantly aesthetic heritage values with postcolonial ethical considerations. To what extent should the biggest sources of historical emissions step up to rescue heritage in their former colonies? Think, for example, of Jakarta as it floods.

In 1970 the first Earth Day took place. The Burmese secretary-general of the United Nations, U Thant (1900–74), addressed the General Assembly:

> As we watch the sun go down, evening after evening, through the smog across the poisoned waters of our native earth, we must ask ourselves seriously whether we really wish some future universal historian on another planet to say about us: 'With all their genius and with all their skill, they ran out of foresight and air and food and water and ideas.'[10]

Looking back after more than half a century, we are forced to conclude that his speech was prophetic. Too little has been done to tackle climate change. To quote Margaret Atwood (b. 1939), these days it is more a matter of 'everything change'.[11] This book has therefore attempted, by focusing on heritage, to offer a different perspective on the most important story of our time. In valuing heritage, after all, a variety of concerns are relevant in addition to the criteria used by Riegl and by UNESCO, including historical sensation, beauty, aura, mineral affinities, solastalgia, *lieux de mémoire*, *Ruinenlust* and dark euphoria. I hope these multilayered musings will help people to find new ways of looking the monster that is the climate crisis in the eye, and take action.

# List of Figures

19. Matthias Withoos, *Repair of the Zuiderzee Dyke at Schardam after the All Saints' Flood of 1675*, 1676, oil on canvas, 65 × 115 cm, Westfries Museum, Hoorn. Bought with support of the Hoogheemraadschap Hollands Noorderkwartier, De Nederlandse Waterschapsbank, Hendrik Muller's Vaderlandsch Fonds, Kerkmeijer-de Regt Stichting & Vrienden van het Westfries Museum. Copyright © Westfries Museum.

20. Jacob van Ruisdael, *A Panoramic View of Amsterdam*, *c.* 1679, oil on canvas, 42 × 41 cm, National Gallery, London, on loan from a private collection. Copyright © Getty/The Picture Art Collection.

21. Pieter and François Hemony, Atlas on the west facade of the Amsterdam Town Hall (now Royal Palace), 1663, Amsterdam. Photo: iStock.

22. Wim T. Schippers, *The Steeple of Drienerlo*, 1979, Universiteit Twente, Enschede. Photo: Wikimedia Commons.

23. Jan Gossaert (attributed), *Madonna van Leuven*, *c.* 1516, oil on panel, 45 × 39 cm, Museo del Prado, Madrid. Copyright © Alamy/Artefact.

24. The Great Acceleration, after W. Steffen et al., *The Anthropocene: Conceptual and Historical Perspectives* (Cambridge, MA: Harvard University Press, 2011).

25. Jan Gossaert, *St Luke Painting the Madonna*, *c.* 1520, oil on panel, 110 × 84 cm, Kunsthistorisches Museum, Vienna. Copyright © incamerastock/Alamy.

26. Jan Lievens, *Brinio, Leader of the Kaninefaten, Raised on a Shield*, 1661, oil on canvas, 546 × 538 cm, Royal Palace, Amsterdam. Photo: Google Arts and Culture.

27. Lake Reschen. Photo: iStock.

# Notes

All web links were last consulted on 13 January 2026.

## Prologue

1 Anna Somers Cocks, 'Enjoy the Venice Biennale, Everyone – but Be Aware It's Taking Place in a Dying City', *The Art Newspaper*, 15 April 2024.

2 In Venice the ground has sunk by 15 cm over the past century, as a result of both natural soil subsidence and human activity (extraction of groundwater).

3 Davide Zanchettin et al., 'Sea-level Rise in Venice: Historic and Future Trends (Review Article)', *Natural Hazards and Earth System Sciences* 21, no. 8 (2021), pp. 2643–78, esp. p. 2643; see also Julius Schlumberger et al., 'Developing a Framework for the Assessment of Current and Future Flood Risk in Venice, Italy', *Natural Hazards and Earth System Sciences* 22, no. 7 (2022), pp. 2381–400.

4 Mario Piana, 'This is How Venice Will Fall: Conservation Expert Shares Day-by-Day Destruction Caused by Rising Water Levels', *The Art Newspaper*, 29 October 2021.

5 Steve Schaft, *Venetië, een aanzet tot verbeelding. Afstudeerproject voor de Academie van Bouwkunst Amsterdam*, thesis, Amsterdam, 2023.

## Chapter 1: Historical heritage threatened by the climate crisis

1 Naomi Oreskes and Erik Conway, *The Collapse of Western Civilization* (New York: Columbia University Press, 2014).

2 'Homeowners Face a $25trn Bill from Climate Change', *The Economist*, 11 April 2024.

3 Twenty-six per cent of the Netherlands lies below the average sea level. Since the level of the sea varies between high and low tide by 1.5 metres, and during spring tides by even more, 59 per cent of the Netherlands is vulnerable to flooding by the sea.

4 Johannes Pontanus, *Rerum et urbis Amstelodamensium historia* (Amsterdam: Hondius, 1611); cited in Dutch in Pieter Scheltema, *Aemstel's oudheid of gedenkwaardigheden van Amsterdam* (Amsterdam: J.H. Scheltema, 1855), vol. I, p. 10.

5 William Aglionby, *The Present State of the United Provinces of the Low-Countries* (London: Starkey, 1669), p. 276.

6 William Bray (ed.), *The Diary of John Evelyn* (London and New York: Dunne, 1901), 2 vols, vol. I, p. 27.

7 Roemer Visscher, *Sinnepoppen* (Amsterdam: Jansz, 1614), p. 121, no. LX.

8 A comparable technique, with shorter piles placed closer together, was used in Venice. The Basilica of Santa Maria della Salute, for example, is supported by 1,156,672 piles of oak and larch.

9 *KNMI 14-klimaatscenario's voor Nederland: leidraad voor professionals in klimaatadaptatie* (De Bilt: KNMI, 2015), p. 5.

10 Rolf Schuttenhelm, 'Hoeveel zeespiegelstijging kan Nederland aan?', *De Correspondent*, 7 February 2020, https://decorrespondent.nl/10947/hoeveel-zeespiegelstijging-kan-nederland-aan/16952361133488-c5ceac77.

11 LOLA Landscape Architects (Rotterdam) and Metropolisfilm (Utrecht), *Gouda Atlantis*, Museum Gouda, 2021, www.youtube.com/watch?v=Lxyl13gSAGo.

12 David Teruel Cano, Sandra Fatorić and Martijn Manders, *The Impacts of Climate Change on Cultural Heritage in the Netherlands: A Preliminary Assessment of Exposure* (Delft: TU Delft, 2020); Sandra Fatorić and Robbert Biesbroek, 'Adapting Cultural Heritage to Climate Change Impacts in the Netherlands: Barriers, Interdependencies, and Strategies for Overcoming Them', *Climatic Change* 162 (2020), pp. 301–20.

13 IPCC (Valérie Masson-Delmotte et al., eds.), *Climate Change 2021: The Physical Science Basis. The Working Group I Contribution to the Sixth Assessment Report of the Intergovernmental Panel on Climate Change* (Cambridge: Cambridge University Press, 2021), pp. 21, 286.

14 Jules Beersma et al. (eds.), *KNMI Klimaatsignaal '21: hoe het klimaat in Nederland snel verandert* (De Bilt: KNMI, 2021). The rise in sea level that the Netherlands will face in the long term is at least around 10 metres, assuming the target of the Paris Accords is achieved and global temperatures increase by a maximum of 2°C, or preferably 1.5°C. At the time of writing, we are heading for an increase of more than 3°C. Warming of more than 4 or 5°C will result in a rise in sea levels of around 55 metres. That full 55-metre rise will be reached only after thousands of years, but we will notice the effects of this scenario long before that, with a rise of 2 metres by 2100 and another 5 metres on top of that during the century that follows.

15 Wereld Natuur Fonds (Wouter Helmer et al., eds.), *Meegroeien met de zee: naar een veerkrachtige kustzone* (Zeist: Wereld Natuur Fonds, 1996), p. 4.

16 Maarten Kleinhans, cited in Rolf Schuttenhelm, 'In Face of Rising Sea Levels the Netherlands "Must Consider Controlled Withdrawal"', *Vrij Nederland*, 7 February 2019, www.vn.nl/rising-sea-levels-netherlands/.

17 Dick Butijn and Rob van den Haak, 'De Haakse Zeedijk', haaksezeedijk.nl; Sjoerd Groeskamp and Joakim Kjellsson, 'NEED: The Northern European Enclosure Dam for if Climate Change Mitigation Fails', *Bulletin of the American Meteorological Society* 101, no. 7 (2020), pp. E1174–89.

18 World Heritage Committee, *Decisions of the 29th Session of the World Heritage Committee, Durban, South Africa, 10–17 July 2005, WHC-05/29.COM/22* (Paris: UNESCO, 2005), p. 36. The meeting in Durban was followed by a separate climate session in 2006 in Vilnius; see the report by Augustin Colette (ed.), *Climate Change and World Heritage: Report on Predicting and Managing the Impacts of Climate Change on World Heritage and Strategy to Assist States Parties to Implement Appropriate Management Responses. Publication Based on Document WHC-06/30.COM/7.1 Presented*

*to the World Heritage Committee at its 30th Session, Vilnius, Lithuania, 8–16 July 2006* (Paris: UNESCO World Heritage Centre, 2007). One of the first publications to look at the consequences of climate change for heritage was M.J. Rowland, 'Climate Change, Sea-Level Rise and the Archaeological Record', *Australian Archaeology* 34, no. 1 (1992), pp. 29–33, DOI: 10.1080/03122417.1992.11681449.

19 ICOMOS, 'Resolution 20GA/15 – Cultural Heritage and the Climate Emergency', 5 December 2020, www.icomos.org/images/DOCUMENTS/Secretariat/2020/Cultural_Heritage_and_the_Climate_Emergency-Resolution_20GA_15_.pdf.

20 For other examples and a review of the literature on the subject, see Elena Sesana et al., 'Climate Change Impacts on Cultural Heritage: A Literature Review', *WIREs Climate Change* 12, no. 4 (2021), DOI: 10.1002/wcc.710.

21 Justin Rowlatt, 'Climate Change Threatening Buried UK Treasures', *BBC News*, 25 January 2022, www.bbc.com/news/science-environment-60091485.

22 Edoardo Zanchini, Gabriele Nanni and Andrea Minutolo, *Il clima è già cambiato. Rapporto 2019 dell'Osservatorio di Legambiente CittàClima* (Rome: Legambiente, 2019), p. 36.

23 ISPRA (Istituto Superiore per la Protezione e la Ricerca Ambientale) (A. Trigila et al.), *Dissesto idrogeologico in Italia: pericolosità e indicatori di rischio (ISPRA Rapporti 356/2021)* (Rome: ISPRA, 2021).

24 Hannah Lynch, 'Iraq's Ancient Buildings are Being Destroyed by Climate Change', *The Guardian*, 15 April 2022.

25 Islam Kamal et al., 'Climate Change Mitigation and Adaptation Strategies and Policies for Cultural Heritage in Egypt', *Journal of the Faculty of Tourism and Hotels, University of Sadat City* 5, no. 1/2 (2021), pp. 21–38; Vivian Yee, 'Climate Change and Human Activity Erode Egypt's Treasured Antiquities', *The New York Times*, 12 November 2022.

26 Boris Radosavljevic et al., 'Erosion and Flooding – Threats to Coastal Infrastructure in the Arctic: A Case Study from Herschel Island, Yukon Territory, Canada', *Estuaries and Coasts* 39 (2016), pp. 900–15.

27 Augustin Colette et al. (eds.), *Case Studies on Climate Change and World Heritage* (Paris: UNESCO, 2007), pp. 58–9.

28 Joseph B. Treaster, 'Art Museums in Puerto Rico Face Long and Expensive Recovery', *The New York Times*, 8 March 2018.

29 In Africa seventy-one heritage locations are threatened by rising sea levels: see Michalis I. Vousdoukas et al., 'African Heritage Sites Threatened as Sea-level Rise Accelerates', *Nature Climate Change* 12 (2022), pp. 256–62; see also Caridad Ballesteros and Luciana S. Esteves, 'Integrated Assessment of Coastal Exposure and Social Vulnerability to Coastal Hazards in East Africa', *Estuaries and Coasts* 44 (2021), pp. 2056–72.

30 Colette, *Climate Change and World Heritage*, pp. 23–4.

31 Zanchettin et al., 'Sea-level Rise in Venice'; Julius Schlumberger et al., 'Developing a Framework for the Assessment of Current and Future Flood Risk in Venice, Italy', *Natural Hazards and Earth System Sciences* 22, no. 7 (2022), pp. 2381–400.

32 Lena Reimann et al., 'Mediterranean UNESCO World Heritage at Risk from Coastal Flooding and Erosion due to Sea-level Rise', *Nature Communications* 9 (2018), article 4161, DOI: 10.1038/s41467-018-06645-9.

33 David G. Anderson et al., 'Sea-level Rise and Archaeological Site Destruction: An Example from the Southeastern United States Using DINAA (Digital Index of North American Archaeology)', *PLOS One*, 29 November 2017, DOI: 10.1371/journal.pone.0188142.

34 Colette et al., *Case Studies on Climate Change*, p. 74; United Nations Human Settlements Programme (Nguyen Quang et al.), *Hoi An, Viet Nam – Climate Change Vulnerability Assessment* (Nairobi: UN-Habitat, 2014); Scott A. Kulp and Benjamin H. Strauss, 'New Elevation Data Triple Estimates of Global Vulnerability to Sea-level Rise and Coastal Flooding', *Nature Communications* 10 (2019), article 4844, DOI: 10.1038/s41467-019-12808-z.

35 Nadja Sayej, 'Fearing Climate Change, the Louvre's New Conservation Center Will Hold One-third of the Museum's Entire Art Collection', *Architectural Digest*, 5 February 2021, www.architecturaldigest.com/story/fearing-climate-change-louvre-new-conservation-center.

36 Christopher Flavelle, 'Saving History with Sandbags: Climate Change Threatens the Smithsonian', *The New York Times*, 25 November 2021; George Marshall, *Don't Even Think About It: Why Our Brains Are Wired to Ignore Climate Change* (London: Bloomsbury, 2015), pp. 99–104.

37 Bruno Meyerfeld, 'Au Brésil, les peintures rupestres de la Serra da Capivara menacées', *Le Monde*, 16 October 2023.

## Chapter 2: Why heritage?

1 Anthony D. Barnosky et al., 'Has the Earth's Sixth Mass Extinction Already Arrived?', *Nature* 471 (2011), pp. 51–7; Elizabeth Kolbert, *The Sixth Extinction: An Unnatural History* (New York: Picador, 2015).

2 'Shelling of Monte Cassino', British Pathé, video undated (1944), www.youtube.com/watch?app=desktop&v=7g8jci-s1j8.

3 Sir Harold Nicolson, 'Marginal Comment', *The Spectator*, 25 February 1944.

4 Benedict Nicolson, *The International Caravaggesque Movement: Lists of Pictures by Caravaggio and His Followers Throughout Europe from 1590 to 1650* (Oxford: Phaidon, 1979), 2 vols.

5 Thomas Mann, *Listen, Germany!* (New York: Knopf, 1943), p. 85.

6 Lucia Allais, *Designs of Destruction: The Making of Monuments in the Twentieth Century* (Chicago: University of Chicago Press, 2018), pp. 71–112.

7 Nathan Ruser et al., 'Cultural Erasure: Tracing the Destruction of Uyghur and Islamic Spaces in Xinjiang', *Australian Strategic Policy Institute*, 24 September 2020, www.aspi.org.au/report/cultural-erasure.

8 Edward L. Shaughnessy, 'Chronologies of Ancient China: A Critique of the "Xia-Shang-Zhou Chronology Project"', in Clara Wing-chung Ho (ed.), *Windows on the Chinese World: Reflections by Five Historians* (Lanham, MD: Lexington Books, 2009), pp. 15–28.

9 David Lowenthal, *The Heritage Crusade and the Spoils of History* (Cambridge: Cambridge University Press, 1996).

10 Lucia Allais, 'Integrities: The Salvage of Abu Simbel', *Grey Room* 50 (2013), pp. 6–45, esp. p. 7.

11 *Convention Concerning the Protection of the World Cultural and Natural Heritage, Adopted by the General Conference at its Seventeenth Session, Paris, 16 November 1972* (Paris: UNESCO World Heritage Centre, 1972), p. 1.

12 *Operational Guidelines for the Implementation of the World Heritage Convention, WHC 05/2, 2 February 2005* (Paris: UNESCO World Heritage Centre, 2005), pp. 19–20.

13 Kadir van Lohuizen, *After Us the Deluge: The Human Consequences of Rising Sea Levels* (Tielt: Lannoo, 2021), pp. 178–9.

14 Kini Dunn, 'Climate Witness: Kini Dunn, Togoru, Fiji', *World Wide Fund for Nature*, 30 November 2004, wwf.panda.org/wwf_news/?16711/Climate-Witness-Kini-Dunn-Togoru-Fiji.

15 Anne Dunn, cited in Pascal Laureyn, 'Nowhere to Hide from Climate Change', *Reliefweb*, 2 January 2018, reliefweb.int/report/fiji/nowhere-hide-climate-change.

16 Frans Grijzenhout (ed.), *Erfgoed: de geschiedenis van een begrip* (Amsterdam: Amsterdam University Press, 2007).

17 Patricia Blake and Max Hayward (eds.), translated by the editors, *Dissonant Voices in Soviet Literature* (New York: Pantheonl Books, 1962), pp. 246, 251.

18 *Declaration on the Responsibilities of the Present Generations Towards Future Generations*, UNESCO General Conference, Paris, 21 October–12 November 1997, 29th session, www.unesco.org/en/legal-affairs/declaration-responsibilities-present-generations-towards-future-generations.

19 Emilie Gaillard, 'The Rights of Future Generations, A New Legal Humanism', *Sustainable Development News*, 29 November 2021, https://icmglt.org/the-rights-of-future-generations-a-new-legal-humanism/.

20 Sam Varvastian, 'Children's Climate Change Case at the European Court of Human Rights: What's at Stake?', *The Conversation*, 4 December 2020, theconversation.com/childrens-climate-change-case-at-the-european-court-of-human-rights-whats-at-stake-151417.

21 Zhiwa Woodbury, 'Climate Trauma: Toward a New Taxonomy of Trauma', *Ecopsychology* 11, no. 1 (2019), pp. 1–8.

22 Jeff Goodell, *The Water Will Come: Rising Seas, Sinking Cities, and the Remaking of the Civilized World* (Boston: Little, Brown & Co., 2017); see also Marshall, *Don't Even Think About It.*

23 Meehan Crist, 'Besides, I'll be Dead', *London Review of Books*, 22 February 2018.

24 Glenn Albrecht et al., 'Solastalgia: The Distress Caused by Environmental Change', *Australasian Psychiatry* 15, supplement 1.1 (2007), pp. S95–8.

25 Nick Watts et al., 'Health and Climate Change: Policy Responses to Protect Public Health', *The Lancet* 386, no. 10006 (2015), pp. 1861–914.

26 Sigmund Freud, 'Das Unheimliche', in Alexander Mitscherlich and Angela Richards (eds.), *Sigmund Freud: Studienausgabe* (Frankfurt am Main: Fischer, 1982), vol. 4, p. 258; Amitav Ghosh, *The Great Derangement: Climate Change and the Unthinkable* (Chicago: University of Chicago Press, 2016), pp. 30–1; Amitav Ghosh, *The Nutmeg's Curse: Parables for a Planet in Crisis* (Chicago: University of Chicago Press, 2021), pp. 251–7; Nicholas Gallie, *The Sublime of Climate Change*, PhD thesis, University of Sussex, 2017.

27 Timothy Morton, *Hyperobjects: Philosophy and Ecology After the End of the World* (Minneapolis: University of Minnesota Press, 2013).

28 Emily Elhacham et al., 'Global Human-made Mass Exceeds All Living Biomass', *Nature* 588 (2020), pp. 442–4.

29 Greta Thunberg to the EU Parliament, Strasbourg, 16 April 2019.

**Chapter 3: Art and nature: fertile cross-pollination?**

1 Peter Frankopan, *The Earth Transformed: An Untold History* (London: Bloomsbury, 2023).

2 Lucas Stephens, Erle Ellis and Dorian Fuller, 'The Deep Anthropocene', *Aeon*, 1 October 2020, aeon.co/essays/revolutionary-archaeology-reveals-the-deepest-possible-anthropocene.

3 William F. Ruddiman, 'The Anthropogenic Greenhouse Era Began Thousands of Years Ago', *Climatic Change* 61, no. 3 (2003), pp. 261–93; Ruddiman's hypothesis was much criticized.

4 Leopold George Heath, *View of a Coal Seam on the Island of Labuan*, lithograph, from James Augustus St. John, *Views in the Eastern Archipelago: Borneo, Sarawak, Labuan, &c* (London: Thomas McClean, 1847).

5 Simon Evans et al., 'Revealed: How Colonial Rule Radically Shifts Historical Responsibility for Climate Change', *Carbon Brief*, 26 November 2023, www.carbonbrief.org/revealed-how-colonial-rule-radically-shifts-historical-responsibility-for-climate-change/.

6 Andreas Malm, *The Progress of This Storm: Nature and Society in a Warming World* (London: Verso, 2018), p. 20.

7 David Wallace-Wells interviewed by Amy Goodman for *Democracy Now!*, 28 June 2023, www.democracynow.org/2023/6/8/wildfires_climate_crisis.

8 Barbara W. Tuchman, 'Mankind's Better Moments', *The American Scholar* 49, no. 4 (1980), pp. 449–63, esp. pp. 450–1.

9 Roman Krznaric, *The Good Ancestor: How to Think Long Term in a Short-Term World* (London: Penguin, 2020), pp. 114–15.

10 UNESCO World Heritage List, Netherlands, https://whc.unesco.org/en/list/818/.

11 Ibid., https://whc.unesco.org/en/list/739/.

12 Dagomar Degroot, *The Frigid Golden Age: Climate Change, the Little Ice Age, and the Dutch Republic, 1560–1720* (Cambridge: Cambridge University Press, 2018).

13 Ibid., p. 288.

14 Dagomar Degroot, 'Little Ice Age Lessons', *Aeon*, 11 November 2019, aeon.co/essays/the-little-ice-age-is-a-history-of-resilience-and-surprises.

15 Willem Frijhoff and Marijke Spies, *1650: bevochten eendracht* (The Hague: Sdu Uitgevers, 1999), pp. 70–136.

16 Hier vraagt men naer geen stand, hier is men vranck en vrij,
Hier heeft een boeren-maegd een edelman op zij,
Daer ziet m'n boeren-zeun aen't hoofd der joffren reyen,
Ginds ziet m'een hoofsche kwant een borgeres geleyen,
Want dat geen groot Monarch, geen wysgeer zelfs vermocht,
Dat ziet men door het nat tot ys gestolt gewrocht;

Vraeght men uyt 's herten grondt wie is er waerlyck wys,
Ick seg uyt 's herten grond: dat is alleen het ys

Cited in Jan Buisman, *Duizend jaar weer, wind en water in de Lage Landen, deel 4: 1575–1675* (Franeker: Van Wijnen, 1995), p. 252.

17 Eric Jan Sluijter, 'Ownership of Paintings in the Dutch Golden Age', in Ronni Baer (ed.), *Class Distinctions: Dutch Painting in the Age of Rembrandt and Vermeer* (Boston: Museum of Fine Arts, 2015), pp. 89–111 and 286–91.

18 Thijs Weststeijn, *The Visible World: Samuel van Hoogstraten's Art Theory and the Legitimation of Painting in the Dutch Golden Age*, trans. Beverley Jackson and Lynne Richards (Amsterdam: Amsterdam University Press, 2008), pp. 242–3.

19 Samuel van Hoogstraten, *Inleyding tot de hooge schoole der schilderkonst* (Rotterdam: Van Hoogstraten, 1678), p. 24. Quotations in English taken from Weststeijn, *The Visible World*, p. 111.

20 Van Hoogstraten, *Inleyding*, p. 346; Weststeijn, *The Visible World*, p. 111.

21 Boudewijn Bakker, *Landscape and Religion from Van Eyck to Rembrandt* (Farnham: Ashgate, 2012); Eric Jorink, *Reading the Book of Nature in the Dutch Golden Age, 1575–1715* (Leiden: Brill, 2010).

22 Oliver Kik, *Children of Mercury: Studies on the Transmission of Geometrical Design Knowledge in the Netherlandish Workshop Practice: 1480–1560*, PhD thesis, Utrecht University, 2021, pp. 130–53.

23 Lytle Shaw, *New Grounds for Dutch Landscape* (Stockholm: OEI, 2021).

24 Richard W. Unger, 'Energy Sources for the Dutch Golden Age: Peat, Wind, and Coal', *Research in Economic History* 9 (1984), pp. 221–53.

25 Paul Hendrix, *Henri Deterding: De Koninklijke, de Shell en de Rothschilds* (The Hague: Sdu, 1996).

26 Shell has announced that it wants to withdraw from this project, but at the time of writing it has not yet succeeded in doing so.

27 Nathaniel Rich, *Losing Earth: The Decade We Could Have Stopped Climate Change* (New York: MCD/Farrar, Straus and Giroux, 2019); Jelmer Mommers, *Hoe gaan we dit uitleggen: onze toekomst op een*

*steeds warmere aarde* (Amsterdam: De Correspondent, 2019), p. 85; Thorfinn Stainforth and Bartosz Brzezinski, 'More than Half of All $CO_2$ Emissions since 1751 Emitted in the Last 30 Years', *Institute for European Environmental Policy*, 29 April 2020, ieep.eu/news/more-than-half-of-all-co2-emissions-since-1751-emitted-in-the-last-30-years.

28 Van Lohuizen, *After Us the Deluge*, p. 246.

29 EUROSTAT, 'Share of Energy from Renewable Sources', last updated 9 January 2026, https://doi.org/10.2908/NRG_IND_REN.

30 Jean Domen, 'Oliegigant Shell is staat in de staat', *Elsevier Weekblad*, 26 June 2018, www.ewmagazine.nl/economie/achtergrond/2018/06/oliegigant-shell-is-staat-in-een-staat-136892w/.

31 Rick Bosman and Sem Oxenaar, 'De staat speelt een veel grotere rol in olie en gas dan gedacht', *De Correspondent*, 1 February 2018, decorrespondent.nl/7888/de-staat-speelt-een-veel-grotere-rol-in-olie-en-gas-dan-gedacht/992085875968-5ac18d1c.

32 According to the registration of emissions by the Dutch national government, in 2021 the country's greenhouse gas emissions amounted to 168 megatonnes $CO_2$-equivalent: 'Overzicht broeikasgassen', as determined in September 2022, www.emissieregistratie.nl/data/overzichtstabellen-lucht/broeikasgassen. According to figures from the Climate Accountability Institute, emissions by Shell (in 2018) amounted to 550 megatonnes $CO_2$-equivalent; see Serena Frijters, 'Hoeveel $CO_2$-uitstoot scheelt het intomen van Shell?', *De Volkskrant*, 28 May 2021.

33 Paul Griffin, *The Carbon Majors Database: CDP Carbon Majors Report 2017*, July 2017, cdn.cdp.net/cdp-production/cms/reports/documents/000/002/327/original/Carbon-Majors-Report-2017.pdf?1501833772. Eighty-three fossil fuel companies are responsible for two thirds of all emissions of greenhouse gases. After Saudi Aramco, Gazprom and ExxonMobil, Shell is in ninth place. The company was responsible for 1.7 per cent of all industrial emissions of greenhouse gases from 1988 to 2015.

34 Mommers, *Hoe gaan we dit uitleggen*, p. 83.

35 Royal Dutch Shell, *Climate of Concern* (documentary from 1991), www.youtube.com/watch?v=0VOWi8oVXmo.

36 Ben van Beurden, *Nieuwsuur* (NPO2), 4 February 2016.

37 Jelmer Mommers, 'De pr-praatjes van Shell zijn een stuk groener dan de investeringen', *De Correspondent*, 2 February 2017, decorrespondent.nl/6082/de-pr-praatjes-van-shell-zijn-een-stuk-groener-dan-de-investeringen/79b9dd9e-6876-0576-2172-0609118128a3.

38 Court of Justice, The Hague, 26 May 2021, Case number C/09/571932 / HA ZA 19-379.

39 'Met vertrek benadrukt Shell vooral zijn eigen existentiële probleem', *NRC Handelsblad*, 17 November 2021.

40 Ghosh, *The Great Derangement*.

41 It has since been put to Ghosh that novelists did sometimes write about the fossil fuel industry: Elizabeth Carolyn Miller, *Extraction Ecologies and the Literature of the Long Exhaustion* (Princeton, NJ: Princeton University Press, 2021).

42 Charles Baudelaire, 'Le peintre de la vie moderne', in *Œuvres complètes de Charles Baudelaire, vol. III* (Paris: Calmann Lévy, 1885 [orig. 1863]), p. 69. English translation of quotation is taken from Charles Baudelaire, *The Painter of Modern Life and Other Essays*, trans. and ed. Jonathan Mayne (New York: Da Capo Press, 1986).

43 Willem van der Ham, *Reuzenarbeid: de bouw van het moderne Nederland in beeld 1861–1918* (Rotterdam: NAI, 2021).

44 Letter from Vincent van Gogh to Theo van Gogh, sent from Wasmes between Tuesday 1 and Wednesday 16 April 1879, https://vangogh letters.org/vg/letters/let151/letter.html#translation, Amsterdam, Van Gogh Museum, inv. no. b149 V/1962.

45 Vincent van Gogh, *Coke Factory in Flénu* (1879), pencil and gouache, Van Gogh Museum, Amsterdam.

46 An aerial photo of the artwork can be seen at www.flevolandsgeheugen.nl/page/8043/richard-serra-en-sea-level.

47 Thijs Weststeijn, *Art and Antiquity in the Netherlands and Britain: The Vernacular Arcadia of Franciscus Junius (1591–1677)* (Leiden: Brill, 2015). The financial contribution by the Getty Center is mentioned at the start.

48 Gert-jan Plets and Marin Kuijt, 'Gas, Oil and Heritage: Well-oiled

Histories and Corporate Sponsorship in Dutch Museums (1990–2021)', *BMGN – Low Countries Historical Review* 137, no. 1 (2022), pp. 50–77.

49 Marian Kent, *Moguls and Mandarins: Oil, Imperialism and the Middle East in British Foreign Policy, 1900–1940* (London: Frank Cass, 1993).

50 Greg Muttitt, *Fuel on the Fire: Oil and Politics in Occupied Iraq* (New York: New Press, 2011).

51 Visit of President George W. Bush to Northern Ireland, 7–8 April 2003.

52 Lawrence Rothfield, *The Rape of Mesopotamia: Behind the Looting of the Iraq Museum* (Chicago: University of Chicago Press, 2009); Milbry Polk and Angela M.H. Schuster (eds.), *The Looting of the Iraq Museum, Baghdad: The Lost Legacy of Ancient Mesopotamia* (New York: Harry N. Abrams, 2005).

53 www.britishmuseum.org/exhibitions/i-am-ashurbanipal-king-world-king-assyria#supporters. The exhibition *I am Ashurbanipal: king of the world, king of Assyria* ran from 8 November 2018 to 24 February 2019.

54 Chris Julien, *Alledaags activisme* (Amsterdam: Podium, 2024), p. 26.

55 Glenn Albrecht in a LinkedIn post, July 2024.

56 Greenpeace UK, 'Artists, Art Workers and Historians' Open Letter to Judge Hehir', 24 September 2024, www.greenpeace.org.uk/resources/open-letter-to-judge-hehir/.

57 Global Witness, 'More than 2,100 Land and Environmental Defenders Killed Globally between 2012 and 2023', press release, 10 September 2024, www.globalwitness.org/en/press-releases/more-2100-land-and-environmental-defenders-killed-globally-between-2012-and-2023/.

58 Markus Ostarek et al., 'Radical Climate Protests Linked to Increases in Public Support for Moderate Organizations', *Nature Sustainability* 7 (2024), pp. 1626–32.

## Chapter 4: The historical sensation in the Anthropocene

1 Cited in Dipesh Chakrabarty, *The Climate of History in a Planetary Age* (Chicago and London: University of Chicago Press, 2021), p. 157. The term 'Anthropocene', coined in 1926 by Vladimir Vernadski, was popularized by Paul J. Crutzen and Eugene F. Stoermer, 'The

"Anthropocene"', *International Geosphere-Biosphere Programme Newsletter* 41 (2000), p. 17.

2 Paul J. Crutzen, 'Geology of Mankind', *Nature* 415, no. 23 (2002), p. 23.

3 Dipesh Chakrabarty, 'The Climate of History: Four Theses', *Critical Inquiry* 35, no. 2 (2009), pp. 197–222.

4 Stephens, Ellis and Fuller, 'The Deep Anthropocene'.

5 J. Huntley et al., 'The Effects of Climate Change on the Pleistocene Rock Art of Sulawesi', *Scientific Reports* 11 (2021), article 9833, DOI: 10.1038/s41598-021-87923-3.

6 Reimann et al., 'Mediterranean UNESCO World Heritage at Risk', p. 3.

7 Van Lohuizen, *After Us the Deluge*, pp. 178–9.

8 Johan Huizinga, 'Het historisch museum', in *Verzamelde Werken* (Haarlem: H.D. Tjeenk Willink, 1948–1953), 9 vols, vol. 2, p. 566. Quotation in English taken from E.H. Kossmann, 'Postscript', in W.R.H. Koops et al. (eds.), *Johan Huizinga 1872–1972. Papers delivered to the Johan Huizinga Conference Groningen, 11–15 December 1972* (The Hague: Nijhoff, 1973), p. 226. Note that an English translation of Huizinga's *Herfsttij der Middeleeuwen* was first published in 1924 as *The Autumn of the Middle Ages* (UK) and *The Waning of the Middle Ages* (US).

9 Immacolata Forino, 'Living in "The Sense of the Past": Solipsistic Impulses in the Domesticscapes of Edmond de Goncourt and Mario Praz', *Interiors* 2, no. 1 (2011), pp. 7–26; Jo Tollebeek, 'De waarheid van de geschiedenis, Mario Praz, Lord Byron en de historische sensatie', *Feit & Fictie* 1, no. 1 (1993), pp. 53–74.

10 Frank Ankersmit, *De sublieme historische ervaring* (Groningen: Historische Uitgeverij, 2007), p. 116; Frank Ankersmit, *Sublime Historical Experience* (Stanford, CA: Stanford University Press, 2005), pp. 121 and 223.

11 The oldest source on the Batavians, an eleventh-century copy of Tacitus' *The Histories*, was kept in the monastery library at the aforementioned Monte Cassino (and rediscovered in 1362 by Giovanni Boccaccio).

12 Ankersmit, *De sublieme historische ervaring*, p. 141; Ankersmit, *Sublime Historical Experience*, p. 323.

13 G.W.F. Hegel, *Vorlesungen über die Philosophie der Weltgeschichte* (Hamburg: Felix Meiner, 1976), Part 2, vols II–IV, p. 926; G.W.F. Hegel, *The Philosophy of History*, trans. J. Sibree (New York: Dover, 1956), p. 447.

14 Francis Fukuyama, *The End of History and the Last Man* (New York: Free Press, 1992).

15 Arthur Danto, 'The End of Art', in *The Philosophical Disenfranchisement of Art* (New York: Columbia University Press, 1984), pp. 81–113, esp. p. 111.

16 Kathryn Yusoff, *A Billion Black Anthropocenes or None* (Minneapolis: University of Minnesota Press, 2018), p. xiii.

17 Crutzen, 'Geology of Mankind', p. 23.

18 Intergovernmental Panel on Climate Change (IPCC), *IPCC Sixth Assessment Report: Climate Change 2022: Mitigation of Climate Change* (Geneva: IPCC, 2022), chapter 5, p. 520, www.ipcc.ch/report/ar6/wg3/.

19 Chakrabarty, *The Climate of History*, p. 16; Carolyn Merchant, *The Anthropocene and the Humanities: From Climate Change to a New Age of Sustainability* (New Haven, CT: Yale University Press, 2020), pp. 15–16.

20 Matt Ridley, *The Rational Optimist: How Prosperity Evolves* (New York: Harper, 2010), pp. 214–17.

21 Jean-François Mouhot, 'Past Connections and Present Similarities in Slave Ownership and Fossil Fuel Usage', *Climatic Change* 105, no. 1 (2011), pp. 329–55.

22 Laetitia Laubscher, 'Between the Devil and the Deep Blue: Marshall Islanders Face Nuclear Fallout and Rising Seas', *Vice*, 7 March 2017, www.vice.com/en/article/between-the-devil-and-the-deep-blue-marshall-islanders-face-nuclear-fallout-and-rising-seas/.

23 Van Lohuizen, *After Us the Deluge*, pp. 118–123, 283.

24 Giorgio Vasari, *Le vite de' più eccellenti pittori, scultori, e architettori* (Florence: Giunti, 1568).

25 Rens Bod, *De vergeten wetenschappen: een geschiedenis van de humaniora* (Amsterdam: Bert Bakker, 2010), pp. 37–46, 132.

26 Sunil Amrith, *Crossing the Bay of Bengal: The Furies of Nature and the Fortunes of Migrants* (Cambridge, MA and London: Harvard University Press, 2015), p. 88.

27 Chakrabarty, *The Climate of History*, p. 4.

28 Will Steffen, Jacques Grinevald, Paul Crutzen and John McNeill, 'The Anthropocene: Conceptual and Historical Perspectives', *Philosophical Transactions of the Royal Society A* 369 (2011), pp. 842–67; John McNeill and Peter Engelke, *The Great Acceleration: An Environmental History of the Anthropocene since 1945* (Cambridge, MA: Harvard University Press, 2014).

29 One of the first people to elaborate upon geological time as a philosophical concept was Scottish geologist James Hutton (1726–97); see Robert Kubicek, 'Ages in Chaos: James Hutton and the Discovery of Deep Time', *The Historian* 70, no. 1 (2008), pp. 142–3.

30 David Wallace-Wells, *The Uninhabitable Earth: A Story of the Future* (London: Penguin, 2019), pp. 78–9.

31 Jilt Jorritsma, 'Haunted by Historicism', *History of Humanities* 6, no. 2 (2021), pp. 669–77, esp. p. 677.

32 Jacob Burckhardt, *Reflections on History* (1868), trans. M.D.H. (Indianapolis: Liberty Classics, 1979), p. 31.

33 Alessandro Antonello and Mark Carey, 'Ice Cores and the Temporalities of the Global Environment', *Environmental Humanities* 9, no. 2 (2017), pp. 181–203, esp. p. 184.

34 Alexander Nagel and Christopher Wood, *Anachronic Renaissance* (New York: Zone Books, 2019), cover text.

35 Weststeijn, *Art and Antiquity in the Netherlands and Britain*, pp. 181–7.

36 Constantijn Huygens, 'Geluck aen de H.G. heeren regeerders van Amstelredam in haer nieuwe stadt huys', in *Koren-bloemen* (The Hague: Vlacq, 1658), vol. XII, p. 820.

## Chapter 5: Transformation

1 Friedrich Nietzsche, *Vom Nutzen und Nachteil der Historie für das Leben* (Leipzig: E.W. Fritzsch, 1874); Friedrich Nietzsche, *On the Advantage and Disadvantage of History for Life*, trans. Peter Preuss (Indianapolis: Hackett, 1980).

2 Alois Riegl, *Der moderne Denkmalkultus: sein Wesen und seine Entstehung* (Vienna and Leipzig: Braumüller, 1903). Translated as 'The Modern Cult of Monuments: Its Essence and its Development', trans. Karin Bruckner with Karen Williams, in *Historical and Philosophical Issues in the Conservation of Cultural Heritage*, edited by Nicholas Stanley-Price et al. (Los Angeles: Getty Conservation Institute, 1996), pp. 69–83.

3 Erica Avrami, Randall Mason and Marta de la Torre, *Values and Heritage Conservation* (Los Angeles: Getty Conservation Institute, 2000); Mohammad S. Taher Tolou Del, Bahram Saleh Sedghpour and Sina Kamali Tabrizi, 'The Semantic Conservation of Architectural Heritage: The Missing Values', *Heritage Science* 8 (2020), article 70, DOI: 10.1186/s40494-020-00416-w.

4 Ante Baric, Branka Grbec and Danijela Bogner, 'Potential Implications of Sea-level Rise for Croatia', *Journal of Coastal Research* 24, no. 2 (2008), pp. 299–305, esp. p. 302; Reimann et al., 'Mediterranean UNESCO World Heritage at Risk', p. 3, fig. 1, no. 97.

5 Eric Hobsbawm and Terence Ranger (eds.), *The Invention of Tradition* (Cambridge: Cambridge University Press, 1983).

6 Alessandro Pergoli Campanelli, *La nascita del restauro: dall'antichità all'Alto Medioevo* (Milan: Jaca Book, 2015).

7 Lowenthal, *The Heritage Crusade*, p. 20.

8 *The Nara Document on Authenticity, WHC-94/CONF.003/INF.008* (Paris: UNESCO, 1994).

9 Cited in C. Scott Littleton, *Understanding Shinto* (London: Duncan Baird, 2002), p. 76.

10 Byung-Chul Han, 'The Copy is the Original', *Aeon*, 8 March 2018, aeon.co/essays/why-in-china-and-japan-a-copy-is-just-as-good-as-an-original; Cassandra Adams, 'Japan's Ise Shrine and its Thirteen-

Hundred-Year-Old Reconstruction Tradition', *Journal of Architectural Education* 52, no. 1 (1998), pp. 49–60.

11 Peter Brimblecombe, Mikiko Hayashi and Yoko Futagami, 'Mapping Climate Change, Natural Hazards and Tokyo's Built Heritage', *Atmosphere* 11, no. 7 (2020), DOI: 10.3390/atmos11070680.

12 Dhrubajyoti Sahariah et al., 'Majuli at the Crossroads: A Study of Cultural Geomorphology', *Space and Culture, India* 1, no. 2 (2013), pp. 12–20; Ashima Sharma, 'The Mising and the Miyah Have Learnt to Live with the Brahmaputra. Can Assam?', *The Third Pole*, 30 September 2021, www.thethirdpole.net/en/livelihoods/adapting-to-brahmaputra-floods-assam-mising-miyah/; Vidya Vijayaraghavan, 'The Mising Tribe of Assam's Unique Approach to Climate Change Adaptation and Mitigation', *Nomomente*, 19 November 2021, www.nomomente.org/post/mising-tribe-of-assam-climate-change-adaptation-and-mitigation; Mitul Baruah, *Slow Disaster: Political Ecology of Hazards and Everyday Life in the Brahmaputra Valley, Assam* (Abingdon: Routledge, 2022).

13 Bruce Sterling, 'Reboot 11 Closing Talk, Copenhagen, 25 June 2009', *Wired*, 25 February 2011, www.wired.com/2011/02/transcript-of-reboot-11-speech-by-bruce-sterling-25-6-2009/.

14 Frederico M. Mazzolani, Beatrice Faggiano and Giulio Martire, 'Design Aspects of the AB Prototype in the Qiandao Lake', *Procedia Engineering* 4 (2010), pp. 21–33.

15 Rose Macaulay, *Pleasure of Ruins* (London: Thames & Hudson, 1966 [1953]), pp. xv–xvi; see also Christopher Woodward, *In Ruins: A Journey Through History, Art, and Literature* (London: Vintage, 2002); Andreas Huyssen, 'Nostalgia for Ruins', *Grey Room* 23 (2006), pp. 6–21; Julia Hell and Andreas Schönle (eds.), *Ruins of Modernity* (Durham, NC: Duke University Press, 2010); and Alain Schnapp, *Une histoire universelle des ruines: Des origines aux Lumières* (Paris: Seuil, 2020).

16 Wu Hung, *A Story of Ruins: Presence and Absence in Chinese Art and Visual Culture* (Princeton, NJ: Princeton University Press, 2012).

17 Wereld Natuur Fonds, *Meegroeien met de zee*, p. 4.

**Chapter 6: Digitization**

1 Delf Rothe et al., 'Digital Tuvalu: State Sovereignty in a World of Climate Loss', *International Affairs* 100, no. 4 (2024), pp. 1491–509.

2 Hugh Denard (ed.), *The London Charter for the Computer-based Visualization of Cultural Heritage*, 7 February 2009, www.londoncharter.org.

3 Patricia S. Lulof, 'Recreating Reconstructions: Archaeology, Architecture and 3D Technologies', in S. Dupré et al. (eds.), *Reconstruction, Replication and Re-enactment in the Humanities and Social Sciences* (Amsterdam: Amsterdam University Press, 2020), pp. 253–74.

4 'Heritage on the Edge', artsandculture.google.com/project/heritage-on-the-edge.

5 Wallace-Wells, *The Uninhabitable Earth*, p. 184.

6 David J. Chalmers, *Reality+: Virtual Worlds and the Problems of Philosophy* (London: Allen Lane, 2022).

7 Weststeijn, *The Visible World*, pp. 130–70.

8 Walter Benjamin, *The Work of Art in the Age of its Technological Reproducibility, and Other Writings on Media*, edited by Michael W. Jennings et al., trans. Edmund Jephcott et al. (Cambridge, MA: Belknap Press of Harvard University Press, 2008), pp. 19–55, esp. p. 21.

9 Johan Huizinga, 'De taak der cultuurgeschiedenis (1929)', in *Verzamelde werken, deel 7: geschiedwetenschap, hedendaagsche cultuur* (Haarlem: Tjeenk Willink, 1950), pp. 1–85, esp. pp. 71–2. Quotations in English taken from the essay collection Johan Huizinga, *Men and Ideas: History, the Middle Ages, the Renaissance* (New York: Meridian Books, 1959), p. 54.

10 Benjamin, *The Work of Art*, pp. 21–2.

11 Ibid., p. 37.

12 Lisa Robertson, *The Baudelaire Fractal* (Toronto: Coach House Books, 2020), p. 41.

13 Frank Jackson, 'Epiphenomenal Qualia', *Philosophical Quarterly* 32, no. 127 (1982), pp. 127–36.

14 Hans Ulrich Gumbrecht, *Our Broad Present: Time and Contemporary Culture* (New York: Columbia University Press, 2014), pp. xii–xiii; Aleida Assmann, *Is Time Out of Joint? On the Rise and Fall of the Modern*

*Time Regime* (Ithaca, NY and London: Cornell University Press, 2020), pp. 180–3.

15 Gumbrecht summarized in Assmann, *Is Time Out of Joint?*, p. 182.

16 Robert McSweeney, 'Scientists Discuss the Role of Climate Change in the Syrian Civil War', *Carbon Brief*, 2 March 2015, www.carbonbrief.org/scientists-discuss-the-role-of-climate-change-in-the-syrian-civil-war/.

17 https://palmyra-3d.online/. The director of the Hermitage, Mikhail Piotrovsky, was cited in Sophia Kishkovsky, 'New Hope that Ancient Palmyra Will be Rebuilt after Isis Damage', *The Art Newspaper*, 11 January 2021.

## Chapter 7: Reconstruction

1 United Arab Republic, *Assouan: La ville des nouvelles réalisations plus grandioses que les obélisques et les pyramides* (Cairo: Administration de l'information, 1961), p. 18; cited in Allais, 'Integrities', pp. 6–45, esp. p. 12.

2 'Report of the Panel of Experts to Consider the Technical and Archaeological Aspects of Two New Schemes for Saving the Abu Simbel Temples', 7–9 May 1963, UNESCO/65/EX/, Addendum, in the UNESCO Archives; cited in Allais, 'Integrities', p. 20.

3 Michael Press, 'Who Really Owns the Past?', *Aeon*, 27 May 2019, aeon.co/essays/why-cultural-heritage-benefits-the-rich-and-powerful-above-all.

4 John Ruskin, *The Seven Lamps of Architecture* (London: Smith, Elder and Col, 1849), aphorism no. 31.

5 Jordi Lopez-Pujol and Marta Ponseti, 'The Three Gorges Dam Project in China: History and Consequences', *HmiC: història moderna i contemporània* 4 (2006), pp. 151–88.

6 Katiana Le Mentec, 'The Three Gorges Dam Project – Religious Practices and Heritage Conservation: A Study of Cultural Remains and Local Popular Religion in the *Xian* of Yunyang (Municipality of Chongqing)', *China Perspectives* 65 (2006), para. 6, DOI: 10.4000/chinaperspectives.626.

7 Cited in Anthony Kuhn, 'Three Gorges History Drowning in Rising Reservoir', radio programme broadcast on NPR (American public radio), 4 January 2008, www.npr.org/templates/story/story.php?storyId=17810431?storyId=17810431&t=1644319075478.

8 Jerzy S. Majewski and Tomasz Markiewicz, *Budujemy nowy dom: odbudowa Warszawy w latach 1945–1952* (Warsaw: Dom Spotkań z Historią, 2012).

9 ICOMOS, Recommendation for the Inclusion of the Historic Centre of Warsaw on the World Heritage List, 7 June 1978, in the UNESCO archives in Paris, whc.unesco.org/document/153136.

10 *Operational Guidelines for the Implementation of the World Heritage Convention, WHC.05/2*, 2 February 2005, p. 20.

11 *Operational Guidelines for the Implementation of the World Heritage Convention, WHC.19/01*, 10 July 2019 (Paris: UNESCO World Heritage Centre, 2019), paragraph 86.

12 World Heritage Committee, *Decisions of the 29th Session*, p. 36.

13 Sandra Fatorić et al., 'Living with Climate Change Risks: Stakeholders' Employment and Coastal Relocation in Mediterranean Climate Regions of Australia and Spain', *Environment Systems and Decisions* 37, no. 3 (2017), pp. 276–88.

14 In his introduction to an American edition of John Betjeman's poetry, *Slick but Not Streamlined* (1947), cited in Alexandra Harris, *Romantic Moderns* (London: Thames & Hudson, 2010), p. 222.

15 Edward Relph, *Place and Placelessness* (London: Pion, 1976).

16 Lowenthal, *The Heritage Crusade*, p. 24.

17 Felwine Sarr and Bénédicte Savoy, *Rapport sur la restitution du patrimoine culturel africain. Vers une nouvelle éthique relationnelle* (November 2018), www.vie-publique.fr/files/rapport/pdf/194000291.pdf.

18 Monika Stobiecka, 'Archaeological Heritage in the Age of Digital Colonialism', *Archaeological Dialogues* 27, no. 2 (2020), pp. 113–25.

19 *Constitution of the United Nations Educational, Scientific, and Cultural Organization, Adopted in London on 16 November 1945* (London: United Nations, 1945).

20 Cited in Mommers, *Hoe gaan we dit uitleggen*, pp. 103–4.

21 Cited in Allais, *Designs of Destruction*, p. 6.

22 David Wallace-Wells, 'Beyond Catastrophe: A New Climate Reality is Coming into View', *New York Times Magazine*, 26 October 2022.

## Epilogue

1 Franz Lidz, 'As Earth Warms, Old Mayhem and Secrets Emerge from the Ice', *The New York Times*, 2 November 2021.

2 Thijs Weststeijn, 'Heritage at Sea: Must We Simply Accept the Loss of Beloved Buildings and Cities to the Floods and Rising Seas of the Climate Crisis?', *Aeon*, 28 October 2021, aeon.co/essays/must-we-accept-the-loss-of-beloved-heritage-to-the-climate-crisis.

3 Wallace-Wells, *The Uninhabitable Earth*, p. 35.

4 Interview in a television programme by VPRO called *Wintergasten*, broadcast on NPO2, 27 December 2021.

5 Sigmund Freud, *Neue Folge der Vorlesungen zur Einführung in die Psychoanalyse* (Vienna: Internationaler Psychoanalytischer Verlag, 1933), pp. 1–182, esp. p. 80.

6 Anthony Leiserowitz et al., *International Public Opinion on Climate Change* (New Haven, CT: Yale Program on Climate Change Communication and Data for Good at Meta, 2022), p. 50. Only 13 per cent of Dutch people are 'very worried' about climate change; in Greece, for example, the figure is 56 per cent. Only 19 per cent of the Dutch think they may have to move house, as against 46 per cent in China, 51 per cent in Indonesia and 68 per cent in Turkey; see Pippa Bailey and IPSOS, *Global Views on Climate Change: Impact, Information, Action*, November 2023, www.ipsos.com/sites/default/files/ct/news/documents/2023-11/Ipsos-Global-Advisor-Views-on-Climate-Change-COP28-Report.pdf, p. 6.

7 Simon Richter, 'Keeping Retreat on the Table in the Safest Delta in the World', online presentation at the University of Pennsylvania, 26 June 2021, www.youtube.com/watch?v=ysOQAc5RHkc.

8 Kari Norgaard, *Living in Denial: Climate Change, Emotions, and Everyday Life* (Cambridge, MA: MIT Press, 2011).

9 Marshall, *Don't Even Think About It*, p. 24.

10 U Thant, *Closing Statement to the Twenty-fifth Anniversary Commemorative Session of the United Nations*, 24 October 1970.

11 Margaret Atwood, 'It's Not Climate Change – It's Everything Change', *Medium*, 27 July 2015, medium.com/matter/it-s-not-climate-change-it-s-everything-change-8fd9aa671804.

# Index